6

SCOTT'S MIND AND ART

SCOTT'S
MIND AND ART

THOMAS CRAWFORD   WALTER BAGEHOT

DAVID DAICHES   ROBIN MAYHEAD

D. W. JEFFERSON   DONALD CAMERON

D. D. DEVLIN   DAVID MURISON

G. LUKÁCS   F. A. POTTLE

Essays Edited by
A. NORMAN JEFFARES

BARNES & NOBLE, Inc.
NEW YORK
PUBLISHERS AND BOOKSELLERS SINCE 1873

First published in Great Britain, 1969
by Oliver and Boyd, Ltd
First published in the United States, 1970
by Barnes & Noble, Inc.

ISBN 0 389 04000 2

Printed in Great Britain by
Cox & Wyman Ltd., London, Fakenham and Reading

ACKNOWLEDGMENTS

Several of the essays in this collection have already been published elsewhere and for permission to reprint them here the following acknowledgments are due: Thomas Crawford, "Scott's Life and Work", reprinted from the Writers and Critics series title, *Scott* (Oliver & Boyd 1965) by permission of the author and the publishers; David Daiches, "Scott's Achievement as a Novelist", reprinted from *Literary Essays* (Oliver & Boyd 1956) by permission of the author and the publishers; G. Lukács, "Scott and the Classical Form of the Historical Novel", (trs. H. & S. Mitchell) reprinted from *The Historical Novel* (Merlin Press 1962) by permission of the author and the publishers; F. A. Pottle, "The Power of Memory in Boswell and Scott", reprinted from *Essays on the Eighteenth Century Presented to David Nichol Smith* (The Clarendon Press 1945) by permission of the author and the publishers. The essay by Walter Bagehot first appeared in the *National Review* VI (April 1858).

CONTENTS

	Acknowledgments	v
	Introduction	ix
Thomas Crawford	Scott's Life and Works	1
David Daiches	Scott's Achievement as a Novelist	21
D. W. Jefferson	The Virtuosity of Scott	54
D. D. Devlin	Scott and History	72
G. Lukács	Scott and the Classical Form of the Historical Novel	93
Walter Bagehot	The Waverley Novels	132
Robin Mayhead	Scott and the Idea of Justice	167
Donald Cameron	The Web of Destiny: the Structure of *The Bride of Lammermoor*	185
David Murison	The Two Languages in Scott	206
F. A. Pottle	The Power of Memory in Boswell and Scott	230
	Select Bibliography	254
	Index	261

INTRODUCTION

The sheer size and scope of Scott's work may, paradoxically, be responsible for his comparative neglect at the hands of contemporary critics. Yet the interest he aroused in the nineteenth century – both warmly appreciative and occasionally coolly deprecating – was impressive in its volume; its tides have been ably charted for us in James T. Hillhouse's *The Waverley Novels and their Critics*. Scott himself was read widely then. But Thomas Crawford has pointed out that there has been no full-scale modern study of Scott's writings, and rightly remarks that it is quite pointless to have a "Scott industry" for academics if the novels themselves remain unread and if there is no possibility of their once more affecting contemporary writers. The very magnitude of Scott's work tends to put off younger readers who have been harrowed over a pitifully small number of texts (which probably do not include Scott) in their English classes at school. It is possible that their teachers, and they themselves, may need help in appreciating the inclusiveness of a writer of Scott's energy, the "bigness" of whose merits has been neglected because the flaws are, and always have been, easy to pick upon, while appreciation of the virtues may require of the reader some understanding of Scottish history, and a consequent apprehension of Scott's purposes in blending the oral traditions of folklore and the minutiae of antiquarianism with a realisation of some of the often unwelcome facts of nineteenth-century economic and political life. Also needed, perhaps, is a sympathy with Scott's desire to synthesise, as Ralph Fox put it, the poetry and prose of life, because of his sensitive awareness of man in his social, legal, national, and regional society. And the reader requires an ability to appreciate Scott's linguistic subtlety, skill in narrative and inventiveness in presenting men and women against a background of such detail that, once known, they remain in the mind, for, even though they may be caricaturish characters, they are certainly individuals never known before.

This collection of essays has been designed, then, as an introduction to Scott which will stress both his general range and some of his particular merits. It explores some of the aspects of his work which, as Thomas Crawford has suggested in his contribution, need critical examination: Scott's own attitude to the processes of history, his idea of justice, his deployment of the supernatural, his use of language, his ability to recreate. (Hazlitt, usually so sensible, was unreasonable in remarking that while Shakespeare created Scott constructed.) His virtuosity and his achievement are treated by two contemporary critics, David Daiches and D. W. Jefferson, while Bagehot's magisterial survey of the Waverley Novels is also included as an example of how he appeared to a highly intelligent nineteenth-century critic.

Many recent views of Scott's novels seem to have been over-dominated by considerations of *The Heart of Midlothian*. It is time for his other work to be scrutinised with the same degree of attention, and to this end Donald Cameron has discussed *The Bride of Lammermoor* in this volume (we can hope for further reassessments later of such novels as *The Talisman* and *The Pirate*, which have peculiarly subtle virtues not always fully recognised).

The crux of the matter may well lie in a modern fashion for the purely contemporary. The past has to be made to seem relevant to the present before the younger reader will adventure into any account of it. The living concern Scott felt for it is exemplified in Professor Pottle's essay – the capturing of the stuff of human history as it is transmitted orally has an excitement about it not always understood through a purely literary reception of Scott. In this age, where sound matters so much, and oral rather than written communication so often appeals by its immediacy and informality, Scott's interest in the ballad and folk-tale is highly relevant. So too is his attitude to the political struggles which went to make up the age in which he lived. In this he learned much from Maria Edgeworth and her approach to the regional novel: her account of the manners of Ireland before and after the Act of Union is more explicit than his, but then the division of Ireland into landlord and peasant was clearer than the picture of Scotland he intended to draw. But his interpretation can have as much historical and social significance as Maria Edgeworth's, provided an effort is made to see what he was about. For Flora MacIvor, or indeed for Jeanie Deans, substitute Rosa Luxemburg, and ponder on the differing attitudes of George Lukács and

Denis Devlin as they are revealed in this volume. Then read *Old Mortality*, *Rob Roy*, *Redgauntlet*, *Guy Mannering*, and *The Talisman*; or better still, *The Tales of a Grandfather*.

How far was Scott responsible for our ideas about, our imaginative recreations of, say, Richard Coeur de Lion, in *The Talisman*, or of Mary Queen of Scots, in *The Tales of a Grandfather*, or of Elizabeth the First, in *Kenilworth*? How much did he influence the historical thinking of later nineteenth-century historians? It is certain that his influence on Europe was profound: he also had a pervasive effect on American, Australian, and Canadian writers – not least on Whitman – and he may well be affecting his Russian readers of today as much as those of the nineteenth century. However particular and parochial his concern, he is none the less a continental writer, not an insular one, because of his panoramic vision and his romantic conservatism. He strove to preserve and amalgamate – the past, he thought, had to come to terms with the present, and the present had to face a future which, paradoxically, could only be truly romantic through a vision of the realities of life. To portray them he needed his large canvas, his large figures, his chiaroscuro, and his particularly Scottish form of narrative art: often exasperating when prosy and the result of an excessively digressive technique, but in vitality, inventiveness, and sense of style unsurpassed in its creation of an actuality, a framework within which the vagaries and varities of many men and women can be interwoven convincingly. Scott's attitude towards them rests upon an uneasy, often delicately balanced tension between romance and realism. This arose out of his experience of a long established legal system far different from that of England, out of his sharp awareness of the integrity and importance of the individual within a clannish society. He recognised the dour toughness of mind and body engendered by armed conflict, and he reflected the enlightenment as it existed in the professional circles of Edinburgh in his day.

This city valued argument and appreciated rhetoric. Scott's versatility as a writer arose, in part, from his membership of this small society where one intellectual could successfully play many roles. In Scott's case poet and novelist enacted the blending of historian, antiquarian, and patriot with businessman, lawyer, sportsman, amateur soldier, and would-be laird; in him biographer, scholar, and journalist moderated the force of artistic intensity but not sufficiently to destroy his power to create *and* to construct. Though there were flaws he was cast in heroic mould; he saw his novels as dramatised history; and many nineteenth-century critics, *pace* Hazlitt, saw him in terms of Shakespeare. He had indeed an epic sensibility; and this he could indulge by constantly exercising his imagination in the service of his dreams. But he was a man whose dreams encompassed more than litera-ture, and because a reputation in the history of his own literature was not his final goal – he preferred, as has been said, the public's judgment rather than that of the critics – he brought into what he wrote so rapidly, so profusely, and often so poignantly, an exciting awareness of both the complexity of human life and its potenti-alities. Both remain in his work for the pleasure of the dis-criminating, imaginatively receptive reader who learns how to come to terms with and in the process to enjoy Scott's particular vision of what was worth preserving and what was worth develop-ing in a post-revolutionary age of change.

Leeds 1969   A. NORMAN JEFFARES

ABBREVIATED TITLES USED IN REFERENCES

A.	=	*The Antiquary.*
Ab.	=	*The Abbot.*
B.L.	=	*The Bride of Lammermoor.*
F.N.	=	*The Fortunes of Nigel.*
G.M.	=	*Guy Mannering.*
H.M.	=	*The Heart of Midlothian.*
I.	=	*Ivanhoe.*
K.	=	*Kenilworth.*
L.L.	=	*Lady of the Lake.*
L.M.	=	*A Legend of Montrose.*
O.M.	=	*Old Mortality.*
P.	=	*The Pirate.*
R.	=	*Redgauntlet.*
R.R.	=	*Rob Roy.*
Wav.	=	*Waverley.*

Thomas Crawford

SCOTT'S LIFE AND WORKS[1]

I

Scott's work arose out of a conflict between two traditions, family and national, in a period of Scottish history when both gentlemen and people had either to give way before the power of money, or allow themselves to be re-made by it, for better or worse. From his father, an Edinburgh solicitor or "Writer to the Signet", he got his practicality, his habits of sober calculation and diligent labour, his attachment to the Hanoverian establishment and therefore, in the last resort, to Anglicisation; from his mother came his obsession with the tales and legends of a heroic past, including stories connected with his father's ultimate ancestors, the Scotts of Buccleuch. Before his second birthday, in 1773, he fell victim to a form of poliomyelitis that left him lame for life. In order to recuperate he was sent off to his grandfather's farm at Sandyknowe, some forty miles from the capital, where he made contact with the strongest of all the formative elements that were later to mould his work – the oral tradition of the Borders, and, beyond that, of Scotland as a whole. From the shepherds he heard folk-tales and legends; from his grandmother, stories of the old days of the reivers and freebooters; from his uncle, eye-witness accounts of the Forty-Five and its aftermath; from servants and labourers, the songs and ballads that were still alive on the lips of the people. In later life he was to draw on popular literature of all kinds – broadside ballads, chapbooks, and published songs: but his first introduction to such material was *oral* and he never lost

[1] Reprinted from Thomas Crawford, *Scott*, Writers and Critics. Edinburgh (Oliver & Boyd) 1965, pp. 1–17, 109–14.

the sense of popular tradition as being not simply a matter of documents shut up in dusty archives, but rather a living record on the lips of successive generations. Many have claimed that there is a fundamental contradiction between Scott's romantic attachment to the past and his prosaic respect for the Hanoverian régime. Yet there are two things that should not be forgotten here – first, that his Toryism belonged just as much to the utilitarian present as to his dreams of Jacobite and feudal glories, and second, that because of the folk sources on which it fed, his love of "old, forgotten, far-off things" had its democratic as well as its conservative side.

In 1778 he began attending the High School in Edinburgh, where he first met with the rudiments of that classical, Anglicised, cosmopolitan, yet in some ways still obscurely national culture which was the distinctive creation of the upper classes in eighteenth-century Scotland. Between his thirteenth and fifteenth years, he attended classes at the University of Edinburgh only to be suddenly stricken with an internal haemorrhage that kept him in bed for many weeks.[2] He whiled away the time by omnivorous reading in the literature of fantasy and romance. The folk culture which he had absorbed at Sandyknowe began to coalesce with his sick-bed day-dreams, with orally transmitted stories about his own Border ancestors, and above all with the written account left by one of his forbears, Minstrel Scott of Satchells, who published in 1688, in verse, *A True History of Several honourable Families of the Right Honourable Name of Scott.* To Walter, the entire history of the Borders seemed but a heroic projection of the epic deeds of the clan Scott, and at first he viewed the history of the whole Scottish nation as simply an extension of Border history and therefore of the annals of his own family.[3] Thus the most vital experiences of his first sixteen years came together in an imaginative synthesis of the aristocratic and the folk, the epical and the romantic; and he had already established a reputation amongst his schoolfellows as a born storyteller.

In 1786 he entered his father's office as an apprentice Writer to

[2] J. G. Lockhart, *The Life of Sir Walter Scott,* 10 vols. Edinburgh (T. C. & E. C. Jack) 1902–3.
[3] C. F. Fiske, *Epic Suggestion in the Waverley Novels.* New Haven (Yale University Press) 1940, p. xi.

the Signet. Here he was exposed to the bourgeois side of his inheritance – to money values, worldly ambition, and sober calculation. The first step upwards was taken in 1788 when it was
decided that he should aim at the very highest branch of the legal
profession – that of advocate, the Scottish (and European) term
for what the English call a barrister. Soon Walter was mixing
freely with the Edinburgh élite and the social circle dominated by
the younger advocates and the officers of the garrison. There
followed another period of university study, which began with his
attendance at the class of Civil Law, and he took other classes
between 1788 and 1792, including Moral Philosophy from Dugald
Stewart. The good sense and refined sentiment which were
Stewart's supreme values mingled and contrasted with Scott's
other reading, and the two strands were present together in his
mind all the days of his life.

He early attended a class in German, which led directly to his
first literary attempts – translations of ballads, and, a few years
later, of Goethe's *Goetz von Berlichingen*.[4] During all this period, he
read omnivorously in the novel, in medieval romances, in Ariosto,
in Spanish literature. In 1792 he was admitted to the Scottish
Bar, and became a hard-drinking *habitué* of Edinburgh clubs, a
participant in anti-Jacobin riots, and, in 1797, an officer in the
local volunteers. These were the years of Revolutionary war, and
the young quartermaster – who always felt that he was a soldier
manqué – compensated for his frustrated longings for a life of
action by drilling on Portobello sands.[5] An unknown advocate's
life at this time was both leisured and precarious. In order to
gain a brief, he had to appear in the Parliament Buildings at nine
in the morning and hang about till two in the afternoon, walking
the boards, hoping against hope that some Writer to the Signet
would ask him to take part in his case. It was a calling that put a
premium on verbal fluency, in which men of various ages, all
trained in formal rhetoric, while away the long hours of waiting
in discussion or narration. The more eminent lawyers of Edinburgh had their own particular style, with its own cadences, its
own tricks of diction, its own fondness for facetious polysyllabic
circumlocution, its own pithiness and pawkiness, its own tendency
to make use of all the linguistic resources open to it, including the

[4] Lockhart, I, 144 ff., 229 ff., II, pp. 12, 16.   [5] Lockhart, I, 253 ff., 297 ff.

B

ability to modulate into the vernacular when the deeds and characters of the lower orders were in question. Above all, it was the style of men to whom time was no object, to whom it was natural to begin a story slowly and deliberately; and then, when once it was fairly under way, to digress into the minute description of attendant circumstances.[6] Walter Scott soon became well known in this society as an interesting *raconteur*, and he was later to carry its style, and even its very tone of voice, into his own prose. That style and that tone of voice were, at one level, emanations and survivals of the Edinburgh of thirty years before, when the towering "lands" of the old town still dominated the city, and all ranks daily intermingled on causeway and in close; at another level, they were style and tone of Jeffrey's *Edinburgh Review* – judicial, ponderous, and English, moving like a see-saw from one position to the other, but generally ending on a note of finality.[7]

Scott's nature was a highly emotional one beneath the gentlemanly veneer, and perhaps more akin to Burns's than is generally realised. When John Murdoch read *Titus Andronicus* to William Burnes's family circle, the children could not bear its mounting atrocities, and nine-year old Robert burst out that if the play were left in the house he would burn it.[8] Similarly, when an older cousin of Scott's had wrung the neck of Walter's pet starling, "I flew at his throat like a wild cat and was torn from him with no little difficulty."[9] From this, and one or two other scattered hints, it is tempting to surmise that the hereditary make-up of Burns and Scott was surprisingly alike. It is Scott's misfortune, however, that he succumbed to the spirit of "catch-the-plack" without much of a struggle. Though he turned against his father's Calvinism, Scott retained to the end the habits of diligence fostered by that creed, and the values of rational control and moral restraint which it shared with both Augustan ethics and utilitarianism. His most vivid experiences took place in the world of the historic imagination, not in personal relations.

We know little of his first love for the daughter of a small

[6] H. Cockburn, *Memorials of his Time*. Edinburgh & London (T. N. Foulis) 1909, Introd. and *passim*.

[7] *Westminster Review*, I (1824), pp. 206-49.

[8] *Works of Robert Burns*, ed. J. Currie, Liverpool, 1800, I, p. 63.

[9] H. J. C. Grierson, *Sir Walter Scott, Bart*. London (Constable) 1938.

tradesman in Kelso, except that he seems to have dropped her for snobbish reasons in 1788.[10] His second love for Williamina Belsches has always been something of a mystery, and the subject of legend since Lockhart's *Life*.[11] Williamina, a conventional and rather passive girl from a higher social position than Scott's own, gave him considerable encouragement, but became engaged to a banker's son (whom she later married) in October 1796. Scott certainly believed he had been jilted, and an interesting comment on the deep passions that smouldered beneath his self-discipline is provided by one of his friends in a contemporary letter: "I always dreaded there was some self-deception on the part of our romantic friend, and I now shudder at the violence of his most irritable and ungovernable mind."[12] Evidently, it was feared that he might commit suicide. Once more, we feel ourselves in the presence of a man whose innate temper seems much more volatile, even volcanic, than anything we normally associate with the Laird of Abbotsford. His less immediate reaction was to marry on the rebound – almost within the year – Charlotte Carpenter; and there seems to have been something hysterical, perhaps even factitious, about his feeling for her. Thus his friend Robert Shortreed reported that "Scott was *sair* beside himself about Miss Carpenter; – we toasted her twenty times over – and sat together, he raving about her, until it was one in the morning."[13] Even so, the marriage was soon qualified by the spirit of mercenary common sense, and it began to cool when Scott was able to measure Charlotte against the aristocratic women he met in London. One should put Shortreed's remark beside what Scott himself wrote to Lady Abercorn on 21 Jan. 1810:

> Mrs Scott's match and mine was of our own making and proceeded from the most sincere affection on both sides which has rather increased than diminished during twelve years' marriage. But it was something short of love in all its fervour which I suspect people only feel *once* in their lives.

[10] Grierson, pp. 17–18; *Letters of Sir W. Scott*, ed. H. J. C. Grierson and others, 12 vols., London (Constable) 1932, I, pp. 1–8.

[11] Lockhart, I, 182 ff. 275 ff.; A. Scott, *The Story of Sir Walter Scott's First Love*. Edinburgh, 1896, *passim*.

[12] Lockhart, I, p. 278.   [13] Lockhart, I, p. 312.

Folks who have been nearly drowned in bathing rarely venturing a second time out of their depth.[14]

The interpretation generally placed on this passage is that Scott believed he had already experienced a much more intense type of love – for Williamina: but Dame Una Pope-Hennessy has argued in favour of Charlotte Carpenter as Scott's one *real* love, maintaining that some of the original events and emotions of the courtship can be deduced from his poem, *The Bridal of Triermain*.[15] Certainly, there are passages in the *Journal* which show his distress when Williamina's name was mentioned – over thirty years after the jilting and seventeen years after her death: but his final remark, on 10 Nov. 1827, was: "To me these things are now matter of calm and solemn recollection, never to be forgotten, yet scarce to be remembered with pain."[16] The implication is that they *did* cause him considerable pain at the time: a deduction which is borne out by several incidents in the novels, such as his making Jonathan Oldbuck a victim of youthful unrequited love,[17] or his authorial comment on Tressilian's hopeless longing for Amy Robsart:

> Nothing is perhaps more dangerous to the future happiness of men of deep thought and retired habits than the entertaining an early, long, and unfortunate attachment. It frequently sinks so deep into the mind that it becomes their dream by night and their vision by day, mixes itself with every source of interest and enjoyment; and, when blighted and withered by final disappointment, it seems as if the springs of the spirit were dried up along with it.[18]

Some critics, following Adam Scott[19] and Lockhart,[20] have seen in certain of Scott's heroines re-creations of Williamina – Margaret

---

[14] *Letters of Sir Walter Scott*, II, p. 287.

[15] U. Pope-Hennessy, *The Laird of Abbotsford*. London & New York (Putnam) 1932, pp. 55 ff., 70–1.

[16] *The Journal of Sir Walter Scott*, eds. J. G. Tait and W. M. Parker. Edinburgh (Oliver & Boyd) 1950, p. 427.

[17] *A*. Dryburgh edn., London, 1892–5, p. 13 and *passim*.

[18] *K*. Dryburgh edn. London, 1892–5, pp. 306–7.

[19] A. Scott, *op. cit.*, p. 15 ff.   [20] Lockhart, II., p. 183.

of Branksome in *The Lay of the Last Minstrel*, Greenmantle in *Redgauntlet*, Matilda in *Rokeby*, and Diana Vernon in *Rob Roy*. But these are active, strong-willed, positive creatures who resemble Charlotte much more than the shadowy Williamina, and there seems little evidence for Edwin Muir's suggestion that

> his resolute burial of Williamina probably crippled his imagination on one side and made him incapable of portraying love in his novels. Certain of his women were drawn from Williamina, but they are remote and bloodless versions. It may be that he could not afford to resurrect her, or perhaps the ghost of his father forbade him.[21]

All that can be said is that Scott once loved Williamina; that he once felt pain at her rejection, which his phenomenal memory kept alive for years; that he quite probably also loved Charlotte; and that their marriage cooled off – perhaps also deepened into friendship. But what connexion this really had with his creative life, or with his reluctance or inability to portray sexual passion, must always remain a matter of speculation.

After 1797, Scott's main interests were work and business. His emotional, even vehement nature turned inward to the imaginative re-creation of the past, then outward to the risks and speculations made possible by the embodiment of that re-creation in works of literature sold on a favourable market. At the present time, Scott is often regarded as primarily an eighteenth-century survival,[22] as a writer who, whatever his innovations, looked backwards to Johnson, Swift, and even Dryden rather than towards such contemporaries as Coleridge and Keats. But this is to underestimate the complexities of literary history. Scott was the culmination of the antiquarian movement of the eighteenth century and the counterpart of his colleagues John Leyden, Joseph Ritson, and C. K. Sharpe, yet at the same time he represented the transformation of that movement by a type of imagination that was both "romantic" and historical. Just as Wordsworth's perception of external nature involved not a simple mirror image but a union of

[21] *From Anne to Victoria*, ed. B. Dobrée. London (Cassell & Co.) 1937, p. 534.

[22] P. Cruttwell, in *From Blake to Byron*, ed. B. Ford. Hammondsworth (Penguin) 1957, pp. 110–11.

subject and object that led to the transcendence of both by "a sense of something far more deeply interfused", so Scott's perception of an antiquarian object – manuscript, broadside, bartisan, or artifact – could in favourable circumstances lead to the bodying forth in fantasy of a past historical environment and social group. And just as the young Blake actually *saw* angels and shepherds, so the young Scott, I am sure, actually *saw* warlike clansmen, feudal lords, and ladies gay, as he wandered in historic places. We have his own admission that he gave himself an active role in these imaginings. "Since I was five years old I cannot remember the time when I had not some ideal part to play for my own solitary amusement," he wrote in his *Journal* for 27 Dec. 1825.[23] In the Introduction to Canto III of *Marmion* Scott answers the question "Why do you write as you do?" by attributing the characteristic cast of his mind to early childhood; his inclination for his own style and subjects is so powerful that he sometimes thinks it innate, and sometimes asks whether it is

> . . . fitlier term'd the sway
> Of habit, form'd in early day?
> Howe'er derived, its force confest
> Rules with despotic sway the breast,
> And drags us on by viewless chain,
> While taste and reason plead in vain.

That Scott realised his narrative poems were attempts to re-create and develop further the visual imaginings of a historically minded child is made clear by the continuation:

> And still I thought that shatter'd tower
> The mightest work of human power;
> And marvell'd as the aged hind
> With some strange tale bewitch'd my mind. . . .
> Methought that still, with trump and clang,
> The gateway's broken arches rang;
> Methought grim features, seam'd with scars,
> Glared through the window's rusty bars. . . .
> While stretch'd at length upon the floor,
> Again I fought each combat o'er,

[23] *The Journal of Sir Walter Scott*, p. 59.

Pebbles and shells, in order laid,
The mimic ranks of war display'd;
And onward still the Scottish Lion bore,
And still the scatter'd Southron fled before[24]

Not only the poems, but the Waverley novels themselves, were created by the visual intensity of Scott's historical imagination. That imagination, however, did not feed on emotions and sensations alone. Intellect also played its part – the intellect of that historicism which was one of the greatest achievements of eighteenth-century Scotland, which gave Scott a critical awareness of social history as a process and underlay, one suspects, the paper he read to the Speculative Society in 1791, "On the Origin of the Feudal System". Two other papers he read at the same time reveal an equally intellectual interest in history: "On the Authenticity of Ossian's Poems" and "On the Origins of the Scandinavian Mythology". The type of causation which he favoured – a necessary connexion – is indicated by a summary of the paper on Feudalism which he sent to his uncle, Captain Robert Scott, of Kelso:

> You will see that the intention and attempt of the essay is principally to controvert two propositions laid down by the writers on the subject; – 1st, That the system was invented by the Lombards; and, 2dly, that its foundation depended on the king's being acknowledged the sole lord of all the lands in the country, which he afterwards distributed to be held by military tenures. I have endeavoured to assign it a more general origin, and to prove that it proceeds upon principles common to all nations when placed in a certain situation.[25]

At its best, Scott's intellectual historicism – the historicism of the enlightenment – was fused with the "romantic-historical" perception of the past, but the way in which it found expression was determined in part by the state of the literary market. Scott, the dreamer, is an almost clinical example, not of the hero as man of letters, but of the man of letters as hero of industry (the phrase is

[24] *Poetical Works*, Dryburgh edn. London, 1892–5, I, pp. 203–5.
[25] Lockhart, I, p. 193.

Benedetto Croce's),[26] enslaved by a system of commodity production which he tried in vain to bend to his will. In satisfying the demands of his public, he provided them with images of virtue and the realisation in fantasy of their more decorous desires. But the value of the novels does not reside in the coincidence of certain private and public wish-fulfilments; it consists in their contribution to knowledge, to the methodology of history.[27] In a hackneyed phrase, "they make the past live"; and whatever lasting artistic significance they possess is connected with their "epistemological" worth.

Scott's first publications (1796), translations of Bürger's "Lenore" and of "Der Wilde Jäger", showed that he was alive to fashionable literary influences, and a meeting with "Monk" Lewis stimulated him to publish a collection of ballads which finally grew into the two volumes of *Minstrelsy of the Scottish Border*, published in Kelso in 1802. In 1799 he became Sheriff-depute of Selkirkshire, a post that brought him £300 a year till the end of his life, and in 1806 he was appointed one of the Clerks of the Court of Session at a salary of £800 a year. Although these posts involved him in a certain amount of routine work, they gave him security; anything that he might earn by writing would be additional to his salary. In 1802 he began his career as a literary capitalist by lending £500 to enable James Ballantyne, the Kelso printer, to set himself up in Edinburgh, and in 1805 he invested £5,000, the proceeds of an inheritance, in Ballantyne's business. In 1809, with the establishment of James's brother John as a publisher, Scott became the secret and effective controller of two complementary businesses.

In the intervening years, Scott turned from ballad-editing to romance-editing (*Sir Tristrem*, 1804), the writing of ballad-epics, and miscellaneous literary works, such as his edition of Dryden, with its fine introductory biography. *The Lay of the Last Minstrel* (1805), the first of the ballad-epics, was followed by *Ballads and Lyrical Pieces* (1806) and *Marmion* (1808), the latter being sold to Constable for 1,000 guineas down. His next poem, *The Lady of the*

[26] B. Croce, *European Literature in the Nineteenth Century*. London (Chapman & Hall) 1924, p. 68.

[27] G. M. Young in *Walter Scott Lectures*, ed. W. L. Renwick. Edinburgh (University Press) 1950, pp. 81–107.

Lake (1810), was even more profitable, for it was published by his own firm, John Ballantyne. Not only did the firm make a handsome profit, but the author himself drew 2,000 guineas directly. For *Rokeby* (1813) he was given £3,000, but it did not sell well, and the Ballantynes were hard hit by their loss. A stronger competitor with a new and irresistible line to sell had appeared on the scene – Lord Byron. After the general market trend had been confirmed by the poor reception given *The Vision of Don Roderick* (1811) and *The Bridal of Triermain* (1813), Scott moved into the field of the prose historical novel with the publication of *Waverley* (1814). There were still three longish poems to come – *The Lord of the Isles* (1815), the journalistic *Field of Waterloo* (1815) and *Harold the Dauntless* (1817): but apart from these, Scott's main endeavours were henceforth in prose – not only the novels, but works like his great edition of Swift (1814), *The Border Antiquities of England and Scotland* (1814–17), the nine volume *Life of Napoleon* (1827), the *Letters on Demonology and Witchcraft* (1830), and his child's history of Scotland and France, *Tales of a Grandfather* (1828–30). Though his plays were unsuccessful [*Halidon Hill* (1822), *Macduff's Cross* (1822), *The Doom of Devorgoil* (1830) and *Auchindrane, or the Ayrshire Tragedy* (1830)][28] his periodical criticism was both sane and acute,[29] the *Lives of the Novelists* (1821–4) and the essays on Chivalry, the Drama, and Romance contributed to the Encyclopaedia Britannica in 1814 and 1822 are still worth reading today.

What was the reason for the anonymity of the Waverley Novels? Why did Scott publish some of them as "by the Author of Waverley";[30] others, by an apparently different author, as *Tales of my Landlord*,[31] allegedly communicated by Jedediah Cleishbotham, schoolmaster and parish clerk of Gandercleugh, in the form of manuscripts written up by his assistant dominie Peter Pattieson

---

[28] Lockhart and Grierson, *passim*.

[29] M. Ball, *Sir Walter Scott as a Critic of Literature. Columbia University Studies in English*, ser. 2., vol. 2. No. 1. New York 1907, *passim*.

[30] *Guy Mannering* (1815); *The Antiquary* (1816); *Rob Roy* (1818); *Ivanhoe* (1819); *Kenilworth* (1821); *The Pirate* (1822); *The Fortunes of Nigel* (1822); *Peveril of the Peak* (1822); *Quentin Durward* (1823); *St. Roman's Well* (1824); *Redgauntlet* (1824); *Woodstock* (1826); *Anne of Geierstein* (1829).

[31] 1st series: *The Black Dwarf, Old Mortality* (1816). 2nd series: *The Heart of Midlothian* (1818). 3rd series: *The Bride of Lammermoor, A Legend of Montrose* (1819). 4th series: *Count Robert of Paris, Castle Dangerous* (1832).

from material orally supplied by the landlord of the village inn; others still as *Tales from Benedictine Sources*,[32] *Tales of the Crusaders*[33] and *Chronicles of the Canongate?*[34] Scott's motives were certainly mixed: the remnants of a snobbish feeling that novel-writing was not a suitable occupation for a gentleman; an apparent diffidence masking a morbid sensitivity to criticism; appreciation of the value of mystery as a publicity device; a shrewd estimate that if all the novels were unequivocally presented to the public as the work of a single man, they would be immediately dismissed as hurriedly produced pot-boilers; a mischievous love of anonymity for its own sake; and finally, the psychological need for a *persona* and the artistic desirability of a formal frame within which the narrative could be enclosed.

Still another reason for anonymity has been suggested – the wish to conceal the fact that the novels and poems were not written in the order in which they were published, and that some of them were composed many years before they were printed. Dame Una Pope-Hennessy claims that Scott had written the drafts of many novels between 1799 and 1805, and cites *Castle Dangerous* (1832), *The Betrothed* (1825), and *The Fair Maid of Perth* (1828) as early works hastily refurbished to meet the financial crisis. *Redgauntlet* (1824) too, in her opinion, "was an early experimental work".[35] Sir Herbert Grierson finds the hypothesis that there existed in 1814 a store of completed manuscripts to draw upon a most attractive one, but points out that "if there was any such reserve to fall back on, it was clearly unknown to his publishers, for they are constantly in a state of waiting for work long overdue". Grierson also remarks that, since the manuscript of *Redgauntlet* exists in Scott's handwriting "on paper manufactured by Cowan in 1822", it is unlikely that Dame Una's conjecture about that novel is a valid one.[36] More recently, R. D. Mayo[37] has demonstrated from an examination of the manuscripts

---

[32] *The Monastery, The Abbot* (1820).　　[33] *The Betrothed, The Talisman* (1825).
[34] 1st series: "The Two Drovers", "The Highland Widow", "The Surgeon's Daughter" (1827). 2nd series: *The Fair Maid of Perth* (1828).

[35] U. Pope-Hennessy, *Sir Walter Scott*. London (Home and Van Thal) 1946, pp. 20, 59, 64–9, 99.

[36] Grierson, pp. 152, 132.

[37] *P.M.L.A.*, LXIII (1948), pp. 935–49.

and above all of their watermarks that it is extremely unlikely that *any* of the novels were written much earlier than Lockhart and tradition would have us believe, unless we are prepared to hold that in each case Scott copied out the older drafts with his own hand and then carefully destroyed the earlier manuscripts. But Scott's penmanship was so rapid, and his facility at composition so remarkable, as to render this latter possibility quite unnecessary. Unless and until early drafts of these novels come to light in Scott's own hand, it must be assumed that Scott really did work at the phenomenal rate indicated by the dates of publication.

It is easy to make out a case for Scott as potentially the greatest of all our novelists, who failed to be so simply because of his enormous output. The size of that output was dictated by his need for money, which in its turn was determined by his middle-class dream of becoming a landed gentleman – an interpenetration of romance with reality more disastrous than any that occurs in the novels. There were two principal periods of monetary strain. The first took place in the years around 1813, when the two Ballantynes increasingly became "front men" for Scott's financial manipulations. The profits of James's printing house went to shore up John's business, while John's profits were eaten up by Scott's royalties. The situation was saved by Archibald Constable, whose fortunes were henceforth inextricably involved with Scott's. The publishing firm of Ballantyne went into liquidation in 1817 with debts amounting to some £10,000; James was confirmed as a printer, but John was transformed into an auctioneer. In 1812 Scott had moved to Abbotsford on the Tweed, and from then on was obsessed with buying more and more land and the over-decoration of his "castle". After the success of *Waverley*, he was able to maximise profits by having one publisher bid against another for his wares,[38] but in the end Constable won. In Grierson's judgment, the prices Scott asked from Constable were "fair and moderate". Nevertheless, "Scott put an undue strain on his publishers by his demands for payment in advance by bills, and on the printing business by the loans which he raised from it for expenditure on land and Abbotsford". Grierson points out that the firm of Constable was itself in a shaky condition during the whole period of Scott's connexion with it, and suggests that if it

[38] Grierson, pp. 133 ff.

had not been for Scott and the Waverley Novels Constable would
have crashed long before 1826.[39] Lady Scott died in the year of
the bankruptcy – the second and worse financial crisis, involving
the failure of Constable & Co. – and by Christmas 1827, less than
two years after the *débâcle*, Scott had driven his pen to earn almost
£40,000. His last years were ones of literary decline – apart from
his moving and noble *Journal* – and he died at Abbotsford on 21
Sep. 1832 after his return from a melancholy tour of Italy and
Germany, begun at the end of 1831. His creditors were paid off by
the posthumous sale of his copyrights.

Most commentators have praised Scott the man even when they
condemned Scott the poet and Scott the novelist.[40] Scott's
heroism, however, is not the heroism of a great creative writer,
but part of a mask, just as his gentlemanliness, his ease in society,
even his love of sport and social entertainment were also part of a
disguise. He had little of the artist's dedication to perfection
which characterises the literary hero of modern times, and none of
the ruthlessness which will sacrifice wife and children, wealth and
success to satisfy creative needs. Instead, he became a slave to the
business man's neurotic compulsion to work, and to the dreams
behind that compulsion. Scott's tragedy was that, as a creative
artist, he "sold out". His successes, great though they were, were
less than they ought to have been, for the simple reason that he
would not regard his obligations to literature as having precedence
over all other duties. He was a Lost Leader right from the time of
the *Lay of the Last Minstrel*. Yet behind the façade of the successful
gentleman and honest bankrupt there lay stoicism, melancholy,
and resignation; these were the end results of all his innate
passion. One is reminded of Ruskin's judgment that Scott's
poetry was the saddest that he knew,[41] and of the fact that Scott's
own favourite poems were *London* and *The Vanity of Human
Wishes*.[42] It is surely wrong to ascribe such abiding despondency
solely to memories of Williamina Belsches, and a misreading of
history to trace Scott's failure, as Edwin Muir does, to the idea

[39] *Op. cit.*, pp. 147–8, 220 ff.

[40] T. S. Eliot, "Byron", in *From Anne to Victoria*, p. 603.

[41] J. Ruskin, *Modern Painters*, 5 vols. London (Routledge) n.d., III, pp.
235–6.

[42] Lockhart, III, pp. 235–6.

that he "lived in a community which was not a community, and set himself to carry on a tradition which was not a tradition". Muir continues:

> His picture of life had no centre, because the environment in which he lived had no centre . . . Scotland did not have enough life of its own to nourish a writer of his scope; it had neither a real community to foster him nor a tradition to direct him . . . If the life he knew had had a real framework, if it had not been melting and dissolving away before him, he would have had a theme worthy of his powers, and he would have had no need to stuff his head with "the most nonsensical trash".

Muir thinks that when, towards the end of his life, Scott wrote, "What a life mine has been! half-educated, almost wholly neglected or left to myself," he was expressing "a sense of something lacking in the whole life of his country".[43] But a similar consciousness of neglect and national deficiency did not prevent James Joyce, originally the citizen of a small and backward country oppressed by a powerful neighbour, from writing great fiction. What was there in the Scotland of the early nineteenth century that absolutely prohibited a writer from becoming acutely aware of his country's real deficiences, as Joyce was later, or from taking up an uncompromising attitude towards his art? It would have been difficult, but not impossible, for a Scottish novelist of 1810–30 to express the fundamental contemporary tensions between Scotland and England; and this, as David Craig has pointed out, would have meant his doing justice "to both the inevitability of a process and the losses involved, while minimising or evading neither".[44] Scott's difficulties as an artist were due not so much to the ambiguous position of his nation, or any defect of life in the Scottish people – this was an age of industrial expansion and political and social ferment – as to a refusal to put art first, and a disastrous compromise with the market.

[43] E. Muir, *Scott and Scotland*. London, (Routledge) 1936, pp. 12–13, 173, 141–3.
[44] D. Craig, *Scottish Literature and the Scottish People 1680–1830*. London (Chatto and Windus) 1961, p. 152.

2

For many decades, readers of Scott have tended to be either contemptuously hostile or enthusiastically apologetic,[45] and he has been the target for generations of aesthetes. In E. M. Forster's opinion, Scott had a "trivial mind and a heavy style. He cannot construct. He has neither artistic detachment nor passion," but only "a temperate heart and gentlemanly feelings, and an intelligent affection for the countryside: and this is not basis enough for great novels." All he had was "the primitive power of keeping the reader in suspense and playing on his curiosity", of addressing his readers in "the voice of the tribal narrator, squatting in the middle of the cave, and saying one thing after another until the audience falls asleep among the offal and bones. . . . Yes – oh dear yes – the novel tells a story."[46] This last characteristic, which seems tiresome and irrelevant to Forster, is in fact Scott's chief formal quality, the aesthetic consequence of his antiquarian and folklorist interests. It would be interesting to have a study of Scott that made full use of Northrop Frye's concept of "low mimetic art" and the new respect for "romance" that is one result of Frye's method.[47]

Scott has also come under attack from recent Scottish writers. Edwin Muir once said that his novels mark "a definite degeneration" of the critical tradition of the eighteenth-century novel; they helped "to establish the mediocre and the trivial" as the main concern of the novel. "All that Scott wrote is disfigured by the main vice of gentility," says Muir; and he speaks of "Scott's inveterate indifference to truth" and "inability to recognize that truth is valuable in itself. . . . Scott was the first writer of really great powers to bow the knee unquestioningly to gentility and abrogate his responsibility."[48] C. M. Grieve (Hugh MacDiarmid) quotes Muir's judgment with approval, yet both Muir and Grieve are

[45] J. T. Hillhouse, *The Waverley Novels and their Critics*, Minneapolis and London, 1936, pp. 263 ff., 287.

[46] E. M. Forster, *Aspects of the Novel*. Harmondsworth (Penguin) 1962, pp. 38–49.

[47] N. Frye, *Anatomy of Criticism*, Princeton, N.J. (University Press) 1957 *passim*.

[48] E. Muir, quoted in C. M. Grieve, *Lucky Poet*, London (Methuen) 1943, pp. 197–8.

aware of Scott's "real bigness"; for Grieve, Scott's positive value consists "only" in "his objective treatment of parts of Scottish history and the partial revivification by his influence" of Flemish, Catalan, and other minority literatures.

> The whole direction of Scott's line was his regret for the quite needless passing of Scottish institutions, mannerisms, etc., into English . . . Properly, Scott can only be used as a battering-ram to drive home the failure of nineteenth-century and subsequent Scottish writers to crystallize phases of Scotland's developing history in the way Scott, though only poorly, did for certain previous periods . . . Where Scott is strong is in the way in which his work reveals that for a subject nation the firm literary bulwark against the encroaching Imperialism is concentration on the national language and re-interpretation of the national history. Scott's work has real value where a stand is being made against Imperialism.[49]

Most recent critics of Scott note the two features seized on by Forster, Muir, and Grieve – gentility, and the celebration of life in time. Unlike Muir, Ralph Fox thinks Scott marks a positive advance on his predecessors:

> He was a revolutionary innovator in one sense . . . his astonishing and fertile genius attempted to make the synthesis which the eighteenth century had failed to produce, in which the novel should unite the poetry as well as the prose of life, in which the naturelove of Rousseau should be combined with the sensibility of Sterne and the vigour and amplitude of Fielding.

Though Scott did not succeed, he was, according to Fox, "a glorious failure". His attempt miscarried for two main reasons, because he idealised the past and because

> he was unable to see man as he is. His characters are not the real men and women of history, but rather his own idealizations of the early nineteenth century English upper middle-class and commercialized aristocracy.[50]

[49] *Op. cit.*, pp. 202–3.
[50] R. Fox, *The Novel and the People*, London (Laurence and Wishart) 1937, pp. 65–6.

Fox also drew attention to Scott's historicism, a position which has been further developed by Arnold Kettle; and a similar attitude has been ably expounded from a non-Marxist point of view by David Daiches. Emery Neff is one of several who have tried to assess Scott's contribution to the growth of the historical outlook, not just in Britain but in Europe as a whole;[51] Donald Davie is the last of a long line of scholars who have demonstrated Scott's enormous contribution to Continental literature;[52] Una Pope-Hennessy follows Newman and some other nineteenth-century writers in demonstrating how Scott furthered a more tolerant attitude to Catholicism;[53] and Russell Kirk groups Scott with Burke as one of the two great inspirers of modern Conservatism.[54]

Scott's "idealisations of the early nineteenth-century upper middle class and commercialised aristocracy" occur mainly in his heroes and heroines, whose connexion with the social ideals and realities of the day has been explored by Alexander Welsh. For Welsh, Scott's fiction is projective rather than historical. "In the Waverley novels," he says, "by adhering steadfastly to the law of the land – so steadfastly that they may hardly act in any direction – the passive hero and blonde heroine demonstrate their respect for property and their fitness to possess and perpetuate the title to property for future generations."[54] Many readers would consider the minor- and lower-class characters in the Scottish novels exempt from Fox's strictures on idealisation, but David Craig has recently challenged this view. Like Grieve, but less intemperately, Craig sets limits to Scott's historical accuracy, for he claims that the Cameronian peasants and preachers in *Old Mortality* are as it were idealisations in reverse – at once caricatures of real Puritans and projections back into the past of Scott's conservative anti-Calvinism.[56] Can the novels be "true" if so many of their charac-

---

[51] E. Neff, *The Poetry of History*, New York and London 1961, pp. 117–18.

[52] D. Davie, *The Heyday of Sir Walter Scott*. London (Routledge and Kegan Paul) 1961, *passim*.

[53] U. Pope-Hennessy, *op. cit.*, pp. 73 ff.

[54] R. Kirk, *The Conservative Mind*, London (Faber and Faber) 1954, pp. 106–14.

[55] A. Welsh, *The Hero of the Waverley Novels* New Haven, Conn. (Yale University Press) 1963, p. 94.

[56] D. Craig, *op. cit.*, pp. 185–8.

ters are prejudiced distortions? Can they be genuine historical models if they contain "projective" heroes and heroines? The answer lies in Georg Lukács's insight that Scott's view is identical with the real logic of English history, which in its turn is nothing more nor less than the famous "English compromise".[57] Because of this, Scott pillories the extremists of both right and left, brings the moderates of both sides together, and makes the "eye" of his novels a middle of the road gentleman who is at all times the soul of honour. A society which could demand such an ideal representative was, indeed, the unheroic result of all the heroism before Scott's day – of 1588, 1649, 1660, 1688, 1715, and 1745. Now that same real logic of British history, as it had unfolded up to Scott's time, entailed the ingestion of Scottish nationality. It is therefore hardly surprising that the *littérateurs* of the Scottish Renaissance feel in duty bound to dismiss as so much pro-Union treachery that side of the novels which is the main source of their thematic unity.

Despite the enormous amount of critical analysis in our age, there has as yet been no full-scale modern study of Scott's writings. A definitive work is hardly possible until the debate on *The Heart of Midlothian* has been extended to all the Scottish novels, and until we have many more essays like Gordon's "*Waverley* and the Unified Design"[58] and Daiches' treatment of *Redgauntlet*.[59] There is also need for a fuller examination of Scott's ballad editing than any yet available; for a good book on the narrative poems; for an up-to-date study of Scott's criticism; for a monograph on his work as a historian and antiquarian; for an analysis of his prose style, using the techniques and insights of modern linguistics; for articles or monographs that would "place" his Journal and his Lives of Swift and Dryden in relation to recent discussion of the development of English biography and autobiography; and for a series of area studies, such as Alexander Welsh's *The Hero in the Waverley Novels*, or Coleman Parsons's forthcoming book on Scott's use of supernatural *motifs*.

[59] G. Lukács, *The Historical Novel* (1937), tr. H. & S. Mitchell, London (The Merlin Press) 1962, p. 37.

[58] S. Stewart Gordon, "Waverley and the 'Unified Design'", in *English Literary History* XVIII (1951) pp. 107–22.

[59] D. Daiches, "Scott's *Redgauntlet*", in *Essays Collected in Memory of James T. Hillhouse* eds. R. C. Rathburn and M. Steinman Jr., Minneapolis, 1958, pp. 49–59.

C

And what of the general reader? It is quite pointless to have a "Scott industry" for academics if the novels themselves are unread and if there is no possibility of their once more affecting contemporary writers. C. M. Grieve's suggestion that Scott's work is of value "wherever a stand is made against Imperialism" needs further development and qualification: for example, it was of greater use to small European nations in the nineteenth century than it can ever be in Africa today. Scott can still be a living influence upon those writers who wish to come to terms with all the contradictory forces in their country's history. In Latin America or European Spain, such an impulse may well be "anti-Imperialist"; in Hungary or Poland it may have an anti-Soviet content; and in Russia itself, it may even contribute to the liberation of Soviet literature by inspiring writers to re-create Whites and Reds, anarchists and social revolutionaries, Trotskyites and Stalinists, Kulaks and the leaders of punitive detachments, exactly as Scott tried to re-create the opposing factions of the century and a half before his time. A Russian Scott may be not only possible but necessary as the prelude to genuinely unfettered writing in his country. Moreover, tendencies that derive ultimately from Scott, or that he helped to transmit, remain valid for the literature of Europe and the English-speaking countries. I am referring to the play of the historical imagination upon the conflicts that have made us what we are, and to an art rooted in folk and popular traditions. If criticism leads to a new interest in Scott, and if a Scott revival helps writers and readers to a genuinely historical understanding of their own condition, then criticism will not have been in vain: it will have helped, not hindered, invention.

David Daiches

SCOTT'S ACHIEVEMENT AS A NOVELIST[1]

In the minds of too many teachers of English and in the pages of too many histories of English literature, Scott is an ultraromantic figure who began his literary career under the influence of a rather extravagant German romanticism, moved from there to a general passion for antiquities, ballads, and everything that was old, quaint, "gothic" or picturesque, and then proceeded to embody this passion in a series of historical novels full of scenes of heroism, chivalry, and general "tushery". In justice to those who present this distorted picture, it must be admitted that there is an element of truth in it: in his youth Scott *was* inclined to be romantic in this attitude, and in later life, when inspiration flagged, he fell back on "tushery" more often than his admirers would like to admit. But Scott's best and characteristic novels are a very different matter. They might with justice be called "antiromantic" fiction. They attempt to show that heroic action, as the typical romantic writer would like to think of it, is, in the last analysis, neither heroic nor useful, and that man's destiny, at least in the modern world, is to find his testing time not amid the sound of trumpets but in the daily struggles and recurring crises of personal and social life. The courageous and passionate Jacobite rebel of *Redgauntlet* is dismissed at the end of the novel with a smile and a shake of the head, all his heroics reduced to a kind of posturing that one pities rather than admires: but humble Jeanie Deans in *The Heart of Midlothian*, who has led her life among simple folk and walks to London to try to get a reprieve for a sister whose offence, after all,

[1] Reprinted from *Literary Essays*. Edinburgh (Oliver & Boyd) 1956; reprinted 1968, pp. 88–121. First published in *Nineteenth Century Fiction*, September 1951.

was both commonplace and sordid, *is* granted her heroic moment, her "crowded hour of glorious life", and she finds it when, against all the laws of romance and chivalry, she pours out her heart in her humble Scots diction before a queen who is less a queen than a normally sensitive woman. And when Jeanie tries to find out how she can repay the kindness of the noble duke who had helped her to her interview with the queen, she asks: "Does your honour like cheese?" *That* is the real Scott touch.

It is worth noting that the heroine of the novel considered by most critics to be Scott's best is a humble Scottish working girl. If Scott is to be classed as a romantic (though it is time we abandoned such indefinite and overworked terms), he must be regarded as at least as close to Wordsworth as to Coleridge. In the well-known fourteenth chapter of *Biographia Literaria*, Coleridge described the different parts he and Wordsworth had agreed to play in the production of *Lyrical Ballads*:

> It was agreed that my endeavours should be directed to persons and characters supernatural, or at least romantic; yet so as to transfer from our inward nature a human interest and a semblance of truth sufficient to procure for these shadows of imagination that willing suspension of disbelief for the moment which constitutes poetic faith. Mr Wordsworth, on the other hand, was to propose to himself as his object, to give the charm of novelty to things of every day, and to excite a feeling analogous to the supernatural, by awakening the mind's attention to the lethargy of custom. . . .

If we forget the tapestry figures of Scott's later novels and think of those which we cannot but remember most vividly – Jeanie Deans, Andrew Fairservice, Bailie Nicol Jarvie, Dugald Dalgetty, Saunders Fairford, Caleb Balderstone, Baron Bradwardine, Edie Ochiltree, and a host of others who live in the minds long after the plots of the novels in which they appear are forgotten – we realise that he is at least as successful in "giving the charm of novelty to things of every day" as in the task assigned to Coleridge. It is a well-known fact that the titular heroes of Scott's novels are generally less real than the minor characters who abound in his works. It is, as a rule, the unheroic characters who have the most vitality: the pusillanimous gardener, Andrew Fairservice, is a more real and, fundamentally, a more important character in *Rob Roy* than the theatrical Helen Macgregor.

What does this mean? Are we to conclude that Scott had skill in creating lively minor characters, but failed in the general plan and structure of his novels? The answer to this and other questions lies in an examination of the *kind* of historical novel that Scott wrote, of the part played by the historical element in those novels and its relation to the other elements.

To identify Scott as a historical novelist is to place him in a category too wide to be helpful. A historical novel can be primarily an adventure story, in which the historical elements merely add interest and a sense of importance to the actions described; or it can be essentially an attempt to illustrate those aspects of the life of a previous age which most sharply distinguish it from our own; or it can be an attempt to use a historical situation to illustrate some aspect of man's fate which has importance and meaning quite apart from that historical situation. Stevenson's *Kidnapped* comes into the first category, and here, too, are many of the novels of Dumas; the eighteenth-century "gothic" romances come into the second; and the best of Scott's novels come into the third. Obviously, the least important kind is the second, for it considers the past simply as picturesque, and picturesqueness is merely a measure of the ignorance of the beholder. Cowboys are doubtless picturesque to New Yorkers, but they are not so to themselves or to their immediate associates. Mexicans may be picturesque to North American tourists, and Scottish fishwives to English artists, but their picturesqueness is obviously not an intrinsic quality. It is no exaggeration to say that to treat history as picturesque is the most superficial and least significant way of treating it. Scott did so occasionally, when he was tired or too hard pressed, and occasionally, too, he mingled the first of my two categories with the second and produced a picturesque historical adventure story, as in *The Talisman*, which is reasonably good of its kind but the kind does not stand very high in the hierarchy of literary forms. The work by which he must be judged – for it is only fair to judge a writer by his most characteristic achievement – avoids the picturesque and seeks rather to bring the past nearer than to exploit its remoteness.

The novels on which Scott's reputation as a novelist must stand

or fall are his "Scotch novels" – those that deal with Scottish his-
tory and manners – and not even all of those. *Waverley, Guy
Mannering, The Antiquary, Old Mortality, The Heart of Midlothian,
Rob Roy, The Bride of Lammermoor, A Legend of Montrose,* and
Redgauntlet – all, except *Redgauntlet*, earlier novels – constitute
Scott's list of masterpieces. There are others of the Waverley
Novels of which no novelist need be ashamed, many with excel-
lent incidental scenes and memorable character studies, but this
group of Scottish novels all possess Scott's characteristic virtues,
and they represent his particular kind of fiction at its very best.

The fact that these novels are all concerned with Scottish history
and manners is intimately bound up with the reasons for their
being his best novels. For Scott's attitude to life was derived from
his response to the fate of his own country: it was the complex of
feelings with which he contemplated the phase of Scottish history
immediately preceding his own time that provided the point of
view which gave life – often a predominantly tragic life – to these
novels. Underlying most of these novels is a tragic sense of the
inevitability of a drab but necessary progress, a sense of the impotence of the traditional kind of heroism, a passionately regretful
awareness of the fact that the Good Old Cause was lost forever
and the glory of Scotland must give way to her interest.

Scott's attitude to Scotland, as Edwin Muir pointed out some
years ago in a thoughtful and provocative study,[2] was a mixture of
regret for the old days when Scotland was an independent but
turbulent and distracted country, and of satisfaction at the peace,
prosperity, and progress which he felt had been assured by the
Union with England in 1707 and the successful establishment of
the Hanoverian dynasty on the British throne. His problem, in
one form or another, was the problem of every Scottish writer
after Scotland ceased to have an independent culture of her own:
how to reconcile his country's traditions with what appeared to
be its interest. Scott was always strongly moved by everything
that reminded him of Scotland's past, of the days of the country's
independence and the relatively recent days when the Jacobites
were appealing to that very emotion to gain support for their
cause. He grew up as the Jacobite tradition was finally ebbing
away, amid the first generation of Scotsmen committed once and

[2] *Scott and Scotland.* London (Routledge and Kegan Paul) 1956.

for all to the association with England and the Hanoverian dynasty. He felt strongly that that association was inevitable and right and advantageous – he exerted himself greatly to make George IV popular in Scotland – yet there were strong emotions on the other side too, and it was these emotions that made him Tory in politics and that provided the greater blessing of leading him to literature and history.

Scott was two men: he was Edward Waverley and Baron Bradwardine, Frank Osbaldistone and (say) Mr Justice Inglewood, Darsie Latimer and, if not Redgauntlet himself, some one more disposed to his side than Darsie was. He was both the prudent Briton and the passionate Scot. And in many of his novels he introduces the loyal and respectable Englishman, allows him to be temporarily seduced by the claims of Scottish nationalism in one form or another, and then, reluctantly, sends him back to his respectable way of life again. So Edward Waverley leaves the Highlands and shakes off his associations with the Jacobite Rebellion, and Frank Osbaldistone leaves Rob Roy and returns to his father's London countinghouse.

This conflict within Scott gave life and passion to his Scottish novels, for it led him to construct plots and invent characters which, far from being devices in an adventure story or means to make history look picturesque, illustrated what to him was the central paradox of modern life. And that paradox admitted of the widest application, for it was an aspect of all commercial and industrial civilisations. Civilisation must be paid for by the cessation of the old kind of individual heroic action. Scott welcomed civilisation, but he also sighed after the old kind of individual heroic action. Scott's theme is a modification of that of Cervantes, and, specifically, *Redgauntlet* is Scott's *Don Quixote*.

Many of Scott's novels take the form of a sort of pilgrim's progress: an Englishman or a Lowland Scot goes north into the Highlands of Scotland at a time when Scottish feeling is running high, becomes involved in the passions and activities of the Scots partly by accident and partly by sympathy, and eventually extricates himself – physically altogether but emotionally not quite wholly – and returns whence he came. The character who makes the journey is the more deliberate side of Scott's character, the disinterested observer. His duty is to observe, to register the proper responses, and in the end to accept, however reluctantly, the proper solution. It is not this character but what he becomes involved in that matters: his function is merely to observe, react, and withdraw. To censure Scott for the woodenness of his heroes – characters like Edward Waverley, Frank Osbaldistone, and many others – is to misunderstand their function. They are not heroes in the ordinary sense, but symbolic observers. Their love affairs are of no significance whatsoever except to indicate the nature of the observer's final withdrawal from the seductive scenes of heroic, nationalist passion. Waverley does not marry the passionate Jacobite Flora MacIvor but the douce and colourless Rose Bradwardine; Waverley's affair with these two girls is not presented as a serious love interest, but as a symbolic indication of the nature of his final withdrawal from the heroic emotions of the past. That withdrawal is never quite one hundred per cent: Waverley does marry the daughter of a Jacobite, but of one who has given up the struggle, and Frank Osbaldistone does (we are old in and epilogue, though we are not shown how it happens) marry Di Vernon, but only after she has dissociated herself from her violently Jacobite father and after Frank himself has, for all his earlier rebellion against a life of commerce, returned to his father's business. These pilgrims into Scotland carry back something of older attitudes that must be discarded, but only as a vague and regretful sentiment. Even Rob Roy tells Frank that the wild and heroic life may be all very well for himself, but it won't do for his children – they will have to come to terms with the new world.

The Jacobite movement for Scott was not simply a picturesque historical event: it was the last attempt to restore to Scotland something of the old heroic way of life. This is not the place for a discussion of the real historical meaning of Jacobitism – I am concerned at present only with how Scott saw it and how he used it in his novels. He used it, and its aftermath, to symbolise at once the attractiveness and the futility of the old Scotland. *That* Scotland was doomed after the Union of Parliaments of 1707 and doubly doomed after the Battle of Culloden in 1746; the aftermath of 1707 is shown in *The Heart of Midlothian* and of 1746 in *Redgauntlet*. In both novels, explicitly in the latter and murmuring in an undertone in the former, there is indicated the tragic theme (for it *is* tragic) that the grand old causes are all lost causes, and the old heroic action is no longer even fatal – it is merely useless and silly. One thinks of the conclusion of Bishop Hurd's *Letters on Chivalry and Romance*: "What we have gotten by this revolution, you will say, is a great deal of good sense. What we have lost is a world of fine fabling." But to Scott it was more than a world of fine fabling that was lost; it was a world of heroic ideals, which he could not help believing should still be worth something. He knew, however, even before it was brought home to him by Constable's failure and his consequent own bankruptcy, that in the reign of George IV it was not worth much – certainly not as much as novels about it.

Scott has often been presented as a lover of the past, but that is a partial portrait. He was a lover of the past combined with a believer in the present, and the mating of these incompatible characters produced that tension which accounted for his greatest novels. Writers on Scott have often quoted that passage in the second volume of Lockhart's *Life* describing Scott's outburst to Jeffrey on the question of legal reforms: "He exclaimed, 'No, no – 'tis no laughing matter; little by little, whatever your wishes may be, you will destroy and undermine, until nothing of what makes Scotland Scotland shall remain.' And so saying, he turned round to conceal his agitation – but not until Mr Jeffrey saw tears gushing down his cheek." One might put beside this Scott's description of his purpose in his introduction to the *Minstrelsy of the Scottish Border*: "By such efforts, feeble as they are, I may contribute somewhat to the history of my native country; the peculiar features of whose manners and characters are daily melting and dissolving into those of her sister and ally. And, trivial as may appear such an offering, to the manes of a kingdom, once proud and independent, I hang it upon her altar with a mixture of feelings, which I shall not attempt to describe."

But we must remember that this lover of old traditions engaged heavily in financial speculations with publishers and printers and spent a great deal of his life poring over balance sheets and estimates of probable profit. One might contrast with the above quotations not only many of Scott's own practical activities but such remarks as the one he made in his Journal after dining with George IV: "He is, in many respects, the model of a British monarch. . . . I am sure such a character is fitter for us than a man who would long to head armies, or be perpetually intermeddling with *la grande politique*." He did not seem much worried there about ancient traditions.

It is this ambivalence in Scott's approach to the history of his country – combined, of course, with certain remarkable talents which I shall discuss later – that accounts for the unique quality of his Scottish novels. He was able to take an *odi et amo* attitude to some of the most exciting crises of Scottish history. If Scott's desire to set himself up as an old-time landed gentleman in a large country estate was romantic, the activities by which he financed – or endeavoured to finance – his schemes were the reverse, and there is nothing romantic in James Glen's account of Scott's financial transactions prefixed to the centenary edition of his letters. He filled Abbotsford with historical relics, but they were relics, and they gave Abbotsford something of the appearance of a museum. He thus tried to resolve the conflict in his way of life by making modern finance pay for a house filled with antiquities. This resolution could not, however, eliminate the basic ambivalence in his approach to recent Scottish history: that remained, to enrich his fiction.

This double attitude on Scott's part prevented him from taking sides in his historical fiction, and Sir Herbert Grierson has complained, though mildly, of this refusal to commit himself. "Of the historical events which he chooses for the setting of his story," writes Sir Herbert, "his judgment is always that of the good sense and moderated feeling of his own age. He will not take sides out and out with either Jacobite or Hanoverian, Puritan or Cavalier; nor does he attempt to transcend either the prejudices or the conventional judgment of his contemporaries, he makes no effort to attain to a fresh and deeper reading of the events." Sir Herbert partly answers his own criticism later on, when he concedes that Shakespeare likewise concealed his own views and did not stand clearly for this or that cause. But there are two questions at issue here. One is whether Scott's seeing both sides of an historical situation is an advantage or a disadvantage to him as a novelist; the other is whether, as Sir Herbert charges, he accepts the prejudices or the conventional judgment of his contemporaries and "makes no effort to attain to a fresh and deeper reading of the events". I should maintain that his seeing both sides is a great advantage, and, as to the second point, that, in terms of his art, Scott *does* attain to a fresh and deeper reading of the events. I say in terms of his art, because I of course agree that there is no overt philosophising about the meaning of history in Scott's novels. But the stories as told by Scott not only "attain to a fresh and deeper reading of the events", but also, I submit, do so in such a way as to illuminate aspects of life in general. As this is the crux of the matter, it requires demonstration in some detail.

Let us consider first *Waverley*, Scott's initial essay in prose fiction, and a much better novel, I venture to believe, than most critics generally concede it to be. I have already pointed out that the plot is built around an Englishman's journey into Scotland and his becoming temporarily involved in the Jacobite Rebellion on the Jacobite side. How does he become so involved and how are the claims of the Jacobite cause presented? First he becomes angry with his own side as a result of a series of accidents and misunderstandings (undelivered letters and so on) for which neither side is to blame. In this mood, he is willing to consider the possibility of identifying himself with the other side – the Jacobite side – and does so all the more readily because he is involved in friendly relations with many of its representatives. He admires the heroism and the clan spirit of the Highlanders, and their primitive vigour (as compared with the more disciplined and conventional behaviour of the Hanoverian troops with whom he formerly served) strikes his imagination. He becomes temporarily a Jacobite, then, not so much because he has been persuaded of the justice of the cause, or because he believes that a Jacobite victory would really improve the state of Britain, but because his emotions have become involved. It has become a personal, not a national, matter.

It should be noted further that Waverley goes into the Highlands in the first place simply in order to satisfy a romantic curiosity about the nature of the Highlanders, and it is only after arriving there that he succumbs to the attractions of clan life. Not that his reason ever fully succumbs: though he comes to realise the grievances of the Highland Jacobites, he has no illusions about their disinterestedness or their political sagacity, and even when he does surrender emotionally he remains critical of many aspects of their behaviour. Thus it is emotion against reason, the past against the present, the claims of a dying heroic world against the colder but ultimately more convincing claims of modern urban civilisation.

The essence of the novel is the way in which these conflicting claims impinge on Waverley. It is worth noting that Waverley, though he began his progress as a soldier in the army of King George, did not set out completely free of any feeling for the other side. Though his father had deserted the traditions of his family and gone over completely to the Government, his uncle, who brought him up, was an old Jacobite, and his tutor, too, though an impossible pedant who had little influence on Waverley, supported the old régime in both Church and State. Waverley thus belonged to the first generation of his family to begin his career under the auspices of the new world – specifically, to become a soldier of King George as a young man. That new world was not yet as firmly established in Scotland as it came to be during Scott's own youth: there was still a possibility of successful rebellion in Waverley's day, but none in Scott's. It was too late for Scott to become a Jacobite, even temporarily, except in his imagination, so he let Waverley do it for him. The claims of the two sides are a little more evenly balanced for Waverley than for Scott, yet even in the earlier period the issue is never really in doubt, and Waverley's part in the Jacobite rebellion must be small, and must be explained away and forgiven by the Government in the end. Above all, it must be a part entered into by his emotions on personal grounds rather than by his reason on grounds of national interest.

I have said that the essence of *Waverley* is the way in which the conflicting claims of the two worlds impinge on the titular hero. The most significant action there cannot concern the hero, but involves the world in which he finds himself. It is important, of course, that the hero should be presented as someone sensitive to the environment in which he finds himself; otherwise his function as the responsive observer could not be sustained. To ensure that his hero is seen by the reader as having the proper sensitivity, Scott gives us at the opening of the book several chapters describing in detail Waverley's education and the development of his state of mind. Waverley's education, as described in Chapter Three, is precisely that of Scott himself. By his undisciplined reading of old chronicles, Italian and Spanish romances, Elizabethan poetry and drama, and "the earlier literature of the northern nations", young Waverley was fitted to sympathise with the romantic appeal of the Jacobite cause and its Highland supporters. This, as we know from Lockhart and from Scott's own account, was Scott's own literary equipment, and it qualified Waverley to act for him in his relations with the Scottish Jacobites.

Waverley became involved in the affairs of the Highlands through a visit to his uncle's old friend, Baron Bradwardine, the first in Scott's magnificent gallery of eccentric pedants. The baron remains a sort of half-way house between the two sides: a Jacobite who takes the field in '45, he is nevertheless not as completely committed to the cause as such characters as Fergus MacIvor and his sister Flora, and at the end he is pardoned and restored to his estate. Bradwardine is a Jacobite more from his love of ancient traditions than out of any political feeling, and it is therefore proper that he should survive to indulge his love of the past harmlessly in antiquarian studies and pedantic conversation. Scott can afford to relax with such a character, as with other minor characters who do not serve to symbolise the extremes of one side or the other: and that is why we find so many of Scott's minor characters more real than some of the principals – their function is to live in the story and represent the more realistic, tolerant life of more ordinary folk whose destinies are less affected by changes of dynasty than those of higher rank. This is particularly true of such minor characters as Davie Gellatley and Duncan Macwheeble. Their function is similar to that of Justice Shallow and Master Silence in Shakespeare's *Henry IV*: they illustrate a kind of life that adapts itself easily to changes and is not really implicated in the civil conflicts surrounding it.

The characters in *Waverley* are marshalled with great skill. First we have the protagonists on either side: Fergus and Flora MacIvor represent different aspects of the Jacobite cause, Fergus displaying that mixture of ambition and loyalty which Scott regarded as an important characteristic of Highland chiefs, Flora embodying a purer and more disinterested passion for the cause; and on the other side is Colonel Talbot, the perfect English gentleman, despising the uncouth ways of the wild Highlanders and representing civilised man as Scott thought of him. In between the two sides

stands Baron Bradwardine, the nonpolitical Jacobite, who does
not have to die for his faith but is content to be left in the end
with his antiquities and old-fashioned code of behaviour. Then
there are the minor characters on either side, who represent either
life persisting in ordinary human forms in spite of everything, or,
as in the case of Evan Dhu Maccombich, the humble follower who
does what he considers his duty out of simple loyalty to his ideals
and without any understanding of the issues at stake. And in the
centre is Edward Waverley, registering his creator's reactions to
what goes on around him. He admires courage, honours loyalty
on either side, welcomes the victory of the Hanoverians yet
sorrows over the fate of the fallen – and then returns for good to
the victorious side, taking with him a wife from among the less
fanatical of the Jacobites. His attitude to Fergus MacIvor is not
unlike that of Brutus to Caesar – "there is tears for his love; joy for
his fortune; honour for his valour; and death for his ambition".

If there is no new historical interpretation of the Jacobite Rebellion in this novel, there is certainly a profound interpretation
of what it meant in terms of human ambitions and interests and
in terms of that conflict between the old world of heroic action
and the new world of commercial progress which, as we have
seen, was so central to Scott. It is the same kind of interpretation
that we find in Shakespeare's *Henry IV*: while accepting the most
enlightened contemporary view of the history involved, it uses
that history as a means of commenting on certain aspects of life
which, in one form or another, exist in every age. This is surely
the highest function of the historical novel as of the history play.

The high-ranking characters in the novels are often the most
symbolical, and they cannot therefore easily step out of their
symbolic role in order to act freely and provide that sense of
abundant life which is so essential to a good novel. This is therefore achieved by the minor characters (and here again the comparison with Shakespeare suggests itself). The "humours" of
Baron Bradwardine, the complacent professional zeal of Bailie
Macwheeble, the simple and eloquent loyalty of Evan Dhu – these
give *Waverley* its essential vitality, though I think it is a fault in the
novel (one which Scott corrected in his subsequent work) that
they play too small a part while too large a part is played by the
more rigid actions of the major figures. The tragic sense that

romantic man must compromise with his heroic ideals if he is to survive in the modern world gives way as the book comes to a close to the less elevated sentiments of the realistic common man. Waverley, leaving Carlisle after the execution of Fergus MacIvor makes a motion as though to look back and see his friend's head adorning the battlements, but – here, significantly, that whole episode ends – he is prevented by his Lowland Scots servant Alick Polwarth, who tells him that the heads of the executed men are on the gate at the other side of the town: "They're no there. . . . The heads are ower the Scotch yate, as they ca' it. It's a great pity of Evan Dhu, who was a very well-meaning, good-natured man, to be a Hielandman; and indeed so was the Laird o' Glennaquoich too, for that matter, when he wasna in ane o' his tirrivies." Similarly, when Waverley, now heir to a fortune, communicates to Bailie Duncan Macwheeble his plans to marry Rose Bradwardine, the worthy legal man brings the level of the action effectively down to that of ordinary professional success.

> "Lady Wauverley? – ten thousand a-year, the least penny! – preserve my poor understanding!"
> "Amen with all my heart," said Waverley, "but now, Mr Macwheeble, let us proceed to business." This word had a somewhat sedative effect, but the Bailie's head, as he expressed himself, was still "in the bees". He mended his pen, however, marked half a dozen sheets of paper with an ample marginal fold, whipped down Dallas of St Martin's Styles from a shelf, where that venerable work roosted with Stair's Institutions, Direleton's Doubts, Balfour's Pratiques, and a parcel of old account books – opened the volume at the article Contract of Marriage, and prepared to make what he called a "sma' minute, to prevent parties frae resiling".[3]

Thus the marriage of the heir to the Waverley estates to the daughter of the pardoned Jacobite is made real by a lawyer's jotting down a "sma' minute, to prevent parties frae resiling". Though we may have to abandon our dreams, the author seems to be saying, life goes on in spite of us, with its small daily matters for tears or laughter, of which, in spite of all alarms and excursions, human existence largely consists. It was because, at bottom

[3] *Wav.*, Ch. 66.

Scott had a tremendous feeling for this kind of ordinary daily life that he was able to suppress the implicit tragic note in so many (but not in all) of his novels and leave the reader at the end to put heroic ideals behind him with a sigh and turn with a smile to the foibles of ordinary humanity. And I should add that that smile is always one of tolerant fellow-feeling, never of condescension.

The subtitle of *Waverley* is "'Tis Sixty Years Since", and the phrase is repeated many times throughout the book. It deals, that is to say, with a period which, while distant enough to have an historical interest, was not altogether out of the ken of Scott's own generation. In the preface to the first edition of *The Antiquary*, his third novel, Scott wrote: "The present work completes a series of fictitious narratives, intended to illustrate the manners of Scotland at three different periods. *Waverley* embraced the age of our fathers, *Guy Mannering* that of our youth, and the *Antiquary* refers to the last years of the eighteenth century." (Scott, it will be remembered, was born in 1771.) As Scott comes closer to his own day, the possibilities for heroic action recede and the theme of the lost heir is introduced as a sort of substitute. It was with recent Scottish history that Scott was most concerned, for the conflict within himself was the result of relatively recent history. The Jacobite Rebellion of 1745 was the watershed, as it were, dividing once and for all the old from the new, and Scott therefore began his novels with a study of the relation between the two worlds at that critical time. It was not that the old Scotland had wholly disappeared, but that it was slowly yet inevitably disappearing that upset Scott. Its disappearance is progressively more inevitable in each of the next two novels after *Waverley*.

Guy Mannering is not in the obvious sense a historical novel at all. It is a study of aspects of the Scottish situation in the days of the author's youth, where the plot is simply an excuse for bringing certain characters into relation with each other. Once again we have an Englishman – Colonel Mannering, who, like Edward Waverley, shares many of his creator's characteristics – coming into Scotland and surrendering to the charm of the country. Scott has to get him mixed up in the affairs of the Bertrams in order to keep him where he wants him. Round Guy Mannering move gipsies, smugglers, lairds, dominies, lawyers, and farmers, and it is to be noted that none of these characters, from Meg Merrilies to Dandie Dinmont, belongs to the new world: they are all essentially either relics of an earlier age, like the gipsies, or the kind of person who does not substantially change with the times, like that admirable farmer Dandie. These people are made to move around the Bertram family, or at least are brought into the story through some direct or indirect association with that family, and the family is decayed and impoverished. The lost heir is found and restored, and, largely through the benevolent offices of an English colonel, a Scottish landed gentleman is settled again on his ancestral acres. That is how things happen in the days of Scott's youth: no clash of arms or open conflict of two worlds, but the prophecies of gipsies, the intrigues of smugglers, the hearty activities of farmers, all set against the decay of an ancient family and all put to right in the end with the help of a gipsy, an English officer, and a Scottish lawyer. If the heroic element is less than in *Waverley*, the element of common life is greater, and the two virtues of honesty (in Dinmont) and urbanity (in Counsellor Pleydell) eventually emerge as those most worth while.

Counsellor Pleydell is a particularly interesting character because he represents that combination of good sense and humanity which Scott so often thought of as mediating between extremes and enabling the new world to preserve, in a very different context, something of the high generosity of the old. Pleydell is a lawyer, essentially middle-class and respectable, but he is drawn with such sympathy that he threatens to remove most of the interest from the rather artificial main plot and share with Dandie Dinmont the reader's chief attention. If the gipsy Meg Merrilies provides something of the old-world romantic note – and she does so with great vigour and effectiveness – the lawyer and the farmer between them represent the ordinary man providing comfort for the future. The bluff courage and honesty of the farmer and the kindly intelligence of the lawyer dominate the story at the end.

Scott knew much of rural superstitions from the ballads, and he saw them as part of the ancient Scotland no less than Jacobitism or the feudal system. The gipsy prophetess Meg Merrilies is thus in a way the counterpart in this novel of Fergus MacIvor in *Waverley*. She, too, dies a violent death at the end of the book, and the stage is left to the representatives of the less spectacular virtues. The different strata of dialogue here are as clear as in the earlier novel.

D

First listen to the simple yet eloquent speech of the gipsy:

> "Ride your ways," said the gypsy, "ride your ways, Laird of Ellangowan – ride your ways, Godfrey Bertram! – This day have ye quenched seven smoking hearths – see if the fire in your ain parlour burn the blyther for that. Ye have riven the thack off seven cottar houses – look if your ain roof-tree stand the faster. – Ye may stable your stirks in the shealings at Derncleugh – see that the hare does not couch on the hearth-stane at Ellangowan. – Ride your ways, Godfrey Bertram – what do you glower after our folk for? – There's thirty hearts there, that wad hae wanted bread ere ye had wanted sunkets, and spent their life-blood ere ye had scratched your finger. Yes – there's thirty yonder, from the auld wife of an hundred to the babe that was born last week, that ye have turned out o' their bits o' bields, to sleep with the tod and the black-cock in the muirs! – Ride your ways, Ellangowan. – Our bairns are hinging at our weary backs – look that your braw cradle at hame be the fairer spread up – not that I am wishing ill to little Harry, or to the babe that's yet to be born – God forbid – and make them kind to the poor, and better folk than their father! – And now, ride e'en your ways; for these are the last words ye'll ever hear Meg Merrilies speak, and this is the last reise that I'll ever cut in the bonny woods of Ellangowan."[4]

This is the high note, popular yet passionate, the note that Scott learned from the Border ballads. If one puts beside this the conversation between Counsellor Pleydell and Dandie Dinmont in Chapter Thirty-six and compares again with that the magnificent domestic scene at the Dinmont farm of Charlies-hope in Chapter Twenty-four (both unfortunately too long for quotation), one gets a view of the range of Scott's dialogue – from the passionate outburst of the gipsy to the humorous realism of the talk between Pleydell and Dinmont and the sympathetic domestic scene at Charlies-hope. These three passages illustrate Scott's basic equipment as a realistic "social" novelist.

Finally, one should note a brief remark of Mr Pleydell's which illustrates perfectly his position as a sensible but sensitive man who

[4] G.M., Ch. 8.

had made a proper adjustment between his emotions and his way of life. Colonel Mannering has asked him what he thinks of the points of difference between the passionate old Covenanting clergy and the modern moderates, and this is his reply:

> "Why, I hope, Colonel, a plain man may go to heaven without thinking about them at all – besides, *inter nos*, I am a member of the suffering and Episcopal Church of Scotland – the shadow of a shade now, and fortunately so – but I love to pray where my fathers prayed before me, without thinking worse of the Presbyterian forms, because they do not affect me with the same associations."[5]

I cannot attempt, in the space at my disposal, to give an account of the action of *Guy Mannering* or to illustrate how Scott manipulates his characters in order to produce the required picture of the Scotland of his youth. Nor can any account of the richness and vitality of the novels be given by a few brief quotations. But I must note that here, as so often in Scott, the formal plot is merely a device for bringing the necessary characters and situations into the novel: it is not a plot in the Aristotelian sense at all, but merely a stage contrived to accommodate the appropriate actors. Yet the action is not episodic: it all contributes to a central pattern, which is not, however, that laid down by the external plot.

One further point before I leave *Guy Mannering*. The nearer to the present Scott moves the more likely he is to present men of noble birth simply as fools. Those who think of Scott as the passionate defender of aristocratic privilege should note that the most highly born character in *Guy Mannering* is Sir Robert Hazlewood, whom Scott represents as a pompous ass, so obsessed by the dignity of his ancient lineage that he can talk of little else, and in other respects a selfish and foolish nonentity. Similarly, Sir Arthur Wardour of *The Antiquary*, equally obsessed by his noble ancestry, is shown as a gullible fool, and much less sympathetic than the antiquary himself, who, it should be noted, is of humble origin and a Whig.

The scene of *The Antiquary* is the Scotland of Scott's own day. The external plot, which is once again that of the lost heir, is, as usual, not to be taken seriously: its function is to bring the faintly

[5] *Op. cit.*, Ch. 37.

drawn Englishman Lovel into Scotland and so set the appropriate characters into motion. In three successive novels Scott begins by bringing an Englishman into Scotland, by sending forth an observer to note the state of the country at the time represented by the novel's action. Lovel, of course, is no more the hero of *The Antiquary* than Christopher Sly is the hero of *The Taming of the Shrew*, and his turning out at the end to be the lost heir of Glenallan is the merest routine drawing down of the curtain. The life of the novel – and it has abundant life – centres in the Scottish characters whom the plot enables Scott to bring together, and in their reactions to each other. Jonathan Oldbuck, the antiquary (and it should be noted that there are antiquaries of one kind or another in a great many of Scott's novels) represents one kind of compromise between the old world and the new that is possible in the modern world. A descendant of German printers, a man of no family in the aristocratic sense, and a Whig in politics to boot, Oldbuck is yet fascinated by Scotland's past and spends his life in antiquarian studies. In the modern world the past becomes the preserve of the interested historian, whatever his birth or politics, while those who attempt to live in the past in any other way become, as Sir Arthur Wardour becomes, ridiculous and insufferable. Sir Arthur, continually lording it over the antiquary because of his superior birth, nevertheless knows less of Scottish history and traditions than the antiquary and is so vain and stupid that he falls a prey to the designing arts of an imposter who swindles him out of his remaining money, so that he has to be rescued through the influence of his friends. Sir Arthur is the comic counterpart of the tragic hero of *Redgauntlet*: both illustrate the impossibility of seriously living in the past after 1746. In *The Antiquary* the prevailing atmosphere is comic. This is unusual in Scott, however often he may end his novels with a formal "happy ending" so far as the superficial plot is concerned. The melodramatic Glenallan episode in this novel and the drowning of the young fisherman Steenie Mucklebackit give a sense of depth and implication to the action, but they do not alter its essential atmosphere. In this novel, too, the hero is the character who plays the dominant part – the antiquary himself, the good-humoured, pedantic, self-opinionated, essentially kindly gentleman who is in many respects a latter-day version of Baron Bradwardine. Round

him move Edie Ochiltree, the wandering beggar; the humble
fishing family of the Mucklebackits; Caxon, the comic barber who
deplores the passing of powdered wigs but takes comfort in the
three yet left to him; the foreign imposter Dousterswiver; and
other characters illustrative of the kind of life the east coast of
Scotland (apart from the big cities) had settled down to by the end
of the eighteenth century.

The plot of *The Antiquary* is even less important than that of
Guy Mannering. It is essentially a static novel, in a sense a novel of
manners, and the parts that stand out in the memory are such
scenes as the gathering in the Fairport post office when the mail
comes in, the antiquary holding forth at dinner or at a visit to a
neighbouring priory, Sir Arthur and his daughter trapped by the
tide and rescued by Edie Ochiltree and Lovel, the interior of the
humble fishing cottage after Steenie's drowning, and similar
pictures, many of them admirable genre portraits in the Flemish
style. And as always in Scott, the novel lives by its dialogue, the
magnificent pedantic monologues of Oldbuck, the racy Scots
speech of Edie Ochiltree, the chattering of gossips in the post
office, the naïve babbling of Caxon. No action, in these early
novels of Scott, ever comes to life until somebody talks about it,
whether in the sardonic tones of Andrew Fairservice, the vernacular declamations of Meg Merrilies, or the shrewd observations
of Edie Ochiltree. And it is to be noticed that the dialogue is at
its best when it is the speech of humble people: Scott could make
them live by simply opening their mouths.

The characteristic tension of Scott's novels is scarcely percep-
tible in *The Antiquary*, though I think it can be discerned by those
who look carefully for it. In *Old Mortality* it is present contin-
uously and is in a sense the theme of the story. In this novel Scott
goes back to the latter part of the seventeenth century to deal with
the conflict between the desperate and embittered Covenanters
and the royal armies intent on stamping out a religious disaffection
which was bound up with political disagreements. Though this
was an aspect of Scottish history which, in its most acute phases at
least, was settled by the Revolution of 1689, it represented a type
of conflict which is characteristic of much Scottish history and
which Scott saw as a struggle between an exaggerated royalism
and a fanatical religion. It should be said at the outset that as a

historical novel in the most literal sense of the word – as an accurate picture of the state of affairs at the time – this is clearly Scott's best work. Generations of subsequent research have only confirmed the essential justice and fairness of Scott's picture of both sides. The only scholar ever seriously to challenge Scott on this was the contemporary divine, Thomas McCrie, who made an attack on the accuracy of Scott's portrait of the Covenanters, but posterity has thoroughly vindicated Scott and shown McCrie's attack to have been the result of plain prejudice.

But we do not read *Old Mortality* for its history, though we could do worse. We read it, as Scott wrote it, as a study of the kinds of mentality which faced each other in this conflict, a study of how a few extremists on each side managed, as they so often do, to split the country into warring camps with increasing bitterness on the one side and increasing cruelty on the other. Scott's interest, of course, would lie in the possibilities for compromise, in the technique of adjustment, in the kind of character who can construct a bridge between the two factions. And just as Edward Waverley, the loyal Englishman, became involved in spite of himself on the Jacobite side in 1745, so Harry Morton, the sensible, moderate, good-hearted Scot, becomes involved in similar circumstances on the side of the Covenanters. The Fergus MacIvor of the Covenanters is the magnificently drawn fanatic, Balfour of Burley. The leader of the other side, the famous Claverhouse, "Bonnie Dundee", is introduced in person, and a convincing and powerful portrait it is. Between these extremes are all those whom varying degrees of zeal or loyalty brought into one camp or the other. The novel contains one of Scott's finest portrait galleries. On the Government side there is Claverhouse himself, his nephew Cornet Grahame, the proud Bothwell, descendant of kings, that perfect gentleman Lord Evandale, Major Bellenden, the veteran campaigner, and some minor figures. On the Covenanting side there is a whole array of clergymen, from the fanatical Macbriar to the more accommodating Poundtext, each presented with an individuality and with an insight into the motives and minds of men more profound than anything Scott had yet shown. The realistic, commonsense Cuddie Headrigg trying, in the interests of their common safety, to put a curb on the tongue of his enthusiastic Covenanting mother produces some of the finest tragicomedy (if one may call it that) in English literature: there are many passages here that would be worth quoting if space did not forbid. The pious and kindly Bessie Maclure shows the Covenanting side at its best, while the generous Lord Evandale plays the same part for the other side. It is in the gradations of the characters on either side that Scott shows his greatest insight into the causes of civil conflict. Total conviction is comparatively rare on either side, and when it is, it is either bitter and passionate, as in Balfour of Burley, or nonchalantly self-assured, as in Claverhouse.

If Scotland had not torn itself in two before the issues presented in the eighteenth century were ever thought of, the fate of the country might have been different, and Scott's study of the last of the Scottish civil wars before the Jacobite Rebellions is thus linked with his major preoccupation – the destiny of modern Scotland. If moderate men on both sides could have won, the future would have been very different. But, though there were moderate men on both sides and Scott delighted to draw them, their advice in the moments of crisis was never taken. There is no more moving passage in the novel than the description of Morton's vain attempt to make his fanatical colleagues behave sensibly before the Battle of Bothwell Brigg. There is a passion behind the telling of much of this story that is very different from the predominantly sunny mood of *The Antiquary*. The extremists prevail, the Covenanting army is destroyed, and a victorious Government takes a cruel revenge on embittered and resolute opponents. This is one novel of Scott's where the moderate men do not remain at the end to point the way to the future. Morton goes into exile and can return to Scotland only after the Revolution. Lord Evandale meets his death at the hands of a desperate man. And if the leaders on both sides – the ruthless fanatic Burley and the equally ruthless but gay cavalier Claverhouse – both go to their death before the novel ends, there is no particular hope implied by their elimination.

Morton returns to marry his love, and the prudent Cuddie settles down to be a douce henpecked husband, but the life has gone out of the novel by this time. The dominating figure, Balfour of Burley, may have been an impossible fanatic, but he represented a kind of energy possessed by none of the wiser

characters. Harry Morton, the observer, the man who sees something good on both sides and is roped into the Covenanting side
by a series of accidents, represents the humane, intelligent liberal
in a world of extremists. *Old Mortality* is a study of a society which
had no place for such a character: it is essentially a tragedy, and
one with a very modern ring.

If *Old Mortality* is, from one point of view, Scott's study of the
earlier errors which made the later cleavage between Scotland and
her past inevitable (for it is true to say that after the Covenanting
wars the English saw no way but a union of the two countries to
ensure the perpetual agreement of the Scots to the king chosen by
England and to prevent the succession question from being a
constant bugbear), *Rob Roy* is a return to his earlier theme, a study
of eighteenth-century Highland grievances and their relation to
Scotland's destiny. It is, in a sense, a rewriting of *Waverley* and
the main theme is less baldly presented. The compromise character here is the ever-delightful Bailie Nicol Jarvie, the Glasgow
merchant who is nevertheless related to Rob Roy himself and,
for all his love of peace and his commercial interests, can on
occasion cross the Highland line into his cousin's country and
become involved in scenes of violence in which, for a douce
citizen of Glasgow, he acquits himself very honourably.

Rob Roy represents the old heroic Scotland, while the worthy
Bailie represents the new. The Union of 1707 may have been a
sad thing for those who prized Scotland's independence, but to
the Bailie and his like it opened up new fields for foreign trade,
and brought increased wealth. "Whisht, sir! – whisht!" he cried
to Andrew Fairservice when the latter complained of the Union.
"It's ill-scraped tongues like yours that make mischief between
neighbourhoods and nations. There's naething sae gude on this
side o' time but it might have been better, and that may be said o'
the Union. Nane were keener against it than the Glasgow folk,
wi' their rabblings and their risings, and their mobs, as they ca'
them nowadays. But it's an ill wind that blaws naebody gude –
let ilka ane roose the ford as they find it. – I say, let Glasgow
flourish! whilk is judiciously and elegantly putten round the
town's arms by way of by word. Now, since St Mungo catched
herrings in the Clyde, what was ever like to gar us flourish like the
sugar and tobacco trade? Will anybody tell me that, and grumble

at a treaty that opened us a road west-awa' yonder?" Rob Roy is courageous and sympathetic, and Helen Macgregor, his wife, is noble to the verge of melodrama, but they represent a confused and divided Highlands and are, after all, nothing but glorified freebooters. Scott, in the person of Frank Osbaldistone, pities their wrongs and feels for their present state, but he knows that they and what they stand for are doomed – indeed, they admit it themselves – and throws in his lot with the prudent Bailie.

It is, of course, grossly to simplify a novel of this kind to present its main theme in such terms. For Scott's sympathy with both sides leads him to produce scene after scene in which one group of characters after another moves to the front of the stage and presents itself in the most lively fashion. And the dialogue is some of the best Scott ever wrote. The Bailie is a perpetual delight, with his garrulity, prudence and essential generosity. The scene in the Glasgow prison, where he encounters his Highland relative; the episode at the clachan at Aberfoyle where he defends himself in a fierce tavern brawl with a red-hot poker; and his dialogue with the proud Helen Macgregor when she threatens him with instant death – no reader of *Rob Roy* can fail to feel the vitality and, what is more, the essential preoccupation with those aspects of human character which make men interesting and diverse enough to be worth contemplating at all which are manifest in these chapters. And the humour – for the books abounds in humour – is the rich humour of character, not mere superadded wit or cleverness. When the Bailie stands before the melodramatic Helen in imminent danger of being bundled into the lake on her hysterical orders, his conversation is absolutely central to his character:

> "Kinswoman," said the Bailie, "nae man willingly wad cut short his thread of life before the end o' his pirn was fairly measured off on the yard-winles – And I hae muckle to do, an I be spared, in this warld – public and private business, as well that belanging to the magistracy as to my ain particular – and nae doubt I hae some to depend on me, as puir Mattie, wha is an orphan – She's a farawa' cousin o' the Laird o' Limmerfield – Sae that, laying a' this thegither – skin for skin, yea all that a man hath will he give for his life."[6]

6 R.R., Ch. 32.

That is the Bailie in danger; and here he is in the comfort of his own home, explaining the virtues of his brandy punch:

> "The limes," he assured us, "were from his own little farm yonder-awa' (indicating the West Indies with a knowing shrug of his shoulders), "and he had learned the art of composing the liquor from auld Captain Coffinkey, who acquired it," he added in a whisper, "as maist folks thought, amang the Buccaniers. But it's excellent liquor," said he, helping us round; "and good ware has often come frae a wicket market. And as for Captain Coffinkey, he was a decent man when I kent him, only he used to swear awfully – but he's dead, and gaen to his account, and I trust he's accepted – I trust he's accepted."[7]

The Bailie dominates the book, and Andrew Fairservice, the dour Lowland gardener, comes a close second. One of Scott's most unattractive characters (he is the degenerate scion of the Covenanting tradition, while the Bailie is its more attractive heir: Calvinism and commerce often went together), Andrew has a flow of insolent, complaining, and generally irritating conversation which is nevertheless irresistible. As Lord Tweedsmuir has said, "he never opens his mouth but there flows from it a beautiful rhythmic Scots." He is a constant irritant to the nominal hero, whose servant he is, and a constant joy to the reader. That ability to make an offensive character attractive through the sheer literary quality of his offensiveness, as it were, is surely the mark of the skilful artist. And such, I would maintain, Scott at his best, and in spite of certain obvious faults, always is.

There are two pivots to this novel; one is the relations between Frank Osbaldistone and his friends with Rob Roy and *his* friends, and the other is Frank's relations with his uncle and cousins. It is, I believe, a mistake to regard the family complications in *Rob Roy* as mere machinery designed to provide a reason for young Osbaldistone's journey into Scotland: they loom much too largely in the novel for that. They represent, in fact, a statement of the theme on which the Rob Roy scenes are a variation – the impossibility of the old life in the new world. Frank's uncle is an old-fashioned Tory Jacobite squire, completely gone to

[7] *Op. cit.*, Ch. 26.

seed, and his sons are either fools or villains. This is what has become of the knights of old – they are either freebooters like Rob Roy, shabby remnants of landed gentry like Sir Hildebrand, or complete villains like Rashleigh. Frank's father had escaped from this environment to embrace the new world wholeheartedly and become a prosperous London merchant. He is at one extreme, Bailie Nicol Jarvie is the middle figure, and Rob Roy is at the other extreme. But the pattern is more complicated than this, for the novel contains many variations on each type of character, so much so, in fact, that it is an illuminating and accurate picture of Scottish types in the early eighteenth century. And through it all runs the sense of the necessity of sacrificing heroism to prudence, even though heroism is so much more attractive.

It is interesting to observe that Scott tends to lavish most of his affection on the middle figures, those who manage to make themselves at home in the new world without altogether repudiating the old. Such characters – Jonathan Oldbuck, Counsellor Pleydell, Bailie Nicol Jarvie – are always the most lively and the most attractive in the novels in which they occur. They represent, in one way or another, the kind of compromise which most satisfied Scott.

Of *The Heart of Midlothian*, which most critics consider the best of Scott's works, I shall say nothing, since I have analysed it in accordance with the view of Scott here developed in the introduction to my edition of the novel.[8]

The Bride of Lammermoor, which followed *The Heart of Midlothian*, presents the conflict between the old and the new in naked, almost melodramatic terms: the decayed representative of an ancient family comes face to face with the modern purchaser of his estates. The book is stark tragedy, for the attempted compromise – the marriage between the old family and the new – is too much for circumstances, and the final death of hero and heroine emphasises that no such direct solution of the problem is possible. Too few critics have observed the note of grim irony in this novel, which goes far to neutralise the melodrama. The portrait of the Master of Ravenswood is bitterly ironical, and there is irony too in the character of his faithful servant, Caleb Balderstone. The pride of both master and servant, which has no

[8] New York (Rinehart) 1948.

justification in their present circumstances or achievements, is a grim mockery of that heroic pride which motivated the knights of old. Ravenswood is a tragic counterpart of Sir Arthur Wardour of *The Antiquary*: both retain nothing of value from the past except an unjustified pride.

A Legend of Montrose – the companion piece of *The Bride of Lammermoor* in the third series of "Tales of My Landlord" – is a slighter novel than those I have been discussing: it lives through one character only, Captain Dugald Dalgetty, the only military figure in English literature beside whom Fluellen looks rather thin. But this one character is sufficient to illuminate the whole story, since, in a tale concerning the Civil War of the 1640s, he represents the most complete compromise figure – the mercenary soldier, trained in the religious wars of the Continent, willing to fight on and be loyal to any side which pays him adequately and regularly. This is another novel of a divided Scotland – divided on an issue foreshadowing that which divides the two camps in *Old Mortality*. Here again we have Highland heroism presented as something magnificent but impossible, and the main burden of the novel falls on Dugald Dalgetty, mercenary and pedant (a most instructive combination to those interested in Scott's mind), the man of the future who, ridiculous and vulgar though he may be, has a firm code of honour of his own and performs his hired service scrupulously and courageously.

After *The Bride of Lammermoor* and *A Legend of Montrose* Scott turned to other fields than relatively recent Scottish history, and in *Ivanhoe* he wrote a straight novel of the age of chivalry without any attempt to relate it to what had hitherto been the principal theme of his prose fiction – the relations between the old heroic Scotland and the new Anglicised, commercial Britain. A novel like *Ivanhoe*, though it has qualities of its own, is much more superficial than any of the Scottish novels, and is written throughout on a much lower plane. Scott did not, in fact, know the Middle Ages well and he had little understanding of its social or religious life. But he returned later to the theme which was always in his mind, and in *Redgauntlet* produced if not certainly the best, then the most illuminating of his novels.

Redgauntlet is the story of a young Edinburgh man who becomes involved against his will in a belated Jacobite conspiracy some twenty years after the defeat of Prince Charlie at Culloden. The moving spirit of the conspiracy turns out to be the young man's own uncle (for, like so many of Scott's heroes, young Darsie Latimer is brought up in ignorance of his true parentage), who kidnaps him in order that, as the long-lost heir to the house of Redgauntlet, he may return to the ways of his ancestors and fight for the Pretender as his father had done before him. Darsie, of course, has no liking for this role so suddenly thrust upon him, and is saved from having to undertake it by the complete collapse of the conspiracy. That is the barest outline of the plot, which is enriched, as so often in Scott, with a galaxy of characters each of whom takes his place in the complex pattern of late eighteenth-century Scottish life which the novel creates.

As with most of the Scottish novels, the story moves between two extremes. On the one hand, there is the conscientious lawyer Saunders Fairford, his son Alan, who is Darsie's bosom friend and with whom Darsie has been living for some time before the story opens, and other characters representing respectable and professional Edinburgh. Saunders Fairford is Scott's portrait of his own father, and the figure is typical of all that is conventional, hard-working, middle class, unromantic. At the other extreme is Darsie's uncle, a stern fanatical figure reminiscent of Balfour of Burley. Between the two worlds – that of respectable citizens who are completely reconciled to the new Scotland and that of fanatical Jacobites engaged in the vain task of trying to recreate the old – Scott places his usual assortment of mediating figures, from the blind fiddler, Wandering Willie, to that typical compromise character, the half-Jacobite Provost Crosbie. This is the Scotland in which Scott himself grew up and in which he recognised all the signs of the final death of the old order. For most of the characters Jacobitism is now possible only as a sentiment, not as a plan of action. But to Redgauntlet, who has dedicated his life to the restoration of the Stuarts, it is a plan of action, and the tragedy – for the novel is essentially a tragedy – lies in the manner of his disillusion.

The story opens with the usual pilgrim's progress. Darsie, tired of his law studies and happily possessed of an independent income, decides to leave the Fairfords', where he has been staying, and take a trip to south-west Scotland for diversion. We are presented first

with a series of letters between Darsie and his friend Alan Fairford,
the former on his travels, the latter at home in his law studies preparing himself to be called to the Bar. These letters are written
with a speed and deftness and with a lively fidelity to character
that carry the reader easily into the story. Darsie becomes involved in a series of adventures which bring him into contact with
a number of characters whom Scott needs to present in order to
round out his picture, then is kidnapped by his uncle, and finally
discovers his real birth and the destiny his uncle intends for him.
The story, opened by letters, is continued in Scott's own person,
with the help of the journal Darsie keeps while held in confine-
ment by his uncle. This technique is not in the least clumsy, but
keeps the emphasis at each point just where Scott needs it. Alan
goes off to rescue his friend, but not before Scott has given us a
brilliant picture of Scottish legal life, a perfect epitome of the
professional activity which then was and to a certain extent still
is the basis of Edinburgh's existence. Edinburgh and its worthy
citizens are in no danger of losing their heads over an impossible
and reactionary ideal. We move from there to Darsie and his
uncle, and gradually the two sets of characters get nearer each
other, until the climax, which is the end of the novel. Nowhere
else (as Mr Edwin Muir has pointed out) did Scott express so
explicitly and so vigorously his sense of the doom of the old
heroic life. In the modern world such ideals were not even
dangerous, they were only silly, and though Scott accepted this,
it was with the deepest reluctance and with all his instincts out-
raged. Consider the climax of *Redgauntlet*, after the pathetic little
conspiracy has been discovered and the Government representative enters the room where the conspirators are arguing among
themselves. As General Campbell, the Government emissary,
enters, Redgauntlet challenges him in the old style:

> "In one word, General Campbell," said Redgauntlet, "is it
> to be peace or war? – You are a man of honour and we can
> trust you."
> "I thank you, sir," said the General; "and I reply that the
> answer to your question rests with yourself. Come, do not be
> fools, gentlemen; there was perhaps no great harm meant or
> intended by your gathering together in this obscure corner,

for a bear-bait or a cock-fight, or whatever other amusement you may have intended, but it was a little imprudent, considering how you stand with government, and it has occasioned some anxiety. Exaggerated reports of your purpose have been laid before government by the information of a traitor in your councils; and I was sent down to take command of a sufficient number of troops, in case these calumnies should be found to have any real foundation. I have come here, of course, sufficiently supported both with cavalry and infantry, to do whatever may be necessary; but my commands are – and I am sure they agree with my inclination – to make no arrests, nay, to make no further inquiries of any kind, if this good assembly will consider their own interests so far as to give up their immediate purpose, and return quietly home to their own houses."

"What! – all?" exclaimed Sir Richard Glendale – "all, without exception?"

"ALL, without one single exception," said the General; "such are my orders. If you accept my terms, say so, and make haste; for things may happen to interfere with his Majesty's kind purposes towards you all."

"His Majesty's kind purposes!" said the Wanderer [i.e., Charles Edward, the Pretender, himself]. "Do I hear you aright, sir?"

"I speak the King's very words, from his very lips," replied the General. "'I will,' said his Majesty, 'deserve the confidence of my subjects by reposing my security in the fidelity of the millions who acknowledge my title – in the good sense and prudence of the few who continue, from the errors of education, to disown it.' His Majesty will not even believe that the most zealous Jacobites who yet remain can nourish a thought of exciting a civil war, which must be fatal to their families and themselves, besides spreading bloodshed and ruin through a peaceful land. He cannot even believe of his kinsman, that he would engage brave and generous, though mistaken men, in an attempt which must ruin all who have escaped former calamities; and he is convinced, that, did curiosity or any other motive lead that person to visit this country, he would soon see it was his wisest course to return

to the continent; and his Majesty compassionates his situation
too much to offer any obstacle to his doing so."

"Is this real?" said Redgauntlet. "Can you mean this? –
Am I – are all, are any of these gentlemen at liberty, without
interference, to embark in younder brig . . . ?"

"You, sir – all – any of the gentlemen present," said the
General. . . .

"Then, gentlemen," said Redgauntlet, clasping his hands
together as the words burst from him, "the cause is lost for
ever."[9]

It is important for a proper understanding of Redgauntlet's
character to note that his zeal is not only for the restoration of the
Stuarts; it is, in some vague way, for the restoration of an independent Scotland, and his dominant emotion is Scottish nationalism rather than royalism. Scott made him a symbol of all that the
old, independent Scotland stood for, and that is why his fate was
of so much concern to his creator. No reader can mistake the
passion of the scene from which I have just quoted: Scott, who
burst into tears when he heard of old Scottish customs being
abolished and who protested in horror when, at the uncovering of
the long-hidden crown jewels of Scotland, one of the com-
missioners made as though to place the old Scottish crown on the
head of one of the girls who were present – the Scott who, in his
heart, had never really reconciled himself to the Union of 1707
(though he never dared say so, not even in his novels), was portraying in the character of Redgauntlet something of himself,
something, perhaps, of what in spite of everything he wished to
be. But as Darsie Latimer – who is clearly a self-portrait, though
a partial one – he only touched the fringe of that tragedy, without
becoming involved in it.

There are other characters and episodes in *Redgauntlet* worth
dwelling on – the character of the Quaker, the episode of the
attack on the fishing nets in the Solway, and that admirable short
story, "Wandering Willie's Tale". One might, too, elaborate on
the structure of the novel, which is perfectly tied together, and
there is the recurring dialogue, which, as always in Scott's
Scottish novels, keeps abundant life continually bubbling.

[9] R., Ch. 24.

Basing Scott's claim on these Scottish novels, what then was his achievement and what is his place among British novelists? It might be said, in the first place, that Scott put his knowledge of history at the service of his understanding of certain basic paradoxes in human society and produced a series of novels which both illuminates a particular period and throws light on human character in general. His imagination, his abundant sense of life, his ear for vivid dialogue, his feeling for the striking incident, and that central, healthy sense of the humour of character, added, of course, essential qualities to his fiction. But it was his tendency to look at history through character and at character through the history that had worked on it that provided the foundation of his art. Scott's might be called a "normal" sensibility, if such a thing exists. He has no interest in aberrations, exceptions or perversions, or in the minutiae of self-analysis – not unless they have played a substantial part in human history. Fanaticism, superstition, pedantry – these and qualities such as these are always with us, and Scott handles them again and again. But he handles them always from the point of view of the ordinary sensitive man looking on, not from their *own* point of view. We see Balfour of Burley through Morton's eyes, and Redgauntlet through Darsie Latimer's. We feel for them, understand them even, but never live with them. That is what I mean when I talk of Scott's *central* vision: his characters and situations are always observed by some one standing in a middle-of-the-road position. That position is the position of the humane, tolerant, informed, and essentially happy man. It is fundamentally the position of a sane man. Scott was never the obsessed artist, but the happy writer.

Scott's abundant experience of law courts, both in Edinburgh and in his own sheriffdom, gave him a fund of knowledge of ordinary human psychology, and he had besides both historical knowledge and imagination. His eccentrics are never as fundamentally odd as Dicken's eccentrics: they are essentially ordinary people, people he had known in one form or another. Most important of all, Scott *enjoyed* people, in the way that Shakespeare must have done. They live and move in his novels with a Falstaffian gusto. There is indeed something of Shakespeare in Scott – not the Shakespeare of *Hamlet* or *Othello*, but the Shakespeare of *Henry IV* or *Twelfth Night*, and perhaps also of *Macbeth*. His gift

E

for dialogue was tremendous, and his use of Scottish dialect to give it authenticity and conviction is unequalled by any other Scottish novelist except very occasionally John Galt, Stevenson in *Weir of Hermiston*, and perhaps Lewis Grassic Gibbon in our own century. In spite of all the tragic undertones in so many of his novels, most of them are redeemed into affirmations of life through the sheer vitality of the characters as they talk to each other. Scott's gallery of memorable characters – characters who live in the mind with their own individual idiom – cannot be beaten by any other British novelist, even if we restrict the selection to some eight of Scott's novels and ignore all the rest. But they are not merely characters in a pageant: they play their parts in an interpretation of modern life. I say of "modern life" to emphasise the paradox: Scott, the historical novelist, was at his best when he wrote either about his own time or about the recent past which had produced those aspects of his own time about which he was chiefly concerned.

Of course Scott was often careless. He wrote fast, and employed broad brush strokes. Sometimes we feel that he wholly lacked an artistic conscience, for he could do the most preposterous things to fill up space or tie up a plot. His method of drawing up the curtain is often clumsy, but once the curtain is up, the life that is revealed is (in his best novels) abundant and true. Scott can be pompous in his own way when his inspiration flags, but he never fools himself into mistaking his pomposity for anything else. Above all, though he is concerned about life he is never worried about it. We read his best novels, therefore, with a feeling of immense ease and satisfaction. We may be moved or amused or excited, but we are never worried by them. His best novels are always anchored in earth, and when we think of Helen Macgregor standing dramatically on the top of a cliff we cannot help thinking at the same time of the worthy Bailie, garrulous and kindly and self-important; Counsellor Pleydell is the perfect antidote to Meg Merrilies, and even Redgauntlet must give way before Wandering Willie and Provost Crosbie. The ordinary folk win in the end, and – paradox again – the Wizard of the North finally emerges as a novelist of manners.

D. W. Jefferson

THE VIRTUOSITY OF SCOTT

Redgauntlet begins with the exchange of letters between Alan Fairford, the son of the Edinburgh lawyer, and Darsie Latimer, who has been living in Alan's home for four years and is now making an excursion into the Border country. The letters supply exposition. We learn that there is a mystery concerning Darsie's ancestry and it is part of the piquancy of his present situation that he has, for some unknown reason, been warned against crossing the Border into England. Alan provides a portrait of his idiosyncratic parent, whose immediate concern is to launch his son upon a legal career, and who, though well-disposed towards the amiable Darsie, sees in him a distracting influence. This opening has perhaps been overpraised. The epistolary style of both heroes is too diffuse, full of trivial pleasantries and redundant literary allusions. When the story begins to move, and Darsie's account of his adventures with the grim gentleman who rescues him on Solway Sands alternates with Alan's story of his meeting in Edinburgh with the saturnine Herries of Birrenswork (he is, of course, the same person and his niece is the elusive heroine of both narratives) the treatment is still disfigured by their jocularities. The criticism can be made with equanimity, because there are triumphs not far ahead which lift the book on to an entirely different level. The early part of Darsie's story – that is, before he is seized by his captors – culminates in the wonderfully rich episode of Wandering Willie; while in the corresponding phase of Alan's story, when anxiety about Darsie begins to develop, his father confronts him with a commitment to the monstrous Peter Peebles, the eternal litigant of the Edinburgh courts, and we are treated to a passage of violently idiosyncratic comedy. The compositional effect of these contrasting gestures is extremely exhilarating. Juxtaposed as they are, reinforcing each other, they give a spectacular impression of Scott's genius.

Wandering Willie is incomparably the more original of these characters. We know, of course, that here is the Scott of the *Border Minstrelsy* in the same sense as the Scott of the Signet office is manifest in the creator of Peter Peebles; and it was a neat device to place the two heroes in these two milieux so that the corresponding sides of his art could come into play. But it would be a mistake to refer to areas of Scott's special experience and knowledge as so much new material for fiction without recognising a newness also in treatment and a vitality beyond anything that the material would seem to offer. In the presentation of Wandering Willie an aspect of Scott which differentiates him from earlier novelists becomes relevant. Whether it is due to the egalitarian sentiment traditional in Scotland, or to the special magnanimity and openness of Scott himself, relations in his novels between people of quality and people of humble status or dubious respectability are more familiar than in the novels even of so generous a writer as Fielding. And these characters exist much more in their own right. (Scott prepared the way for Dickens in this respect: but Dickens had his own species of egalitarianism too, and his social attitudes were different from Scott's.) Darsie and Willie take to each other, and the passage in which each shows off his skill with the violin has great charm and humorous warmth. In conveying the intense joy of the old man in his prodigious artistry Scott is himself the delighted virtuoso. Through Darsie he can share with the reader his pleasure in a creation so novel and humanly appealing:

> He preluded as he spoke, in a manner which really excited my curiosity; and then taking the old tune of Galashiels for his theme, he graced it with a wildness of complicated and beautiful variations; during which, it was wonderful to observe how his sightless face was lighted up under the conscious pride and heartfelt delight in the exercise of his own very considerable powers.
>
> "What think you of that, now, for three-score and twa?" I expressed my surprise and pleasure.

"A rant, man – an auld rant," said Willie; "naething like the music ye hae in your ball-houses and your playhouses in Edinbro'; but it's weel aneugh anes in a way at a dyke-side. – Here's another . . ." He then played your favourite air of Roslin Castle, with a number of beautiful variations, some of which I am certain were almost extempore.

Darsie bribes his "consort" to lend him Willie's second fiddle, at which the latter is at first disconcerted; but when he begins to play the old man concedes that he has "some skill o' the craft":

To confirm him in this favourable opinion, I began to execute such a complicated flourish as I thought must have turned Crowdero into a pillar of stone with envy and wonder. I scaled the top of the finger-board, to dive at once to the bottom – skipped with flying fingers, like Timotheus, from shift to shift – struck arpeggios and harmonic tones, but without exciting any of the astonishment which I had expected.

Willie indeed listened to me with considerable attention; but I was no sooner finished, than he immediately mimicked on his own instrument the fantastic complication of tones which I had produced, and made so whimsical a parody of my performance, that, although somewhat angry, I could not help laughing heartily . . .

At length the old man stopped of his own accord, and, as if he had sufficiently rebuked me by his mimicry, he said, "But for a' that, ye will play very weel wi' a little gude teaching. But ye maun learn to put the heart into it, man – to put the heart into it."[1]

Willie is not sentimentalised. There is a moment, when he enters the hut to find that another musician ("the pipe and tabor bastard") is entertaining the assembly, in which Darsie sees him momentarily as a "fierce, brawling, dissolute stroller". The pipe and tabor are banished, Willie takes over and all is well. Later we hear touching accounts of his fidelity to the Redgauntlet family; and

[1] R., Letter 10. Darsie Latimer to Alan Fairford. All quotations from Scott are from first editions. References are to chapters as numbered in Everyman Library editions.

one of the engaging episodes of the novel is that in which he cheers the imprisoned Darsie by exchanging signals with him in the form of significant Scottish tunes. But Willie and his partner are among the trouble-makers who attack the Quaker's fishing station.

As the story advances and we learn who Darsie is, the value of his encounter with Wandering Willie becomes greatly enhanced. He will be unable to accept the role thrust upon him, as head of his family, by his fanatical Jacobite uncle: but he has achieved this bond with the old family retainer. If Willie represents a sympathetic and romantic aspect of the world with which Darsie is connected by descent, his celebrated tale evokes the harsher and more barbarous side, of which there are still remnants in the laird of Redgauntlet. It is through Wandering Willie that the novel achieves a generous balance. It would have been an impoverishment if the debonair hero's only contact with this eclipsed and dying way of life had been through his uncle's action in kidnapping him.

Professor Daiches, in a valuable essay on *Redgauntlet*, says of Wandering Willie's tale that it is "a device to enable Scott to use more Scots in his novel than he would otherwise have found possible".[2] This remark has interesting implications. Some of Scott's detractors speak of the tale as if it were the only good thing in the book, virtually the only good thing in the Waverley Novels, presumably because colloquial force and sharp, concretely realised narrative transcend all other values in fiction. Clearly this is a kind of writing in which Scott excelled. But we may regard it as characteristic of him – it helps to give the measure of him – that he could keep such a gift in reserve, using it sparingly and subordinating it to larger aims for which the national idiom, with all its great possibilities, would have been inappropriate. Scott was the master of a number of styles. In such episodes as the magnificent scene at the end of *Redgauntlet*, where the Pretender is at variance with his pleading and protesting adherents, the speeches owe something to a style of political oratory perfected in the period of Burke: the ideal medium for the dignified disclaimer,

---

[2] "Scott's *Redgauntlet*", in *From Jane Austen to Joseph Conrad. Essays collected in Memory of James T. Hillhouse*, ed. R. C. Rathburn and Martin Steinmann, Jr. Minneapolis (*University of Minnesota Press*) 1962, p. 58.

for lofty regret or decorous refusal, and for those necessary flourishes of generous sentiment when nothing more can be said or done. Much of the attraction of Scott's historical novels is in the assured tone of the passages that state historical circumstances, where at his best he achieves something of Gibbon's intellectual control and urbanity of style.[3] Scott is often associated with a kind of writing that falls away from the best of the late eighteenth century. But even when he conducts his narrative and exposition in that leisurely, polysyllabic, undistinguished manner which places him on the losing side in so much modern discussion about prose and fiction, it could be argued that the style expresses very well an aspect of the *persona* by which he achieved his great and beneficial hold over so vast a readership. The apparent unconcern about getting the story going, the lack of pressure and the easy-going detachment, the philological asides, became the accepted foibles of a writer of infinite good faith, immense reserves of authority and great power to give pleasure when the time was ripe. It was part of the legend that Scott's readers yawned a little over the early chapters of a novel. His air of being sometimes too much the leisurely verbose scholar and learned companion to be alert to the full requirements of narrative art did him no serious harm – until our own time. Now that the legend can no longer be counted on to exert its spell we must take more deliberate stock of his literary equipment.

There is another splendid, though briefer example of colloquial narrative in *Redgauntlet*: Pate-in-Peril's account of his escape after the Forty-Five. The story is told in circumstances of the greatest piquancy. The bearer of this nickname, Mr Maxwell of Summertrees, is an impenitent Jacobite. His host at dinner, Provost Crosbie, is of the opposite persuasion but a temperate man, unwilling to harm "unfortunate gentlemen" who happened to be "out" in a certain year, and, incidentally, related by marriage to Redgauntlet. Mr Crosbie is on good terms with Summertrees, and

---

[3] The following passages may be cited as good examples: *O.M.*, Ch. 37, the third paragraph ("The triumphant whigs, while they established presbytery . . ."), which captures something of Gibbon's manner on themes relating to religious fanaticism; and *B.L.*, Ch. 2, the fifth paragraph ("The character of the times aggravated these suspicions . . ."), an admirably acute and lucid comment on the ways of monarchs.

presses him to tell the story of his escape for the benefit of the
decidedly Whiggish Alan; and after much entertaining by-play –
expressions of misgiving followed by civil assurances – he does so,
opening with a fine satirical preamble:

> Ye have heard of a year they call the *forty-five*, young gentle-
> man; when the Southrons' heads made their last acquaintance
> with Scottish claymores. There was a set of rampauging
> chields in the country then that they called rebels – I never
> could find out what for – Some men should have been wi'
> them that never came, Provost – . . . Weel, the job was
> settled at last. Cloured crowns there were plenty, and raxed
> necks came into fashion. I dinna mind very weel what I was
> doing, swaggering about the country with dirk and pistol at
> my belt for five or six months, or thereaway; but I had a
> weary waking out of a wild dream. Then did I find myself on
> foot in a misty morning, with my hand, just for fear of going
> astray, linked into a handcuff, as they call it, with poor Harry
> Redgauntlet's fastened into the other; and there we were,
> trudging along, with about a score more that had thrust
> their horns ower deep in the bog, just like ourselves, and a
> sergeant's guard of redcoats, with twa file of dragoons, to
> keep all quiet, and give us heart to the road. Now, if this
> mode of travelling was not very pleasant, the object did not
> particularly recommend it; for you understand, young man,
> that they did not trust these poor rebel bodies to be tried by
> juries of their ain kindly countrymen, though ane would have
> thought they would have found Whigs enough in Scotland to
> hang us all. . . .[4]

If Scott's narrative usually lacks the flavour and gusto of Pate-in-
Peril's account of how he slipped out of the handcuff and ran for
it, the reason lies partly in the larger, more generalised perspectives of his novels, within which the local effect of sharply
realised action is not often very relevant. Scott's favourite local
effects, with which he gives us relief from the larger perspectives,
consist of talk rather than of action – the dialogue of his Scots-
speaking characters, of which there is an overflowing abundance.
But Scott belongs to something bigger than Scottish literature;

[4] *R., Ch. 11.*

and in his novels he belongs to more than the novel. The novel had always contained elements beyond the fictional. It was customary for novelists to be didactic and documentary. Scott could use the arts peculiar to fiction in giving embodiment to those ideas about societies and their history that made the historical novel a new leap forward in nineteenth-century thought. The Pate-in-Peril chapter is a good example. But he saw no objection to the absorption into the novel of materials that could just as well have appeared in a work of history, topography or antiquarian scholarship. Here is a kind of literature in which the factual and the fictitious, with their alternating and contrasting effects, are on very good terms.

Peter Peebles belongs to that tradition of comedy, of which Rabelais, Ben Jonson, and Sterne are among the great masters, the theme of which is some branch of learning or quackery seen as the occasion for human involvements and obsessions. Scott was in a position to give a new lease of life and a new quality to this kind of wit. Scottish law, as Professor Daiches has pointed out, was linked with various kinds of Scottish antiquarianism as a means of keeping patriotic feeling alive. When the immense pokes containing the papers appertaining to *Peebles against Plainstanes* are opened in the presence of Alan's father, it is with "no ordinary glee"[5] that he takes possession of them; and the job he does on them in the next few days, to help Alan in his first case, reflects Scott's own capacity to become very fully engaged with such matters. Much less detail, much less suggestion of the real thing would have sufficed if it had only been a question of furnishing a comic scarecrow of a litigant to embarrass Alan at a moment of crisis. Scott could not forbear to handle the case circumstantially. Peter is not merely obsessed with his rights; he is proud of the importance of his case, and faces the world with his armoury of legal jargon as a man conscious of his traditions. When he turns up at later stages of the novel in pursuit of the defaulting Alan the reader may at first feel some apprehension: the tendency to give such characters too much rope, renewing entertainment to excess, is one of Scott's foibles to which Dickens was also addicted. But actually these reappearances are highly successful, as some recent critics of *Redgauntlet* have noted. It was a happy stroke on Scott's

[5] *Op. cit.*, Letter 13. Alan Fairford to Darsie Latimer.

part to give Peter, in his last scene, a forbearing listener, Joshua
Geddes, who actually invites him to speak about his great and
celebrated lawsuit. This draws from him an outburst of eloquence
which, coming as it does in the interstices between the moving
penultimate and final phases of the Jacobite theme, is a remarkable
example of the buoyancy and largesse of Scott's art:

> "Celebrity? – Ye may swear that," said Peter . . . "And I
> dinna wonder that folk that judge things by their outward
> grandeur, should think me something worth their envying.
> It's very true that it is grandeur upon earth to hear ane's
> name thunnered out along the long-arched roof of the
> Outer-House, – '*Poor* Peter Peebles against Plainstanes, *et per
> contra*'; a' the best lawyers in the house fleeing like eagles to
> the prey; some because they are in the cause, and some
> because they want to be thought engaged (for there are tricks
> in other trades but selling muslins) – to see the reporters
> mending their pens to take down the debate – the Lords
> themselves pooin' in their chairs, like folk sitting down to a
> gude dinner, and crying on the clerks for parts and pendicles
> of the process, who, puir bodies, can do little mair than cry
> on their closet-keepers to help them. To see a' this," con-
> tinued Peter, in a tone of sustained rapture, "and to ken that
> naething will be said or dune amang a' thae grand folk, for
> maybe the feck of three hours, saving what concerns you and
> your business – O, man, nae wonder that ye judge this to be
> earthly glory! . . ."[6]

Scott invented a new kind of novel, and the magnitude of the
innovation, largely as a result of Lukács's analysis, now receives
full recognition. But interest tends to be focused on the new
themes more than on the new compositional techniques they
provided opportunity for. The techniques can often be seen in
very simple terms. There were contrasts implicit in his subject-
matter, the great range of which is supported by a corresponding
range of skills. The fact that he could command the idioms
appropriate to different milieux enabled him to make his transitions stylistically effective. And this command of idioms expresses an imaginative grasp of the varied human scenes that are

[6] *Op. cit.*, Ch. 23.

depicted, so that the splendid contrasts and juxtapositions have the effect of making more vivid our impression of his human richness. As we have seen, their timing can sometimes be artistically very satisfying. Earlier novelists such as Fielding and Smollett had used contrasts of style, but Scott's material gave a different kind of scope.

Let us look briefly at another of the historical novels from this point of view, and then with more detailed attention at a novel which lacks the historical theme.

Turning from *Redgauntlet*, the work of the practised novelist, to *Waverley*, his first venture, one notices a marked difference. But if, on a first impression, one is inclined to describe some of the technique as primitive this judgment soon calls for qualification, if not complete reversal. The shape of the first third of the novel is simply that of the hero's itinerary, with the interest depending on the documentary descriptions and on characters who exemplify the way of life of the various places he visits: a shape very little different from that of a travel book. But, to repeat a point already made, a largely documentary level of interest in a novel had never been regarded as a matter for reproach. *Humphrey Clinker*, Smollett's last and ripest work, owes more than half of its interest to the characters' experiences of real places and real people encountered there. The element of plot and situation is minimal. In Smollett's day picturesque travel was in its infancy and this was not among his interests. Though his travellers go to Scotland they are not in search of wildness or Highland traditions. Scott opens his career in fiction with a novel that reflects developments of the period between Smollett and himself; developments, for the most part, in which he took the lead.

His greatest rival in popularity had also used the travel book as his framework, with a war-ravaged, post-revolutionary Europe as the theatre of his pilgrim's imaginative adventures. It was a good idea of Scott's to make the pattern of the travel itinerary serve also the purpose of introducing history into fiction. Edward Waverley's journey into Scotland takes place in a crucial year of Scotland's past. It is a journey to a war; and some of the people he meets are of the kind who exemplify not only a way of life but also the motivations that bring about events in history. Waverley's role is largely that of a reflector. The interest lies in his interest,

kindled by places and people, and in the interpretations of their
world offered to him by such representatives as Baron Bradwardine, Evan Dhu, Fergus, and Flora. His function is to show
interest, on behalf of novelist and reader; and, of course, his relations with the people he meets enhance the points of manners that
continually arise. Through his response the hamlet of Tully-
Veolan comes to life. In conversation with the sympathetic hero
Rose Bradwardine recalls terrible childhood scenes of feuds with
Highlanders; and in the same chapter he receives from Baillie
Macwheeble an explanation of the phenomenon of "blackmail".
The apparition of Evan Dhu in full national costume has a
novelty for the hero which the reader can enjoy. The charming
account of the Highland girl, Donald Bean Lean's daughter, who
prepares his breakfast and takes leave of him with a curtsey and
the offer of her cheek for a kiss, is as documentary as the dialogue
between Waverley and Evan Dhu that follows, on the important
distinction between a common thief and a gentleman drover like
Donald, who will think it a worthy end to "die for the law", that
is, on the "kind gallows". Waverley, as we realise more fully
later, is important to the people he visits. Donald Bean Lean and
Fergus MacIvor show this, and reveal themselves, by the way they
make their first appearance. The fact that Waverley is addicted to
romanticism enables Scott to be as documentary as he pleases in
the Highland passages. It is part of the plot that Waverley must
go through this phase; and if there is something of the portentous
in such set pieces as that in which Flora sings to the accompani-
ment of the harp in a setting of exemplary picturesqueness, the
shocks that follow provide a sufficient corrective.

It becomes apparent when Waverley receives a severe letter
from his commanding officer and then sees the newspaper giving
the news of his disgrace, that what we have been reading is not the
whole truth about his adventure. Nothing could be more appropriate than the sharp change of atmosphere and local colour as he
then journeys to the Lowlands. We have another Scotland and
another Scott. If the pattern is still that of the itinerary the
reasons are different, and romantic connoisseurship has been left
behind. The episode of the horseshoe is the occasion for an
excellent piece of genre painting with a caustic flavouring of
satire. The village of Cairnvreckan, the hero learns, has a good

blacksmith, but as he is a "professor" he will drive a nail for no man on the sabbath for less than the price of sixpence per shoe. The scene that greets Waverley as he arrives at the smithy is animated in no ordinary fashion, and the effect serves more purposes than that of incidental comedy and change of atmosphere. There are signs of impending events, of military preparation. The plot is moving. Waverley becomes uncomfortably involved in a scene of bustle and threatened hostility, from which he is rescued only to be confronted with a charge of high treason in the next chapter, where the idiom is neither of the Highlands nor of the Lowlands but of a colourless and chilling formality. Eventually, after an escape and much confusion, Waverley joins his Jacobite friends again, and with the collapse of his fortunes and his well-timed presentation to the Chevalier he now finds himself ready to commit himself to the cause. At this point Scott, the historical novelist, with his commanding view of the whole situation, can come fully into his own, and Waverley now occupies the exemplary role about which Lukács[7] has so much to say: that of the hero who becomes involved with one side in a conflict, but not irrevocably, and is allowed to find his way back to the other side with which victory and the future will for the most part lie. He is still a reflector, but less passively. He becomes a person upon whom historical forces converge and who will take decisions of the kind that reflect the direction that history will take. The management of the transition from Waverley's earlier role to this more significant one shows Scott quite impressively in action as a novelist. The scene in which the hero meets the Prince has that grand yet easy manner of which Scott is so satisfying a master. Gradually weaknesses in the cause make themselves felt; Fergus's less admirable side disturbs the hero; and we are eventually prepared for his encounter with Colonel Talbot, who helps him to extricate himself. Scott judges well the occasions for authorial intervention, for those brief stretches of historical narrative which keep the fictional events within their framework of well-digested fact, and for the judgments that could come only from someone for whom the ill-fated rebellion was a chapter of the historical past.

[7] *The Historical Novel*, trs. H. and S. Mitchell. London (The Merlin Press) 1962, p. 37.

The Antiquary has no great national perspectives, no causes in relation to which the characters' lives can acquire an importance beyond the personal and the local. As in the other two novels many chapters pass by before we realise in what kind of plot the hero's destiny has become entangled; but when we come to it, it turns out to be melodrama. Like a number of Scott's heroes he is of mysterious parentage, and the story of the circumstances in which he came into the world provides a macabre recital late in the book. The unravelling of this mystery, together with the eventual thwarting of an unconvincing villainous German, who has fastened himself upon a gullible baronet (the father of the insipid heroine) with absurd schemes of financial gain, furnishes a large part of the action: not very promising material, it would seem. We must look elsewhere for the qualities that make this novel so engaging a masterpiece.

The role of the antiquary himself is central to any account of the book. Monkbarns can readily be placed in the line of those sympathetic eccentrics to whom Stuart Tave[8] has applied the term "amiable humorist". Matthew Bramble, in *Humphrey Clinker*, is one of his predecessors, and it is largely due to his sharp observations on people and places, and his essentially humane though often irritable interest in the world around him, that Smollett's novel succeeds almost without the aid of plot or story. Monkbarns has to carry Scott's novel over a remarkable number of the early chapters by his sheer sociability and hobby-horsical loquacity. The plot takes a long time to develop, and very few of the other characters are brought effectively into play in the first half of the book.

Monkbarns differs in significant ways from earlier figures in the hobby-horsical tradition. In some respects, Sterne is a much greater master of this kind of characterisation than Scott. The rhetorical concentration and sharpness, yet also lightness, of his art with the brothers Shandy gives an intensity of life and a human grace to eccentric preoccupation unequalled in later comic literature. Monkbarns is diffuse and his amiable eccentricities and obsessions are more of the surface. But he belongs to his com-

---

[8] Stuart M. Tave, *The Amiable Humorist. A Study in the Comic Theory and Criticism of the Eighteenth and early Nineteenth Centuries*. Chicago (University Press) 1960.

munity and its people in ways that are not true of the brothers Shandy. The latter are rhetorically conceived, and this has artistic advantages, but the rhetoric excludes a great deal. We cannot step out of Mr Shandy's house and walk into the village, or see him in his various roles as a country squire. We see Monkbarns playing these roles, in a society more fully realised than any in the works of earlier novelists. He is in touch with everybody, and this keeps the story going, even when there is no story. His spirited altercation with Mrs Macleuchar, who dispenses the tickets for the coach between Edinburgh and Queensferry, gives the novel its start; and on the journey he has reason to upbraid the coachman. The second chapter begins with some talk between Monkbarns and the landlord of the inn, with whom he is acquainted, in an idiom that gives them common ground. Monkbarns uses caustic colloquialisms, the landlord can converse on matters of law. In his conversations with those of his own class Monkbarns talks the language of the learned without accent, but with speakers who use a Scots dialect he makes some approximation to their speech, so that in a sparring dialogue there is a certain human equality. The third and fourth chapters are occupied almost totally with Monkbarns's antiquarian and archaeological outpourings to his former companion in the coach, the hero, Lovel, to whom he now extends hospitality: but this is interrupted by Edie Ochiltree, the old Blue-gown, who makes nonsense of his conjectures concerning the remnants of the Roman camp ("I mind the bigging o't"); and the exchange that follows between the outraged enthusiast and his humorous tormentor is remarkable for its familiarity and freedom. With the next two chapters we meet Monkbarns's neighbour, Sir Arthur Wardour, and his daughter Isabella, for whom we learn that Lovel cherishes a hopeless passion. Monkbarns invites them to dinner with Lovel, but this becomes mainly an occasion for learned squabbling. Then comes the episode of the rescue. First Edie, then Lovel, then Monkbarns and others participate in extricating Sir Arthur and Isabella from the danger they incur by walking home by the sands: but if the reader expects that this will advance the plot he soon discovers his error, and in the next few chapters we are back in Monkbarns's abode, where Lovel spends a night and then listens to a great deal more of his host's erudite talk. But towards the end of chapter eleven there is a passage with a new note, which does more perhaps than any other to illustrate Monkbarns's role in the novel and in the community. As he and Lovel walk along the sands they encounter Maggie Mucklebackit:

> Upon the links or downs close to them, were seen four or five huts inhabited by fishers, whose boats, drawn high upon the beach, lent the odoriferous vapours of pitch melting under a burning sun, to contend with those of the offals of fish and other nuisances usually collected round Scottish cottages. Undisturbed by these complicated steams of abomination, a middle-aged woman, with a face which had defied a thousand storms, sat mending a net at the door of one of the cottages. A handkerchief close bound about her head, and a coat, which had formerly been that of a man, gave her a masculine air, which was increased by her strength, uncommon stature, and harsh voice.
>
> "What are ye for the day, your honour?" she said, or rather screamed, to Oldbuck; "caller haddocks and whitings – a bannock-fluke and a cock-padle."
>
> "How much for the bannock-fluke and cock-padle?" demanded the Antiquary.
>
> "Four white shillings and saxpence," answered the Naiad.
>
> "Four devils and six of their imps," retorted the Antiquary; "Do ye think I am mad, Maggie?"
>
> "And div ye think," rejoined the virago, setting her arms a-kimbo, "that my man and my sons are to gae to the sea in weather like yestreen and the day -- sic a sea as it's yet outbye – and get naething for their fish, and be misca'ed into the bargain, Monkbarns? It's no fish, ye're buying – it's men's lives."
>
> "Well, Maggie, I'll bid you fair – I'll bid you a shilling for the fluke and the cock-padle, or sixpence separately – and if all your fish is as well paid, I think your man, as you call him, and your sons, will make a good voyage."[9]

Maggie responds indignantly, and eventually they settle for "half a crown and a dram", to the great annoyance later of Monkbarns's sister. The passage retains some of the familiar rhetoric of

[9] *A.*, Ch. 11.

eighteenth-century fiction, with its transitions from the Augustan
to various levels of the colloquial. Smollett would have written
"Naiad" and "virago", and would have described a scene of
squalor in phrases akin to "odoriferous vapours" and "complicated steams of abomination". But no eighteenth-century
novelist would have written "a face which had defied a thousand
storms". Maggie is endowed with a touch of the heroic, but only
a touch, and her cry, "It's no fish ye're buying – it's men's lives",
in its context, has an element of sales rant. Scott abstains from any
invitation to us to connect this speech with the overwhelming
grief of the Mucklebackits after the drowning of Steenie. The
dangers of a fisherman's life were, no doubt, a topic with which
all buyers of fish would expect to be plied. Monkbarns's immediate response is a niggardly offer, though he allows her to score a
partial victory.

With the greater realism of nineteenth-century fiction, to which
Scott contributed so decisively, the rhetorical felicity and precision
of the earlier novelists declined. But Scott belonged also to the
earlier tradition. He departs from it in passages where he indulges
in prolixity – he or his Scottish talkers. But prolixity is a relative
term. No rule can be produced to prove, in a given case, that we
have had too much. To many readers, of Scott's time and ours,
Monkbarns's learned interests are very much alive. Where he has
a great deal to say artistic shaping and economy tend to disappear,
but there are exceptions. In a highly entertaining episode late in
the novel he outlines, for the benefit of Edie and Hector Mac-
Intyre, the peculiarity of Scots law with respect to imprisonment
for debt. He has a subject worthy of his powers, entertaining in a
Shandean fashion, and relevant to Sir Arthur's situation, and he
handles it in splendid style. The setting of the scene has something
of Sterne's art:

> The uncle and nephew walked together, and the mendicant
> about a step and a half behind, just near enough for his
> patron to speak to him by a slight inclination of his neck, and
> without the trouble of turning round. Petrie, in his Essay on
> Good-breeding, dedicated to the magistrates of Edinburgh,
> recommends, upon his own experience, as tutor in a family of
> distinction, this attitude to all led captains, tutors, dependents,

F

and bottle-holders of every description. Thus escorted, the Antiquary moved along, full of his learning, like a lordly man of war, and every now and then yawing to starboard and larboard to discharge a broadside upon his followers.[10]

The mourning of the Mucklebackits for the death of Steenie shows Scott at his noblest and most moving. But the passage should be read in the light of the previous chapter, where news of the calamity reaches Monkbarns, who asks Caxon the wig-maker whether he is really expected to attend the funeral. The theme leads to antiquarian reflexions on the old custom of the landlord attending the body of the peasant to the grave: a point illustrating the difference between feudal attitudes and those of classical times. He suggests that Hector should also attend: "I assure you, you will see something that will entertain – no that's an improper phrase – but that will interest you, from the resemblances which I will point out betwixt popular customs on such occasions and those of the ancients." When Monkbarns appears at the funeral his behaviour is equal to the occasion, and his offer to assist in carrying the coffin is deeply appreciated. Monkbarns is a good and charitable man, with a true concern for people, but with his cool worldly sense Scott defines the limits of his susceptibility.

It may be felt that Scott takes excessive risks in so delaying the crisis of the novel. We are well past the half-way mark before we begin even to know who the actors were, in the grim story of Lovel's family. But the actual working out of the plot, when we come to it, is brilliant. It exhibits the kind of technique that has already been noted in the other novels, in which contrasts of colouring, milieu and language, enhanced by surprising transitions and felicitous timing, are salient features.

We begin with the mysterious sounds and sights of which the startled Dousterswivel becomes aware during his nocturnal meeting with Edie among the abbey ruins: sounds of vocal music, mingled with the dreary noise of the wind, and then, as he peers through a grate, the solemn ceremonies of a Catholic funeral. This, for the reader also, is a moment of sheer surprise, in its context acutely atmospheric. He has no idea of its relevance until another much more splendid surprise confronts him in the next

[10] *Op. cit.*, Ch. 39.

chapter (twenty-six), which marks a vital transition in the novel, being the first of a number where the Mucklebackit cottage provides the setting. It opens with a sturdy piece of genre painting and some fine fishwives' talk, into which enters a reference to the funeral ceremonies of the previous chapter. It is the Countess of Glenallan who is lying in state. But why must the burial be by candle-light in the abbey ruins? This, for some reason, is a question for the old grandmother, who, "lost in the apathy of age and deafness", has to be appealed to several times and with raised voice before anything happens. Everything is done that could be done to make this a marvellous moment. The style at first maintains the Augustan, half-humorous distance. The grandmother is an "aged sibyl", the grandchild a "little mermaid", or the "lesser querist"; but as the question penetrates a new note enters into the description, and the old woman is transformed into a figure of tragedy. Her realisation that the Countess has died (". . . after her lang race o' pride and power – O God forgie her!") awakens her to an outpouring which, as one of the fishwives expresses it, is "awesome . . . like the dead speaking to the living". Scott exploits the fact that old Elspeth's mental powers come and go. She subsides, the fishwives are heard again, and when she comes to life once more the effect is a blend of the two strains, a renewal of drama but accompanied by homely comedy:

> "Whisht, whisht, Maggie, your gudemither's gaun to speak again."
> "Was na there some ane o' you said," asked the old sibyl, "or did I dream, or was it revealed to me, that Joscelind, Lady Glenallan, is dead an' buried this night?"
> "Yes, gudemither," screamed the daughter-in-law, "it's e'en sae."[11]

Elspeth dispatches Edie to the Earl of Glenallan, an episode which has its entertaining aspects (it irks the old man to discover that he rates only a third-class alms in this Catholic establishment); and the next stage is the Earl's visit to Elspeth, timed to follow upon the funeral of Steenie Mucklebackit. The spectacle of the Earl stepping down from his gloomy aristocratic seclusion to the fisherman's cottage to hear the narrative of the past is strangely

[11] *Op. cit.*, Ch. 26.

stirring, if only because, like Elspeth's awakening, it resembles a return from the dead; and the disturbing of the Mucklebackits, who vacate their cottage while the recital takes place, enhances the solemnity of the visit. The recital itself is in the Gothic vein: but the Mucklebackit setting does wonders for the total effect, and the sharp intersecting of the less real world with the more real enhances the former. Even better than this scene is the piquant episode where Monkbarns, Hector, and Edie call on Elspeth to get from her a repetition of her story. The antiquary opens the door and hears her chanting a wild and doleful ballad of which several stanzas are given: "A diligent collector of these legendary scraps of ancient poetry, his foot refused to cross the threshold when his ear was thus arrested, and his hand instinctively took pencil and memorandum book." It is the genuine article: "'Percy would admire its simplicity – Ritson could not impugn its authenticity.'" So nothing can be done until they hear her out, though Edie and Hector grumble impatiently. She ends her performance, and Monkbarns is on tenterhooks to hear it again to fill in the missing portion: but now they proceed to business, only to be baulked, after some provokingly evasive speeches, by the old woman's sudden death. Edie utters appropriate words, and Monkbarns follows him with:

> "We must call in the neighbours . . . and give warning of this additional calamity – I wish she could have been brought to a confession. And, though of far less consequence, I could have wished to transcribe that metrical fragment. But Heaven's will must be done!"[12]

One is reminded by this sequence of episodes of some excellent words by Percy Lubbock, inspired by Stevenson, on Dickens's method of "dealing with his romantic intrigues"; which was "to lead gradually into them, through well-populated scenes of character and humour; so that his world is actual, its air familiar, by the time that his plot begins to thicken. He gives himself an ample margin in which to make the impression of the kind of truth he needs, before beginning to concentrate upon the fabulous action of the climax."[13] Lubbock applies them to *Bleak House,* but

[12] *Op. cit.*, 40.
[13] *The Craft of Fiction*; London (Jonathan Cape) 1921, p. 213.

they fit *The Antiquary* quite well. The two novels are, of course, very different. Lady Dedlock's descent upon Tom-all-Alones to learn certain facts from Jo has something in common with Lord Glenallan's visit to the Mucklebackits (in both cases the crossing of social boundaries has great force, though more in *Bleak House*); both melodramatic plots come to light in a world full of human idiosyncrasy and comedy; and, in general, Dickens owed something to Scott's methods of composition. But in what he made of them his originality is unassailable. To whom did Scott owe these arts?

If we ask the question so that it need not relate specifically to the narrative techniques mentioned by Lubbock, or even to narrative technique at all, but more generally to Scott's use of transitions and contrasts, and his prodigious variety of colouring, milieu, and idiom, there would seem to be only one answer. Certainly he did not owe this to his predecessors in the novel, masters though they were of variations and transitions within an entirely different compass. But if the name of Shakespeare is to be invoked it should be with the warning that facile comparisons between the two writers have never done Scott much good. If the example of Shakespeare's incredible human and poetic range, his felicitous blending of modes and idioms and the steepness of some of his transitions operated as an example to Scott, we may content ourselves with marvelling at the results, without pursuing comparisons unnecessarily. Influence at such a distance in time leaves an author with all the really crucial problems to settle for himself. What Scott did can be discussed in terms of the themes provided by his age and country, and his special relation to them, together with a literary equipment equally traceable to the ways of writing and speaking in the England and Scotland of his own time. Only Shakespeare could have inspired an art of such spaciousness and variety, but in achieving it with these materials Scott was wholly original.

D. D. Devlin

SCOTT AND HISTORY

"He understood what History meant." (Carlyle)

Carlyle's comment on learning of Scott's death is generous but vague. What, we soon ask, *did* history mean to Scott? If we turn to his essay on Scott for further explanation we find, disappointingly, that Carlyle does not mean very much by his epigraph.

> . . . these Historical Novels have taught all men this truth, which looks like a truism, and yet was as good as unknown to writers of history and others, till so taught: that the bygone ages of the world were actually filled by living men, not by protocols, state-papers, controversies and abstractions of men. Not abstractions were they, not diagrams and theorems; but men, in buff or other coats and breeches, with colour in their cheeks, with passions in their stomach, and the idioms, features and vitalities of very men. It is a little word; inclusive of great meaning![1]

This is, of course, an important part of Scott's achievement; for Victorian critics it was perhaps the most important thing to say about Scott and History, and to contemporary readers it must have been the most radical and exciting element in the Waverley novels. Today this would not be enough to establish Scott's importance, though his ability to make the past vivid still has large appeal. Carlyle's delight is echoed by Professor G. M. Young, who talks of

the revolution effected by Scott in the writing of history, and

[1] Carlyle, "Sir Walter Scott", in *Critical and Miscellaneous Essays*, 7 vols. London, 1888.

72

particularly of medieval history. The secret is to treat every document as the record of a conversation, and go on reading till you hear the people speaking. And that is, or will be, the keyword of the new school. "What happened here?" the older generation might ask. "No battle was fought, no treaty was signed, no council assembled – pass on." Their successors will answer, "People were talking. Let us stop and listen."[2]

Scott's ability to listen, it seems, is his chief historical merit. Professor Young does not suggest that Scott either comments on events or considers the question "Why did it happen?". In the same essay he categorises further and by implication sets a lower value on Scott. He distinguishes two sorts of historical theme, the logical and the psychological:

> One, having set its zero hour, undertakes to show how and why things happened as they did, and the other what did it feel like to be alive when they were happening.[3]

Professor Young is naturally aware that there is more to Scott's attitude towards history than this. He says, very briefly and tantalisingly, that Scott knew the object of history to be "nothing less than the setting forth of an entire culture". He does not expand the remark (except to say that the twelfth chapter of *The Bride of Lammermoor* describes the breakdown of feudal economy at Wolf's hope) but it suggests that Scott's intentions or achievements are not so simple as is still sometimes thought.

"Intentions" is perhaps the wrong word to use about so untheoretic a writer as Scott. He seldom commented on the aims or intentions of his novels, or on what he felt an historical novel should do. We have not much more than a few sentences in the Dedicatory Epistle to *Ivanhoe* and a metaphor in the opening chapter of *Waverley*. Scott's modesty is notorious, and misleading; one of the points he insists on in the Dedicatory Epistle is that he does not aim at total and detailed historical accuracy, and is not at all sure that an historical novelist should.

[2] G. M. Young, "Scott and the Historians", in *Sir Walter Scott Lectures, 1940–1948*, ed. W. L. Renwick. Edinburgh (University Press) 1950, p. 98.
[3] *Op. cit.*, p. 104.

It is true that I neither can nor do pretend to the observation
of complete accuracy, even in matters of outward costume,
much less in the more important points of language and
manners. But the same motive which prevents my writing
the dialogue of the piece in Anglo-Saxon or in Norman-
French, and which prohibits my sending forth to the public
this essay printed with the types of Caxton or Wynken de
Worde, prevents my attempting to confine myself within the
limits of the period in which my story is laid. It is necessary,
for exciting interest of any kind, that the subject assumed
should be, as it were translated into the manners, as well as
the language, of the age we live in.[4]

Scott took liberties in matters of detail. In *Old Mortality* a regiment of redcoats marches at night with kettledrums sounding. It
was pointed out to Scott that drums were never used on night
marches, but he refused to change it because he felt it had a picturesque effect. The reason may not have been serious, and, in
fact, Scott was generally strong in details of this kind: but he
knew they did not matter, and he was right to insist that it was
neither his task nor the task of any historical novelist to achieve
accuracy of this kind. Sir Herbert Grierson brings Aristotle to
Scott's support, and reminds us that "the concern of the poet is
not with what actually did happen, but with what might happen
now or might have happened at such or such a definite period of
history, so far as we have acquired a sufficient knowledge and
understanding of the period in question".[5] A slavish accuracy in
historical detail will be false to the spirit and truth of history and
implies a single and narrow view of what history means.

If the historical novelist regards his duty as being to avoid
anachronisms, history will seem to him a chain. The different
condition of things existing in the period of which he writes
will be a source of labour to him, and a pitfall. But to the
true historical novelist they are a glory, they are the whole
point of his work, and what was a weakness becomes a
strength. If a writer wishes to "work up" a period in order to

---

[4] *I.*, Dedicatory Epistle.
[5] Sir Herbert Grierson, "History and the Novel" in *Sir Walter Scott
Lectures, 1940–1948*, p. 45.

set a story in it, he will feel history a fetter and every unexpected fact may hamper the story he intended to tell. But if he has steeped his mind in some past age, and has lived in that age, turning it over and over in his imagination, realising the conditions of affairs and the relationships of men and pondering over the implications of these and so recasting the life of the age for himself, then that particular age and those special conditions will suggest their own story, and the historical peculiarities of that age will give point to his novel and will become a power. There is all the difference in the world between a man who has a story to tell and wishes to set it in a past age and to adjust it to the demands of history, and the man who has the past in his head and allows it to come forth in story.[6]

We should not expect the historical novelist to retell the story of great events. "What matters is that we should re-experience the social and human motives which led men to think, feel and act as they did in historical reality."[7] The historical novel need have no "real" historical person; no incident in it need ever "really" have happened. "The novelist who seeks to tell 'things that really happened' must clutch at episodes."[8] Only the world in which the characters are placed, "the currents that sweep over their lives, and the movements that overwhelm them need to be real".[9] The historical novel may be "true to history without being true to fact". A more modern way of expressing it is to say that Scott makes "imaginative models of real historical processes and their inner conflicts".[10]

These points are well dramatised in *Redgauntlet*. The main action and the main character in this story (set in 1763 or 1764) are wholly fictional. The Young Pretender never returned to Scotland to make one final attempt for the Crown, and no such person as Redgauntlet ever existed. Scott uses this fiction, this picture of

[6] H. Butterfield, *The Historical Novel*. Cambridge (University Press) 1924, p. 36.
[7] George Lukács, *The Historical Novel*, tr. H. and S. Mitchell. London (Merlin Press) 1962, p. 42.
[8] Butterfield, p. 55.   [9] *Op. cit.*, p. 50.
[10] Thomas Crawford, *Scott*, Writers and Critics. Edinburgh (Oliver & Boyd) 1965, p. 50.

a Jacobite "who still cherished a lingering though hopeless attachment to the House of Stewart" to interpret to us the nature and inevitable decline of Jacobitism, and to say something about the inevitability and necessity of all historical change. He sees Jacobitism less as a political faith than as an older way of life, a different culture. In the "Postscript which should have been a Preface" to *Waverley* he says that this older Scotland has been destroyed, not by military action, but by "the gradual influx of wealth and extension of commerce". (To this we might add, "and by the Law". There is a reference in *Redgauntlet* to the Act of 1748 which abolished vassalage and hereditary jurisdiction. In the Dedicatory Epistle to *Ivanhoe* Scott said that "the attorney is now a man of more importance than the lord of the manor".) In *Waverley* there is no description of the battle of Culloden (what other historical novelist could have resisted this?) since Culloden, however tragic, was historically irrelevant: Jacobitism would have died in any case. In *Redgauntlet* Scott dramatises the social circumstances that have brought about this change; he personifies "the gradual influx of wealth and commerce". Joshua Geddes, a Quaker, represents commerce. He quarrels with Redgauntlet over fishing. Scott vividly describes the excitement and glamour of Redgauntlet and his friends fishing at night with spears. Geddes uses the newer method of stake-nets; fishing is for him a commercial undertaking. Geddes is successful in this novel, and Redgauntlet unsuccessful. The stake-nets come to stay, and the Quaker's richly laid-out home and garden contrast with the hut where Redgauntlet lives. The Quakers in eighteenth-century Scotland had a reputation for piety and business. The future was with them; they had made the change successfully from past to present. The Quaker's ancestors, Scott tells us, had been very like Redgauntlet:

> "Yes, friend Latimer, my ancestors were renowned among the ravenous and bloodthirsty men who then dwelt in this vexed country; and so much were they famed for successful freebooting, robbery and bloodshed that they are said to have been called Geddes, as likening them to the fish called a Jack, Pike, or Luce, and in our country tongue a Ged. . . ."[11]

[11] R., Letter 7, p. 105.

Alan Fairford says in the novel, "My father's industry has raised his family from a low and obscure situation; I have no hereditary claim to distinction of any kind." Alan is a lawyer, and is the hero of the book, a canny successful man. Scotland in 1763 belongs to him and the Quaker Geddes (the Law and Commerce) even though they have no "hereditary claim" to it. Alan, the middle-class lawyer, marries into the great Redgauntlet family. Through the characters and their actions Scott dramatises the gradual changes that he saw in the economy and society of Scotland. But the novel has an even wider reference. In the last and greatest scene the small bunch of half-reluctant conspirators find themselves with the Young Pretender in a small public house on the shores of the Solway. The mood is one of despair and half-hysterical heroics. But the rebellion is not to be destroyed by military action.

> Amid this scene of confusion, a gentleman, plainly dressed in a riding-habit, with a black cockade in his hat, but without any arms except a *couteau-de-chasse* walked into the apartment without ceremony.[12]

The gentleman is General Campbell who has left the government troops some distance and has come with an offer of a free pardon for everyone.

> "Then, gentlemen," said Redgauntlet, clasping his hands together as the words burst from him, "the cause is lost for ever!"[13]

The cause has been lost by something stronger than force of arms, by the mere passage of time. *Redgauntlet*, then, through characters like Alan Fairford, Geddes, Provost Crosbie, Redgauntlet himself, Alan's father, and others, gives us the chance "to re-experience the social and human motives which led men to think, feel and act just as they did in historical reality". But it does more; to go back to Grierson, it shows us what might have happened in history; it offers us the true shape of history; it is not truth of fact but "an imaginative model of a real historical process and its inner conflict". And it is one thing more: a moving comment on the need for change and the price to be paid for it.

[12] *Op. cit.*, Ch. 24.   [13] *Ibid.*

Many of the Waverley novels make a similar comment. Scott did not care for Edward Waverley ("The hero is a sneaking piece of imbecility") and it is hard for the reader to admire him.

> "I cannot permit you, Colonel Talbot," answered Waverley, "to speak of any plan which turns on my deserting an enterprise in which I may have engaged hastily, but certainly voluntarily, and with the purpose of abiding the issue."[14]

But Waverley *does* desert the enterprise. If he is a dull dog; if at the end he willingly adopts (like his father) "a political creed more consonant both to reason and his own interest", we must recognise that, like other Scott heroes he has the essential ability to reject a past, not because it is wrong, but because it is impossible. He survives. He is the new hero who settles for Rose Bradwardine and safety. His marriage is a rejection of the past. Our impression of Waverley is our recognition of the price paid.

But to talk of "the true shape of history" and of "historical process" is to jump ahead. In the Dedicatory Epistle to *Ivanhoe* and in the first chapter of *Waverley* Scott touches on something more important than historical accuracy but connected to it. Is human nature a constant? Have the human passions been the same at all times and in all countries? If it is a constant, then too fussy a concentration on ephemeral detail will detract from that general truth which it is a novelist's task to provide. It is, as Donald Davie says, "one of the most serious questions that can be asked of the whole Waverley series, whether in these novels Scott believes in a constant 'nature' in this sense, or not".[15] If you believe that human nature is unalterable; that "amidst all the disorder and inequality which variety of discipline, example, conversation, and employment, produce in the intellectual advances of different men, there is still discovered . . . such a general . . . similitude as may be expected in the same common nature affected by external circumstances indefinitely varied",[16] then you will not see history as process. What such a question raises is the nature of Scott's historicism.

---

[14] *Wav.*, Ch. 51.

[15] Donald Davie, *The Heyday of Sir Walter Scott*. London (Routledge and Kegan Paul) 1961, p. 26.

[16] Johnson, *The Rambler*, No. 151.

It is, of course, unwise to rely on Scott's explicit references: only the novels themselves can make plain what Scott thought history meant. But his few explicit comments are valuable because they show he is aware of the question and because they make clear, through all the uncertainty with which he discusses it, that there will be no simple answer to it in his novels. In the first chapter of *Waverley* he writes:

> By fixing, then, the date of my story Sixty Years before the present 1st November 1805, I would have my readers understand that they will meet in the following pages neither a romance of chivalry nor a tale of modern manners . . . from this my choice of an era, the understanding critic may further presage that the object of my tale is more a description of men than manners.

(It is interesting that Scott, in echoing Fielding's phrase – "I describe not men, but manners; not an individual, but a species" – should invert it and yet mean what Fielding means. A page later Scott explains that he writes "from the great book of Nature, the same through a thousand editions".)

> Considering the disadvantages inseparable from this part of my subject, I must be understood to have resolved to avoid them as much as possible, by throwing the force of my narrative upon the characters and passions of the actors – those passions common to men in all stages of society, and which have alike agitated the human heart, whether it throbbed under the steel corselet of the fifteenth century, the brocaded coat of the eighteenth, or the blue frock and white dimity waistcoat of the present day. Upon these passions it is no doubt true that the state of manners and laws casts a necessary colouring; but the bearings, to use the language of heraldry, remain the same, though the tincture may be not only different, but opposed in strong contradistinction.[17]

Donald Davie is right to remind us that if this "constitutes a plea for the thoroughly neo-classical principle that the business of the artist is with 'nature', meaning by that the constant elements in human nature to be detected beneath the adventitious distinctions

[17] *Wav.*, Ch. I.

of period, race and trade",[18] the sentences come from one of the chapters written in 1805 and do not aptly describe the rest of the novel written about seven years later. From the reluctant, "Upon these passions it is no doubt true that the state of manners and laws casts a necessary colouring", and from the dismissive "tincture", Scott later came to give "bearings" and "tincture" more equal weight.

For many readers of Scott today Scott's understanding of history was only possible when he began to qualify (the Marxists would say that he shed it) the Enlightenment view that human nature was unchangeable. The qualification is clearer by the time of the Dedicatory Epistle to *Ivanhoe*.

> In point of justice, therefore, to the multitudes who will, I trust, devour this book with avidity, I have so far explained our ancient manners in modern language, and so far detailed the characters and sentiments of my persons, that the modern reader will not find himself I should hope, much trammelled by the repulsive dryness of mere antiquity. In this, I respectfully contend, I have in no respect exceeded the fair license due to the author of a fictitious composition. The late ingenious Mr. Strutt, in his romance of Queen-Hoo-Hall, acted upon another principle; and in distinguishing between what was ancient and modern, forgot, as it appears to me, that extensive neutral ground, the large proportion, that is, of manners and sentiments which are common to us and to our ancestors, having been handed down unaltered from them to us, or which, arising out of the principles of our common nature, must have existed alike in either state of society. . . .
>
> What I have applied to language, is still more justly applicable to sentiments and manners. The passions, the sources from which these must spring in all their modifications, are generally the same in all ranks and conditions, all countries and ages; and it follows, as a matter of course, that the opinions, habits of thinking, and actions, however influenced by the peculiar state of society, must still, upon the whole, bear a strong resemblance to each other. Our ancestors were not more distinct from us, surely, than Jews are

[18] Davie, p. 26.

from Christians; they had "eyes, hands, organs, dimensions, senses, affections, passions"; were "fed with the same food, hurt with the same weapons, subject to the same diseases, warmed and cooled by the same winter and summer", as ourselves. The tenor, therefore, of their affections and feelings must have borne the same general proportion to our own.

Alexander Welsh says of the closing sentences that "Scott hesitates . . . as if he were aware of the impending surge of historicism".[19] It is certainly not the language of someone totally convinced that human nature is the one fixed point in history. As we should expect from a novelist whose characteristic method is to offer the clash of opposing forces, and through his mediocre heroes and comic characters offer us a middle way, Scott's historicism is not simple: it is a compromise and cannot be easily defined. Scott sees the past as inevitably leading to the present, but sees that the present itself is no resting place. The present is not necessarily superior to the past; its importance is simply that it *is* the present. He does not exploit the remoteness of the past but shows its closeness to the present. The nostalgia that Scott might feel for the earlier culture represented by Redgauntlet, or Vich Ian Vohr or Rob Roy is checked by his recognition that history is movement, change, very often progress, and necessarily leads to the present. There is no condescension towards the past; what was of value there was valuable indeed but it is not permanent, it is simply part of a process (battles, as we saw, are irrelevant) which leads to a probably more valuable present. (Scott never tired of praising Sir Humphrey Davy and his safety-lamp). His interest is in the dynamic movement of history. "His best novels," Leslie Stephen said, "might all be described as 'Tales of My Grandfather'."[20] They catch and dramatise history at a moment of critical change. He can make this recent past real more easily than the Middle Ages not because he can supply with accuracy a greater wealth of concrete detail, but because he can show that past to be the necessary "pre-history of the present".

[19] Alexander Welsh, *The Hero of the Waverley Novels*. New Haven and London (Yale University Press) 1963, p. 87.
[20] Leslie Stephen, "Some Words about Sir Walter Scott", in *Hours in a Library*, (First Series).

His knowledge of the recent past was greater than his knowledge of any other. He knew about the recent past in Scotland – its society and politics and economy, the way the people lived and how they felt. His knowledge is not given in a static or analytic way, but comes to us through

> . . . his capacity to give living human embodiment to histori-cal-social types. The typically human terms in which great historical trends become tangible had never before been so superbly, straightforwardly and pregnantly portrayed.'[21]

But Scott cannot be taken over by the Marxists, though his under-standing of the relationship between the individual and society is such that a Marxist interpretation of Scott's historicism can carry conviction. Arnold Kettle rightly says of Jeanie Deans's refusal to perjure herself to save her sister's life that "History is behind it, the history of generations of lowland peasants fighting for the right".[22]

George Lukács writes:

> With the suppression of the uprising of 1745 – which is depicted in Waverley – the real downfall of gentile society in Scotland begins, says Engels. Several decades later [*sic*] (in *Rob Roy*) we see the clans already in a state of complex economic dissolution. One character in this novel, the shrewd merchant and bailiff of Glasgow, Jarvie, clearly sees that it has become a matter of economic necessity for the clans to wage their desperate and hopeless battle on behalf of the Stuarts. They are no longer able to maintain themselves on the basis of their primitive economy. They possess a surplus population, permanently armed and well seasoned who cannot be put to any normal use, who must resort to plunder and pillage, and for whom an uprising of this kind is the only way out of a hopeless situation. Thus we have here already an element of dissolution, the beginnings of class-uprooting which were as yet absent from the clan picture of *Waverley*.
>
> Once more we must admire here Scott's extraordinarily

[21] Lukács, p. 35.
[22] Arnold Kettle, *An Introduction to the English Novel*. London (Hutchinson) 1951, vol. I., p. 115.

realistic presentation of history, his ability to translate these new elements of economic and social change into human fates, into an altered psychology.[23]

The mistake in putting *Rob Roy* at a later date than *Waverley* is interesting. It is because the clans are in a state of economic dissolution that the events of *Waverley* (the 1745 rebellion) and their result are inevitable. But if we can agree with much of what Lukács says, he is false to Scott and the effect of the novels when he relates "economic and social change" so closely to an "altered psychology". Scott's understanding of history is greater – great enough to make so firm a logic impossible.

> Marx, like Hegel, insisted that human history is not a number of different parallel histories, economic, political, artistic, religious, and so on, but one single history. But like Hegel, again, he conceived this unity not as an organic unity in which every thread of the developing process preserved its own continuity as well as its intimate connexion with the others, but as a unity in which there was only one continuous thread (in Hegel the thread of political history, in Marx that of economic history) . . .[24]

Scott offers a different continuous thread. "Without some assumption of basic uniformity [in human nature] neither history nor art is possible."[25] This notion of a basic uniformity is what delights and instructs us in Scott's portrayal of characters. Bailie Nicol Jarvie is, in Lukács's phrase, a "living human embodiment of an historical-social type". He represents the new and growing commercial Scotland; he is the man of the future, a successful man whose success consists in moving from past to present. He is distantly related to Rob Roy; his insistence on this relationship emphasises the difference and distance between them, and suggests how anachronistic is the way of life represented by Rob Roy. (Rob Roy himself sees there is no future for his children in such a

[23] Lukács, p. 58.
[24] R. G. Collingwood, *The Idea of History*. Oxford (The Clarendon Press) 1946, p. 123.
[25] Francis R. Hart, *Scott's Novels, The Plotting of Historic Survival*. Charlottesville (The University Press of Virginia) 1966, p. 182.

G

way of life; and if he spurns Jarvie's well-meant offer to find them jobs in the Glasgow mills, that, after all, is where many sons of Rob Roy have since gone.) The most famous scene in the novel is the fight at the clachan of Aberfoil; and the scene is memorable (though short) because of its symbolic force. Jarvie's sword is "rusty" (the future does not lie with the sword). He attacks his Highland opponent with a firebrand, forces him to retreat and so acts out the defeat of an older, heroic past by a commercial and less glamorous present. The Bailie is for Credit as opposed to Honour – that Honour represented by Rob Roy and towards which Frank Osbaldistone is nostalgically drawn. ("Honour is a homicide and a bloodspiller, that gangs about making frays in the street; but Credit is a decent honest man, that sits at home and makes the pot play.") He proposes, indeed a new equation, that Credit *is* Honour.

All this is true, but it is not quite everything. The bailie is not simply the "embodiment of an historical-social type." He is a type of human being that is always with us – vain, loquacious, smug, kind-hearted – though the "tincture" may be different in different ages. That Scott meant his characters to supply the continuous thread in history is shown by his fondness for giving them names after the manner of Fielding: Fairservice, Mailsetter, Mucklewrath, even Rashleigh and Waverley.

Frank Osbaldistone's father (in *Rob Roy*) may represent the commercial values of eighteenth-century England. Scott's interpretation of him is indeed "a genuine contribution to the understanding of history, to the drawing of a distinction between capitalism in its first expansive and adventurous phase, and the capitalism of a later age that is above all prudent and cautious".[26] But this does not wholly explain our delight in him, or in Bailie Nicol Jarvie, or in Alan Fairford's father in *Redgauntlet*. Our delight is similar in kind (but greater) to the delight which Fielding offers when he draws the lawyer in the stagecoach in *Joseph Andrews*.

> The lawyer is not only alive, but hath been so these four thousand years; and I hope G— will indulge his life as many yet to come. He hath not indeed confined himself to one pro-

[26] Davie, p. 62.

fession, one religion or one country; but when the first mean
selfish creature appeared on the human stage, who made self
the centre of the whole creation, would give himself no pain,
incur no danger, advance no money, to assist or preserve his
fellow-creatures; then was our lawyer born; and, whilst such
a person as I have described exists on earth, so long shall he
remain upon it.[27]

Scott does not try to explain character wholly in terms of social or
economic or other conditions of the time. He follows a complex
middle way between an Enlightenment view of history, with
human nature as the one great and totally fixed point, and an
historicist approach to the past. "His recreated past was peopled
not only by concrete individuals but by historical forces as well";[28]
and his "series of novels . . . illuminates a particular period and
throws light on human character in general . . . it was his tendency
to look at history through character and at character through the
history that had worked on it that provided the foundation of his
art."[29]

Scott then, is supremely the historian of the recent past. He
portrays great crises in (especially) Scottish history and sees each
crisis producing a compromise; the "truth" of the history of
England and Scotland is the middle way, the famous English
compromise: this is, in part, what History meant to him.

> Thus, out of the struggle of the Saxons and Normans there
> arose the English nation, neither Saxon nor Norman; in the
> same way the bloody Wars of the Roses gave rise to the
> illustrious reign of the House of Tudor, especially that of
> Queen Elizabeth; and those class struggles which manifested
> themselves in the Cromwellian Revolution were finally
> evened out in the England of today, after a long period of
> uncertainty and civil war, by the 'Glorious Revolution' and
> its aftermath.[30]

[27] *Joseph Andrews,* Book III, Ch. I.
[28] J. H. Raleigh, "What Scott meant to the Victorians", in *Victorian
Studies,* Vol. VII, No. I (1963) p. 23.
[29] David Daiches, "Scott's Achievement as a Novelist" in *Literary Essays.*
Edinburgh (Oliver & Boyd) 1956, p. 119.
[30] Lukács, p. 32.

But he enlarges the historical crisis to make it both a personal crisis and one of permanent general value. At a time of great change, when Scott could see the transformation from the Scotland of his grandfathers ("There is no European nation, which, within the course of half a century, or little more, has undergone so complete a change as this Kingdom of Scotland.")[31] he saw that the crucial compromise was not between Saxon and Norman, Jacobite and Hanoverian, but between Past and Present. He deals with the recent past because through it he can more easily dramatise the process of change and the need to survive such change.

> Theme is never focused on what is *done* but on what is still alive, still redeemable, still unresolved. Every past scene is the present. The times in such pasts are always out of control; the question is always how to live with, how morally to survive such times, such presents, and how to stabilize the present by redeeming the past.[32]

Scott sees that the process of history forces on the individual the need for adaptation and change. There is no indulged nostalgia in the novels, but only a recognition of the need to move from past to present, and an awareness of the price that has to be paid.

The problem of such survival was a personal one for Scott, and a problem for society, for Scotland. The heroism of Vich Ian Vohr and Rob Roy and Redgauntlet is at last anachronistic; Scott's epic heroes are always defeated. They are either killed, or like Flora Mac-Ivor and Redgauntlet, retire from the world to convent or monastery. (Sir Hilderbrand Osbaldistone and all his sons die; Frank inherits their estate.) But it was something larger – a problem of adjustment of general and permanent and increasing value. "If the Author of Waverley's study in the politics of survival is not still timely, it is hard to know one that is."[33]

Something of all this can be illustrated from *The Bride of Lammermoor*, particularly as it is usual to refer to this novel as a special case and to point to what distinguishes it from Scott's other work. It seems less immediately tied to a particular time. Ravenswood is not interested in politics, although the decline in

---

[31] *Wav.*, Ch. 72. New Century Library, London (Nelson) 1909.
[32] Hart, pp. 337–8.   [33] *Op. cit.*, p. 338.

the family fortunes is owing, at least in part, to political change. The hero's apartness makes the book seem less of an historical novel than any other in the series. Ravenswood is not the usual Scott hero; he is not, finally, the middle-of-the-road solution to some great historical crisis. Unlike the other Scott heroes he does not wander. The point of the book is that Ravenswood, like Redgauntlet, cannot wander; he cannot move away from "the falling tower". Ravenswood's failure is a personal one; Redgauntlet's failure is the failure of something larger and more poignant. The novel is another account by Scott of failure to change with changing times. If in this novel the failure to move from past to present is less evident in political or social terms, we see here more clearly than elsewhere that Scott is not narrowly or only concerned with a great crisis in social or political history, but with a great personal and private crisis which is always with us (even if the "tincture" of the crisis is determined by a political – economic or cultural situation.)

But the private tragedy in *The Bride of Lammermoor* is not divorced from a concrete historical situation. Ravenswood's failure to change and adapt is the obvious one in the novel, but is not the only one; for Caleb Balderstone parodies his master in this, and cannot admit that times have changed, and changed on the whole for the better. Caleb Balderstone, the old family retainer, is zealous for what he believes is the honour of the house. He parodies, and so "places" Ravenswood's fierce attachment to what he, too, considers family honour. Caleb is Scott's comment on Ravenswood just as Peter Peebles is one of his comments on Redgauntlet.

The foolishness of Caleb's concerns is made clearer by the fact that for the people of the neighbourhood, the inhabitants of the village of Wolf's hope, the changing times have brought nothing but gain. They continued to pay "a kind of hereditary respect to the Lords of Ravenswood", but recently, because of the difficulties of the Ravenswood family "most of the inhabitants of Wolf's hope had contrived to get feu-rights to their little possessions . . . so that they were emancipated from the claims of feudal dependence". All this is galling to Caleb, "who had been wont to exercise over them the same sweeping authority in levying contributions which was exercised in former times in England . . ." and

Caleb "loved the memory and resented the downfall of that authority . . ." Caleb attempts to exact produce for Ravenswood by referring to custom and former usage, but all these claims are defeated by the lawyer, Davie Dingwall, employed by the villagers for the very purpose of confirming their complete freedom from all such attempted exactions, or, in Caleb's phrase, "that due and fitting connection between superior and vassal". When Caleb hints that his master may use violence to enforce his claims, the lawyer answers that his clients

> "had determined to do the best they could for their own town, and he thought Lord Ravenswood, since he was a lord, might have enough to do to look after his own castle. As to any threats of stouthrief oppression, by rule of thumb or *via facti*, as the law termed it, he would have Mr. Balderstone recollect that new times were not as old times – that they lived in the south of the Forth, and far from the Highlands – that his clients thought they were able to protect themselves; but should they find themselves mistaken, they would apply to the government for the protection of a corporal and four red-coats, who," said Mr. Dingwall with a grin, "would be perfectly able to secure them against Lord Ravenswood, and all that he or his followers could do by the strong hand".[34]

Like Ravenswood, Caleb dies at the end of the book; like Ravenswood, he dies because he does not want to live in a world that has changed too much for him. Neither he nor Ravenswood can move from past to present; neither can survive a crisis at once historical and personal.

There is no hero in *The Bride of Lammermoor*. Scott's heroes are those who can survive the change from past to present, who can move with the times and profit by them, and who can recognise the inevitability of such change. Scott's heroes are in the fullest sense "historical" heroes, and most historical when they are fictional. They are of different kinds. There are those "wooden" heroes who have never been popular with readers. Professor Daiches has commented on their peripatetic nature.

[34] *B.L.*, Ch. 12.

> Many of Scott's novels take the form of a sort of pilgrim's progress: an Englishman or a Lowland Scot goes north into the Highlands of Scotland at a time when Scottish feeling is running high, becomes involved in the passions and activities of the Scots partly by accident and partly by sympathy, and eventually extricates himself – physically altogether but emotionally not quite wholly – and returns whence he came. . . . It is not this character but what he becomes involved in that matters: his function is merely to observe, react and withdraw.[35]

The implied opposition here, or tension, which runs through all Scott's best novels was first pointed out by Coleridge.

> The essential wisdom and happiness of the subject consists in this, – that the contest between the loyalists and their opponents can never be *obsolete* for it is the contest between the two great moving principles of social humanity; religious adherence to the past and the ancient, the desire and the admiration of permanence on the one hand; and the passion for increase of knowledge, for truth, as the offspring of reason – in short, the mighty instincts of *progression* and *free agency*, on the other.[36]

The "wooden" hero is a passive hero, but he is not neutral; "He stands committed to prudence and the superiority of civil society. . . . He is committed to the civil, and observes the uncivil."[37] He is finally not simply an observer but a critic of what he sees. But his conclusions are not quite Scott's. He is often mocked by Scott, not simply because of the early romantic errors which lead him astray, but because of the ease and speed with which he rejects his romantic views, and because of his failure to see the tragedy and loss that lie behind all such rejection.

But Scott sees them. After the rear-guard action at Clifton, Waverley is separated from the Highland army and finds shelter for a time at the house of a young farmer. In his enforced idleness Waverley has time to reflect on what has happened to him:

[35] Daiches, pp. 92–3.
[36] *Coleridge's Miscellaneous Criticism*, ed. T. M. Raysor. London (Constable) 1936, pp. 341–2.
[37] Welsh, p. 57.

... it was in many a walk by the shores of Ullswater, that he acquired a more complete mastery of a spirit tamed by adversity, than his former experience had given him; and that he felt himself entitled to say firmly, though perhaps with a sigh, that the romance of his life was ended, and that its real history had now commenced.[38]

This "real history" is the "real history" of the Waverley novels; it is the story of survival from past to present. If the words "perhaps with a sigh" suggest no great depth of feeling, no estimate of the price of such change on Waverley's part, it is through the Baron Bradwardine (in spite of his absurdity) that Scott conveys something of his understanding of what the destruction of a heroic past means. The Baron, after the failure of the Forty-Five, recognises the inevitability of change, the facts of "real history". When Waverley returns to the ruined house of Tully-Veolan he hears a voice singing the "Border Widow's Lament". It is the daft gardener, Davie Gellatly. All he can say is "A' dead and gone – a' dead and gone". A page or two later the Baron explains what is dead and gone:

"I did what I thought my duty," said the good old man, "and questionless they are doing what they think theirs. It grieves me sometimes to look upon these blackened walls of the house of my ancestors; but doubtless officers cannot always keep the soldier's hand from depredation and spuilzie; and Gustavus Adolphus himself, as ye may read in Colonel Munro his Expedition with the worthy Scotch regiment called Mackay's regiment, did often permit it. – Indeed I have myself seen as sad sights as Tully-Veolan now is, when I served with the Marechal Duke of Berwick. To be sure we may say with Virgilius Maro, *Fuimus Troes* – and there's the end of an auld sang. But houses and families and men have a' stood lang eneugh when they have stood till they fall with honour; and now I hae gotten a house that is not unlike a *domus ultima*" – they were now standing below a steep rock. "We poor Jacobites," continued the Baron, looking up, "are now like the conies in Holy Scripture (which the great

[38] *Wav.*, Ch. 60.

traveller Pococke calleth Jerboa), a feeble people, that make our abode in the rocks."[39]

Tully-Veolan is, of course, restored. Bailie MacWheeble can gloat that "Mr. Bradwardine, your family estate is your own once more in full property". But it has been bought by an Englishman, Colonel Talbot, and bought from him by another Englishman, Edward Waverley; and something of Scott's complex reaction to the change (this is what happened after 1745) is suggested with dry amusement by the one addition to the furniture of the restored dining parlour, the picture of Edward Waverley and Fergus Mac-Ivor in their Highland dress. Scott's deliberate anachronism is superb. (Is Edward Waverley the first of the hundreds of English-men to be painted in the Kilt?) We cannot forget that as he dines in the rebuilt house the massacres continue in the Highland glens, and the head of Fergus Mac-Ivor rots above the Scotch gate at Carlisle.

Mention of Baron Bradwardine should remind us that these middle-of-the-road heroes are neither Scott's most frequent nor most effective examples of his admiration for those who survive. Professor Daiches claims that the essence of the novel is the way in which conflicting claims impinge on the titular hero.[40] But this is to say too little. It implies that the essential narrative shape of the novel centres on the hero, and ignores the fact that it is generally Scott's comic characters who are the true heroes, who gain Scott's fullest esteem and who carry the meaning of his novels. They recognise that personal and national survival depend on changing with the times, on moving successfully from past to present. In *Rob Roy* there is Bailie Nicol Jarvie. In *Redgauntlet* there is Provost Crosbie, a Justice of the Peace who sympathises with the Jacobites and is distantly related to Redgauntlet. He is a successful merchant; he does not wish the old times back, but he knows that with their passing, something rare and fine and heroic has passed too. In the same novel there is "Wandering Willie's tale", that great story which summarises so much of what Scott says in his novels about history and our reaction to it. Steenie Steenson survives great political changes with skill and safety and

39 *Ibid.*
40 Daiches, p. 96.

even honour. He behaves with courage to get a receipt and lives successfully through a revolution.

Above all there is Dugald Dalgetty in *A Legend of Montrose*. This is Scott's only novel where the chief comic character and the peripatetic hero are the same person. Dalgetty visits an older, heroic way of life. Scott gives it all the glamour and romance he can: but Dalgetty – a bore and a pedant – is not impressed. He sees it as static, anachronistic, and condemned. (Dalgetty is the only character in the novel who travels, who moves). Sir Miles Musgrave says of him, "That fellow is formed to go through the world."

But for the great heroic figures in Scott the world is too much. They make dramatic gestures and simple choices in a world where neither is possible. They do not know what history means, that it is movement and crisis, and that personal and national survival depend on directing the crisis and turning it to account.

G. Lukács

SCOTT AND THE CLASSICAL FORM OF THE HISTORICAL NOVEL[1]

Scott's historical novel is the direct continuation of the great realistic social novel of the eighteenth century. Scott's studies on eighteenth-century writers, on the whole not very penetrating theoretically, reveal an intensive knowledge and detailed study of this literature. Yet his work, in comparison with theirs, signifies something entirely new. His great contemporaries clearly recognised this new quality. Pushkin writes of him: . . . "The influence of Walter Scott can be felt in every province of the literature of his age. The new school of French historians formed itself under the influence of the Scottish novelist. He showed them entirely new sources which had so far remained unknown despite the existence of the historical drama of Shakespeare and Goethe . . ." And Balzac, in his criticism of Stendhal's *La Chartreuse de Parme*, emphasises the new artistic features which Scott's novel introduced into epic literature: the broad delineation of manners and circumstances attendant upon events, the dramatic character of action and, in close connexion with this, the new and important role of dialogue in the novel.

It is no accident that this new type of novel arose in England. We have already mentioned, in dealing with the literature of the eighteenth century, important realistic features in the English novel of this period, and we described them as necessary consequences of the post-revolutionary character of England's development at the time, in contrast to France and Germany. Now, in a period when the whole of Europe, including its progressive

[1] Reprinted from G. Lukács, *The Historical Novel*, trs. H. & S. Mitchell, London (The Merlin Press) 1962, pp. 31–63.

classes and their ideologists, are swayed (temporarily) by a post-revolutionary ideology, these features in England must stand out with more than usual distinctness. For England has now once more become the model land of development for the majority of continental ideologists, though of course in a different sense from that of the eighteenth century. Then, the fact that bourgeois freedoms had actually been realised, served as an example to the Continental Enlighteners. Now, in the eyes of the historical ideologists of progress, England appears as the classic example of historical development in their sense. The fact that England had fought out its bourgeois revolution in the seventeenth century and had from then on experienced a peaceful, upward development, lasting over centuries, on the basis of the Revolution's achievements, showed England to be the practical, model example for the new style of historical interpretation. The "Glorious Revolution" of 1688, likewise, inevitably presented itself as an ideal to the bourgeois ideologists who were combating the Restoration in the name of progress.

On the other hand, however, honest writers, keenly observant of the real facts of social development, like Scott, were made to see that this peaceful development was peaceful only as the ideal of an historical conception, only from the bird's-eye view of a philosophy of history. The organic character of English development is a resultant made up of the components of ceaseless class struggles and their bloody resolution in great or small, successful or abortive uprisings. The enormous political and social transformations of the preceding decades awoke in England, too, the feeling for history, the awareness of historical development.

The relative stability of English development during this stormy period, in comparison with that of the Continent, made it possible to channel this newly-awoken historical feeling artistically into a broad, objective, epic form. This objectivity is further heightened by Scott's conservatism. His world-view ties him very closely to those sections of society which had been precipitated into ruin by the industrial revolution and the rapid growth of capitalism. Scott belongs neither with the ardent enthusiasts of this development, nor with its pathetic, passionate indicters. He attempts by fathoming historically the whole of English development to find a "middle way" for himself between the warring extremes. He finds in English history the consolation that the most violent vicissitudes of class struggle have always finally calmed down into a glorious "middle way". Thus, out of the struggle of the Saxons and Normans there arose the English nation, neither Saxon nor Norman; in the same way the bloody Wars of the Roses gave rise to the illustrious reign of the House of Tudor, especially that of Queen Elizabeth; and those class struggles which manifested themselves in the Cromwellian Revolution were finally evened out in the England of today, after a long period of uncertainty and civil war, by the "Glorious Revolution" and its aftermath.

The conception of English history in the novels of Scott thus gives a perspective (though not explicit) of future development in its author's sense. And it is not difficult to see that this perspective shows a marked affinity with that resigned "positivity" which we observed in the great thinkers, scholars, and writers of this period on the Continent. Scott ranks among those honest Tories in the England of his time who exonerate nothing in the development of capitalism, who not only see clearly, but also deeply sympathise with the unending misery of the people which the collapse of old England brings in its wake; yet who, precisely because of their conservatism, display no violent opposition to the features of the new development repudiated by them. Scott very seldom speaks of the present. He does not raise the social questions of contemporary England in his novels, the class struggle between bourgeoisie and proletariat which was then beginning to sharpen. As far as he is able to answer these questions for himself, he does so in the indirect way of embodying the most important stages of the whole of English history in his writing.

Paradoxically, Scott's greatness is closely linked with his often narrow conservatism. He seeks the "middle way" between the extremes and endeavours to demonstrate artistically the historical reality of this way by means of his portrayal of the great crises in English history. This basic tendency finds immediate expression in the way he constructs his plot and selects his central figure. The "hero" of a Scott novel is always a more or less mediocre, average English gentleman. He generally possesses a certain, though never outstanding, degree of practical intelligence, a certain moral fortitude and decency which even rises to a capacity for self-sacrifice, but which never grows into a sweeping human passion, is never the enraptured devotion to a great cause. Not only are the Waverleys, Mortons, Osbaldistons, and so on correct, decent, average representatives of the English petty aristocracy of this kind, but so, too, is Ivanhoe, the "romantic" knight of the Middle Ages.

In later criticism this choice of hero was sharply criticised, for example by Taine. Such later critics saw here a symptom of Scott's own mediocrity as an artist. Precisely the opposite is true. That he builds his novels round a "middling", merely correct and never heroic "hero" is the clearest proof of Scott's exceptional and revolutionary epic gifts, although from a psychological-bio-graphical point of view, no doubt his own personal, petty aristo-cratic-conservative prejudices did play an important part in the choice of these heroes.

What is expressed here, above all, is a renunciation of Romanti-cism, a conquest of Romanticism, a higher development of the realist literary traditions of the Enlightenment in keeping with the new times. As a form of opposition to the degrading, all-levelling prose of rising capitalism the "demonic hero" makes his ap-pearance even in the writings of politically and ideologically pro-gressive writers who frequently, though unjustly, have been treated as Romantics. This hero type, particularly as he appears in the poetry of Byron, is the literary expression of the social eccen-tricity and superfluity of the best and sincerest human talents in this period of prose, a lyrical protest against the dominion of this prose. But it is one thing to acknowledge the social roots or even the historical necessity and justification of this protest and another to make of it a lyrical-subjectivist absolute. On this latter basis an objective portrayal is impossible. The great realistic writers of a somewhat later period who portrayed this type, such as Pushkin or Stendhal, overcame Byronism differently from Scott and in a higher form. They interpreted the problem of the eccentricity of this type in a social-historical, objective-epic way: that is, they saw the present historically and revealed all the social determinants of the tragedy (or tragi-comedy) of this protest. Scott's criticism and rejection of this type does not go as deep as this. His recog-nition or rather sense of the eccentricity of this type has the result of eliminating him from the sphere of historical portrayal. Scott endeavours to portray the struggles and antagonisms of history by means of characters who, in their psychology and destiny, always represent social trends and historical forces. Scott also extends this approach to the processes of declassing, always regarding them socially and not individually. His understanding for the problems of the present is not sufficiently deep for him to portray the problem of declassing as it affects the present. Therefore he avoids this subject and preserves in his portrayals the great historical objectivity of the true epic writer.

For this reason alone, then, it is completely wrong to see Scott as a Romantic writer, unless one wishes to extend the concept of Romanticism to embrace all great literature in the first third of the nineteenth century. But then the physiognomy of Romanticism, in the proper, narrow sense, becomes blurred. And this is of great importance if we are to understand Scott. For the historical subject-matter of his novels is very close to that of the Romantics proper. However, we shall show subsequently in detail that Scott's interpretation of this subject-matter is entirely opposed to that of the Romantics, as is his manner of portrayal. This contrast has its first, immediate expression in the composition of his novels – with the mediocre, prosaic hero as the central figure.

Naturally, Scott's conservative philistinism is manifest here as well. Already Balzac, his great admirer and successor, took objection to this English philistinism. He says, for example, that with very few exceptions all of Scott's heroines represent the same type of philistinely correct, normal English woman; that there is no room in these novels for the interesting and complex tragedies and comedies of love and marriage. Balzac is right in his criticism, and it applies far beyond the erotic sphere which he stresses. Scott does not command the magnificent, profound psychological dialectics of character which distinguishes the novel of the last great period of bourgeois development. Nor indeed does he reach the heights scaled by the bourgeois novel in the second half of the eighteenth century, by Rousseau, Choderlos de Laclos, and Goethe's *Werther*. His greatest successors in the historical novel, Pushkin and Manzoni, also far surpassed him in this respect by the depth and poetry of their characterisation. But the change which Scott effects in the history of world literature is independent of this limitation of his human and poetic horizon. Scott's greatness lies in his capacity to give living human embodiment to historical-social types. The typically human terms in which great historical trends become tangible had never before been so superbly, straightforwardly, and pregnantly portrayed. And above all, never before had this kind of portrayal been consciously set at the centre of the representation of reality.

This applies to his mediocre heroes as well. They are unsurpassed in their portrayal of the decent and attractive as well as narrow-minded features of the English "middle class". And as central figures they provide a perfect instrument for Scott's way of presenting the totality of certain transitional stages of history. This relationship was most clearly recognised by the great Russian critic, Belinsky. He accepts that the majority of the minor characters are more interesting and significant as human beings than the mediocre main hero, yet he strongly defends Scott. "This has indeed to be the case in a work of purely epic nature, where the chief character serves merely as an external central hub round which the events unfold and where he may distinguish himself merely by general human qualities which earn our human sympathy; for the hero of the epic is life itself and not the individual. In epic, the individual is, so to speak, subject to the event; the event over-shadows the human personality by its magnitude and importance, drawing our attention away from him by the interestingness, diversity and multiplicity of its images."

Belinsky is quite right in emphasising the purely epic character of Scott's novels. In the entire history of the novel there are scarcely any other works – except perhaps those of Cooper and Tolstoy – which come so near to the character of the old epos. This, as we shall see, is very closely linked with the nature of Scott's historical subject-matter. And it is linked not with his interest in history as such, but with the specific nature of his historical themes, with his selection of those periods and those strata of society which embody the old epic self-activity of man, the old epic directness of social life, its public spontaneity. This it is that makes Scott a great epic portrayer of the "age of heroes", the age in and from which the true epic grows, in the sense of Vico and Hegel. This truly epic character of Scott's subject-matter and manner of portrayal is, as we shall later show in detail, intimately linked with the popular character of his art.

Nevertheless, Scott's works are in no way modern attempts to galvanise the old epic artificially into new life, they are real and genuine novels. Even if his themes are very often drawn from the "age of heroes", from the infancy of mankind, the spirit of his writing is nevertheless that of man's maturity, the age of triumphing "prose". This difference must be stressed if only because it is intimately connected with the composition of Scott's novels, with the conception of their "hero". Scott's novel hero is in his way just as typical for this genre as Achilles and Odysseus were for the real epopee. The difference between the two hero types illustrates very sharply the fundamental difference between epic and novel, moreover in a case where the novel reaches its closest point to the epic. The heroes of the epic are, as Hegel says, "total individuals who magnificently concentrate within themselves what is otherwise dispersed in the national character, and in this they remain great, free and noble human characters". Thereby "these principal characters acquire the right to be placed at the summit and to see the principal event in connexion with their individual persons". The principal figures in Scott's novels are also typical characters nationally, but in the sense of the decent and average, rather than the eminent and all-embracing. The latter are the national heroes of a poetic view of life, the former of a prosaic one.

It is easy to see how these contrasting conceptions of the hero spring from the fundamental requirements of epic and novel. Achilles is not only compositionally the central figure of the epic, he is also a head taller than all his fellow actors, he really is the sun round which the planets revolve. Scott's heroes, as central figures of the novel, have an entirely opposite function. It is their task to bring the extremes whose struggle fills the novel, whose clash expresses artistically a great crisis in society, into contact with one another. Through the plot, at whose centre stands this hero, a neutral ground is sought and found upon which the extreme, opposing social forces can be brought into a human relationship with one another.

Scott's simple, yet inexhaustible and superb inventiveness in this respect is generally, especially today, too little appreciated, although Goethe, Balzac and Pushkin clearly recognised this greatness. Scott presents great crises of historical life in his novels. Accordingly, hostile social forces, bent on one another's

H

destruction, are everywhere colliding. Since those who lead these warring forces are always passionate partisans of their respective sides, there is the danger that their struggle will become a merely external picture of mutual destruction incapable of arousing the human sympathies and enthusiasms of the reader. It is here that the compositional importance of the mediocre hero comes in. Scott always chooses as his principal figures such as may, through character and fortune, enter into human contact with both camps. The appropriate fortunes of such a mediocre hero, who sides passionately with neither of the warring camps in the great crisis of his time can provide a link of this kind without forcing the composition. Let us take the best known example. Waverley is an English country squire from a family which is pro-Stuart, but which does no more than quietly sympathise in a politically ineffective fashion. During his stay in Scotland as an English officer, Waverley, as a result of personal friendships and love entanglements, enters the camp of the rebellious Stuart supporters. As a result of his old family connexions and the uncertain nature of his participation in the uprising, which allows him to fight bravely, but never to become fanatically partisan, his relations with the Hanoverian side are sustained. In this way Waverley's fortunes create a plot which not only gives us a pragmatic picture of the struggle on both sides, but brings us humanly close to the important representatives of either side.

This manner of composition is not the product of a "search for form" or some ingeniously contrived "skill", it stems rather from the strengths and limitations of Scott's literary personality. In the first place Scott's conception of English history is, as we have seen, that of a "middle course" asserting itself through the struggle of extremes. The central figures of the Waverley type represent for Scott the age-old steadfastness of English development amidst the most terrible crises. In the second place, however, Scott, the great realist, recognises that no civil war in history has been so violent as to turn the entire population without exception into fanatical partisans of one or other of the contending camps. Large sections of people have always stood between the camps with fluctuating sympathies now for this side, now for the other. And these fluctuating sympathies have often played a decisive role in the actual outcome of the crisis. In addition, the daily life of the nation still goes on amidst the most terrible civil war. It has to go on in the sheer economic sense that if it does not, the nation will starve and perish. But it also goes on in every other respect, and this continuation of daily life is an important foundation for the continuity of cultural development. Of course, the continuation of daily life certainly does not mean that the life, thought and experience of these non- or not passionately participant popular masses can remain untouched by the historical crisis. The continuity is always at the same time a growth, a further development. The "middle-of-the-road heroes" of Scott also represent this side of popular life and historical development.

But still further and very important consequences flow from this manner of composition. For instance what may sound paradoxical to the reader prejudiced by present-day traditions of the historical novel, but is nevertheless true, is the fact that Scott's incomparable ability to recreate the great figures of history was due to precisely this aspect of his composition. In Scott's life-work we meet with the most important personalities of English and even of French history: Richard *Coeur de Lion*, Louis xi, Elizabeth, Mary Stuart, Cromwell, etc. All these figures appear in Scott in their real historical grandeur. Yet Scott is never prompted by a feeling of romantically decorative hero-worship *à la* Carlyle. For him the great historical personality is the representative of an important and significant movement embracing large sections of the people. He is great because his personal passion and personal aim coincide with this great historical movement, because he concentrates within himself its positive and negative sides, because he gives to these popular strivings their clearest expression, because he is their standard-bearer in good and in evil.

For this reason Scott never shows the evolution of such a personality. Instead, he always presents us with the personality complete. Complete, yet not without the most careful preparation. This preparation, however, is not a personal and psychological one, but objective, social-historical. That is to say, Scott, by disclosing the actual conditions of life, the actual growing crisis in people's lives, depicts all the problems of popular life which lead up to the historical crisis he has represented. And when he has made us sympathisers and understanding participants of this crisis, when we understand exactly for what reasons the crisis has arisen, for what reasons the nation has split into two camps, and when we have seen the attitude of the various sections of the population towards this crisis, only then does the great historical hero enter upon the scene of the novel. He may therefore, indeed he must, be complete in a psychological sense when he appears before us, for he appears in order to fulfil his historic mission in the crisis. The reader, however, never has the impression of any-thing rigidly complete, for the broadly drawn social struggles which precede the appearance of the hero show how at just such a time, just such a hero had to arise in order to solve just such problems.

Scott, of course, uses this manner of portrayal not only for the historically authenticated and well-known representative figures. On the contrary. In Scott's most important novels historically unknown, semi-historical or entirely non-historical persons play this leading role. Think of Vich Ian Vohr in *Waverley*, Burley in *Old Mortality,* Cedric and Robin Hood in *Ivanhoe*, Rob Roy and so on. These, too, are monumental historical figures, created according to the same artistic principles as the familiar historical figures. Indeed, the popular character of Scott's historical art manifests itself in the fact that these leader figures, who are directly interwoven with the life of the people, in general are more historically imposing than the well-known central figures of history.

But what is the connexion between Scott's ability to portray the historical greatness of an important figure and the minor composi-tional role which the latter plays? Balzac understood this secret of Scott's composition. Scott's novels, he said, marched towards the great heroes in the same way as history itself had done when it required their appearance. The reader, therefore, experiences the historical genesis of the important historical figures, and it is the writer's task from then on to let their actions make them appear the real representatives of these historical crises.

Scott thus lets his important figures grow out of the being of the age, he never explains the age from the position of its great representatives, as do the Romantic hero-worshippers. Hence they can never be central figures of the action. For the being of the age can only appear as a broad and many-sided picture if the everyday life of the people, the joys and sorrows, crises and confusions of average human beings are portrayed. The important leading figure, who embodies an historical movement, necessarily does so at a certain level of abstraction. Scott, by first showing the complex and involved character of popular life itself, creates this being which the leading figure then has to generalise and concentrate in an historical deed.

Scott's manner of composition here shows a very interesting parallel to Hegel's philosophy of history. For Hegel, too, the "world-historical individual" arises upon the broad basis of the world of "maintaining individuals". "Maintaining individuals" is Hegel's all-embracing term for men in "civil society", it describes society's uninterrupted self-reproduction through the activity of these individuals. The basis is formed by the personal, private, egoistic activity of individual human beings. In and through this activity the socially general asserts itself. In this activity the "maintenance of moral life" unfolds itself. But Hegel does not only think of society in the sense of this self-reproduction, as something stagnant; society also stands amid the current of history. Here the new opposes itself hostilely to the old, and the change "goes hand in hand with a depreciation, demolition and destruction of the preceding mode of reality". There occur great historical collisions in which, while the "world-historical individuals" are conscious bearers of historical progress (or of the "spirit" according to Hegel), they are so only in the sense of granting consciousness and clear direction to a movement already present in society. It is necessary to emphasise this side of the Heglian conception of history, because it is here – despite Hegel's idealism, his over-rating of the role of the "world-historical individuals" – that the contrast with the Romantic hero cult comes out sharply. According to Hegel the function of the world-historical individual is to tell men what they want. "He is," says Hegel, "the hidden Spirit knocking at the door of the present, still subterranean, still without a contemporary existence and wishing to break out, for whom the contemporary world is but a husk containing a different kernel from the old."

Scott's unequalled historical genius shows itself in the individual characteristics which he gives his leading figures so that they really concentrate in themselves the salient positive and negative sides of the movement concerned. The social and historical solidarity of leader and led in Scott is differentiated with extraordinary subtlety. Burley's single-minded, dauntless, heroic fanaticism marks the human summit of the rebellious Scottish Puritans at the time of Stuart Restoration, just as Vich Ian Vohr's peculiar, adventure-some compound of French courtly manners and clan patriar-chalism represents the reactionary side of Stuart Restoration attempts after the "Glorious Revolution" which closely involved backward sections of the Scottish people.

This close interaction, this deep unity between the historical representatives of a popular movement and the movement itself is heightened compositionally in Scott by the intensification and dramatic compression of events. Here again the classical form of narrative must be shielded from modern prejudices. It is a general belief today that because epic portrays more extensively and broadly than drama, therefore it is pure extension, the chronicle-like succession and juxtaposition of all the events of a period which must constitute the essential character of epic art. Yet this is not the case even in Homer. Think of the composition of the *Iliad*. The poem begins with an extremely dramatic situation, the clash between Achilles and Agamemnon. And the actual narra-tive consists only of those events which are the direct consequence of this clash, namely the events up to Hector's death. Even classical aesthetics recognised a conscious principle of composition here. With the rise of the modern social novel such intensification has become even more necessary. For the inter-relationships between the psychology of people and the economic and moral circumstances of their lives have grown so complex that it requires a very broad portrayal of these circumstances and interactions if people are to appear clearly as the concrete children of their age. It is no accident that Scott's growing historical consciousness moved towards this kind of form. To awaken distant, vanished ages and enable us to live through them again he had to depict this concrete interaction between man and his social environment in the broadest manner. The inclusion of the dramatic element in the novel, the concentration of events, the greater significance of dialogue, i.e. the direct coming-to-grips of colliding opposites in conversation, these are intimately linked with the attempt to portray historical reality as it actually was, so that it could be both humanly authentic and yet be reliveable by the reader of a later age. It is a question of the concentration of characterisation. Only bunglers have maintained (and continue to do so) that the historical characterisation of people and events means the accumulation of single, historically characteristic traits.

Scott never underestimated the importance of picturesque, descriptive elements of this kind. Indeed, he used them so much that superficial critics have seen here the essence of his art. But for Scott the historical characterisation of time and place, the historical "here and now" is something much deeper. For him it means that certain crises in the personal destinies of a number of human beings coincide and interweave within the determining context of an historical crisis. It is precisely for this reason that his manner of portraying the historical crisis is never abstract, the split of the nation into warring parties always runs through the centre of the closest human relationships. Parents and children, lover and beloved, old friends, etc., confront one another as opponents, or the inevitability of this confrontation carries the collision deep into their personal lives. It is always a fate suffered by groups of people connected and involved with one another; and it is never a matter of one single catastrophe, but of a chain of catastrophes, where the solution of each gives birth to a new conflict. Thus the profound grasp of the historical factor in human life demands a dramatic concentration of the epic framework.

The great writers of the eighteenth century composed much more loosely. They were able to do so because they took the manners of their time for granted and could assume an immediate and obvious effect upon their readers. But do not forget that this applies to the general structure of composition and not to the manner in which individual moments and happenings are portrayed. These writers also knew quite well that it was not completeness of description that mattered – the enumeration of an object's constituents or of a sequence of events forming a person's life, but the working-out of essential human and social determinants. Goethe's *Wilhelm Meister* is conceived much less dramatically than Scott's or Balzac's novels which come later. But the individual events in this long story show a definite tendency towards intensification. Wilhelm Meister's relationship to Serlo's theatre, for instance, is almost entirely concentrated around the problem of the Hamlet production. In Goethe, too, there is no question of a complete description of the theatre, nor of a complete chronicle of events in the theatre.

The dramatic concentration and intensification of events in Scott is thus in no way a radical innovation. It is merely a special summing-up and extension of the most important artistic principles of the preceding period of development. But because Scott accomplished this extension at a great historical turning-point, in keeping with the real needs of the time, it signifies a turning-point in the history of the novel. For the historical novel presents the writer with a specially strong temptation to try and produce an extensively complete totality. The idea that only such complete-ness can guarantee historical fidelity is a very persuasive one. But it is a delusion, to which Balzac, in particular, drew sharp attention in his critical writings. In a review of Latouche's completely forgotten historical novel *Leo*, he says: "The entire novel consists of 200 pages on which 200 events are dealt with; nothing betrays the incompetence of the author more than the heaping-up of facts. . . . Talent flourishes where the causes which produce the facts are portrayed, in the secrets of the human heart, whose motions are neglected by the historians. The characters of a novel are forced to be more rational than historical characters. The former must be roused to life, the latter have already lived. The existence of the latter requires no proof, however bizarre their actions may have been, while the existence of the former requires general agreement." It is clear that the more remote an historical period and the conditions of life of its actors, the more the action must concern itself with bringing these conditions plastically before us, so that we should not regard the particular psychology and ethics which arise from them as an historical curiosity, but should re-experience them as a phase of mankind's development which concerns and moves us.

What matters therefore in the historical novel is not the re-telling of great historical events, but the poetic awakening of the people who figured in those events. What matters is that we should re-experience the social and human motives which led men to think, feel and act just as they did in historical reality. And it is a law of literary portrayal which first appears paradoxical, but then quite obvious, that in order to bring out these social and human motives of behaviour, the outwardly insignificant events, the smaller (from without) relationships are better suited than the great monumental dramas of world history. Balzac, in his criticism of Stendhal's *La Chartreuse de Parme*, enthusiastically praised Stendhal's genius, because he had undertaken a magnificent picture of court life within the framework of an Italian petty state. Balzac points out how in the petty struggles of the court of Parma all the social and spiritual conflicts which took place, for example, in the big struggles round Mazarin and Richelieu, are clearly manifest. And these struggles, according to Balzac, can be better portrayed in this way because the political content of the intrigues in Parma can be easily surveyed as a whole, can be translated directly into action and because its human spiritual reflexes can be revealed in an obvious, straightforward way, whereas the presentation of the big political problems which formed the substance of the intrigues round Mazarin or Richelieu, would create a dead and heavy ballast in a novel.

Balzac applies his argument to the smallest details involved in the epic treatment of history. He criticises among other things a novel by Eugène Sue which deals with the rebellion in the Cévennes under Louis XIV. Sue gave an extensive description of the entire campaign from fight to fight in a modern dilettantist manner. Balzac attacks this enterprise with the greatest vigour. He says: "It is impossible for literature to go beyond a certain limit in painting the facts of war. To depict the Cévennes mountains, the plains between them, the flat expanse of Languedoc, and troop manoeuvres covering this entire area – this is something that Walter Scott and Cooper felt to be beyond their powers. They never attempted a campaign in their works, but confined themselves to small encounters, revealing through them the spirit of the two contending masses. And even these small skirmishes which they undertook required lengthy preparation in their works." Balzac's description here of the intensive character of Scott's and Cooper's picture of history, applies also to the later development of the historical novel in the work of its great classical exponents.

Thus it would be a mistake to think that Tolstoy, for instance, really depicted the Napoleonic wars *in extenso*. What he does is, every now and then, to take an episode from the war which is of

particular importance and significance for the human development of his main characters. And Tolstoy's genius as an historical
novelist lies in his ability to select and portray these episodes so
that the entire mood of the Russian army and through them of the
Russian people gains vivid expression. Where he attempts to deal
with comprehensive political and strategic problems of the war,
for example in his description of Napoleon, he abandons himself
to historico-philosophical effusions. And he does this not only
because he misunderstands Napoleon historically, but also for
literary reasons. Tolstoy was far too great a writer to be capable
of offering a literary surrogate. Where his material could no
longer be artistically embodied, he radically forsook literary
means of expression and attempted to master his theme by intellectual means. And in so doing he furnishes a practical proof for the
correctness of Balzac's analysis of the Scott novel and his criticism
of Sue.

The historical novel therefore has to *demonstrate from artistic*
means that historical circumstances and characters existed in
precisely such and such a way. What in Scott has been called very
superficially "authenticity of local colour" is in actual fact this
artistic demonstration of historical reality. It is the portrayal of the
broad living basis of historical events in their intricacy and complexity, in their manifold interaction with acting individuals. The
difference between "maintaining" and "world-historical" individuals is expressed in this living connexion with the existential
basis of events. The former experience the smallest oscillations in
this basis as immediate disturbances of their individual lives, while
the latter concentrate the main features of events into motives for
their own actions and for influencing and guiding the actions of
the masses. The closer the "maintaining individuals" are to the
ground, the less fitted they are for historical leadership, the more
distinctly and vividly do these disturbances make themselves felt
in their everyday lives, in their immediate, emotional responses.
Obviously, such responses may easily become one-sided and even
false. But a total historical picture depends upon a rich and graded
interaction between different levels of response to any major
disturbance of life. It must disclose artistically the *connexion*
between the spontaneous reaction of the masses and the historical
consciousness of the leading personalities.

Such connexions are of decisive importance for the understanding of history. One of the distinctive qualities of really great popular political leaders is their unusually sensitive understanding for such spontaneous reactions. Their genius manifests itself in the usual rapidity with which they are able to perceive in quite small and insignificant reactions a change of mood, in the people or a class, and to generalise the connexion between this mood and the objective course of events. This power of perception and generalisation forms the basis of what leaders customarily call "learning from the masses". Lenin in his pamphlet *Will the Bolsheviks Retain State Power?* describes a very instructive instance of this interaction. After the suppression of the July rising of the Petrograd proletariat in 1917 Lenin is forced to live in illegality with a worker's family in the suburbs. He describes the preparation of the midday meal. "The wife brings in the bread. The husband says: 'Look at this lovely bread. They don't dare give us bad bread now. We had almost forgotten that there was good bread to be had in Petrograd.'" Lenin adds: "I was amazed at this class estimate of the July days. My thoughts had revolved round the political significance of the events. . . . As a person who had never known want, I had never given a thought to bread. . . . Thought follows an uncommonly complicated and intricate path to reach, via political analysis, what is at the basis of everything, namely the class struggle for bread."

Here we can see such an interaction in wonderful plasticity. The Petrograd worker reacts with spontaneous class-consciousness to the events of the July days. Lenin learns from these reactions with the greatest sensitivity and turns them to account with remarkable speed and precision in the consolidation, substantiation, and propagation of the correct political perspective.

It would, of course, be historically wrong if interactions of this kind were portrayed in novels dealing with the Middle Ages, seventeenth or eighteenth centuries. Besides, such interactions lay far beyond the horizon of the classical founders of the historical novel. Moreover, this example was only meant to illustrate the general structure of the interaction. But although all Scott's heroes acted with a "false consciousness" this is never a scheme, neither in its content nor its psychology. The difference, both in historical content and psychology, between close-to-life spontaneity and the capacity of generalisation, which exists apart from the immediate necessities of earning a living, runs right through history. It is the task of the historical novelist to portray this concrete interaction, in keeping with the concrete, historical circumstances of the age he represents, as richly as possible. And this is one of Scott's greatest strengths.

The colourful and varied richness of Scott's historical world is a consequence of the multiplicity of these interactions between individuals and the unity of social existence which underlies this richness. The problem of composition already discussed, the fact, that the great historical figures, the leaders of the warring classes and parties are only minor characters in the story, now takes on a new light. Scott does not stylise these figures, nor place them upon a Romantic pedestal; he portrays them as human beings with virtues and weaknesses, good and bad qualities. And yet they never create a petty impression. With all their weaknesses they appear historically imposing. The primary reason for this is, of course, Scott's deep understanding for the peculiarity of different historical periods. But the fact that he is able to combine historical grandeur with genuine human qualities in this way depends upon the manner of his composition.

The great historical figure, as a minor character, is able to live himself out to the full as a human being, to display freely all his splendid and petty human qualities. However, his place in the action is such that he can only act and express himself in situations of historical importance. He achieves here a many-sided and full expression of his personality, but only insofar as it is linked with the big events of history. Otto Ludwig says very perceptively of Scott's Rob Roy: "He can appear all the more significant, because we do not follow his life step by step; we see him only at moments when he is *significant*; he surprises us by his omnipresence, he reveals himself only in the most interesting attitudes."

These remarks not only correctly describe Scott's manner of composition, they also point to general laws of portrayal: to the manner of representing important persons. Here there are deep differences between epic and novel. The all-national character of the principal themes of epic, the relation between individual and nation in the age of heroes require that the most important figure should occupy the central position, while in the historical novel he is necessarily only a minor character.

However, the choice of situation, noted by Otto Ludwig, where the leading figure only appears at significant moments also applies *mutatis mutandis* to epic. Holderlin recognised this, correctly and profoundly, in the case of Achilles. He says: "One has often wondered why Homer who, after all, wanted to sing the anger of Achilles, hardly allows him to appear, etc. . . . He did not wish to profane the divine youth in the tumult outside Troy. The ideal must not appear commonplace. And he really could not sing him more gloriously and tenderly than by withdrawing him into the background . . . , so that every loss of the Greeks from the day the matchless one is missed from the army recalls his superiority over the entire resplendent host of lords and servants, and the rare moments when the poet allows him to appear before us are thrown all the more into relief by his absence."

It is not too difficult to see the common factors here. Since all narrative art has to do with the small and even trivial details of life, it cannot allow the hero to figure personally in the foreground all the time for this would mean reducing him to the general level of the life portrayed; only a forced stylisation could then effect the desired and necessary distance between him and the other charac-ters. But this kind of stylisation runs contrary to the real nature of epic which always seeks to create the impression of life as it normally is *as a whole*. This precisely is one of the many, never-fading charms of the Homeric epics, while the so-called literary epic, which almost consistently stylises the distance between hero and surrounding world, elevating the central figure artificially, is epically lifeless, rhetorical and lyrical. In Homer a character like Achilles always has the same naturalness and human simplicity as any other figure. Homer lifts him from his surroundings by genuinely epic means, that is which are both artistic *and* true to nature: he creates situations where the significant emerges, so to speak, "of its own accord", situations in which the hero steps naturally, "of his own accord", on to a pedestal by contrasting with his own absence.

All these general epic functions are present in Scott, too. But, as we have seen, the relationship of the "world-historical indi-vidual" to the world in which he acts is quite different in the

historical novel. The important features here are not the supreme
manifestations of an essentially unchanging world order (as far as
literature was concerned), but on the contrary the radical sharpening of social trends in an historical crisis. Further, the historical
novel portrays a much more differentiated social world than the
ancient epos. And with the increasing class divisions and class
oppositions the representative role of the "world-historical
individual", who concentrates the most important features of a
society, takes on quite a different significance.

The antagonisms in the old epics are predominantly national
ones. The great national opponents, say, Achilles and Hector,
represent socially, and therefore also morally, very similar orders:
the moral scope of their actions is approximately the same: for the
one, the human assumptions behind the actions of the other are
fairly transparent and so on. All this is quite different in the world
of the historical novel. Here the "world-historical individual" is,
even viewed socially, a *party*, a representative of *one* of the many
contending classes and strata. However, if he is to fulfil his
function as the crowning summit of such an artistic world, then he
must – in a very complex, very indirect way – also render visible
the generally progressive features of the whole of society, of the
whole age. These complicated preconditions of his representative
role are portrayed in Scott by means of that broad prehistory
which everywhere points towards his appearance; and the need
for this prehistory would alone suffice to make him a minor
character in the sense already explained.

This again then, as the reader has no doubt already gathered
from the previous remarks, is not a matter of a clever technical
trick on Scott's part, but of the artistic expression, in compositional terms, of his historical attitude to life. His admiration of the
great personalities of history as decisive factors in the historical
process leads him to this manner of composition. By renewing the
old laws of epic poetry in his original way Scott discovers the only
possible means whereby the historical novel can reflect historical
reality adequately, without either romantically monumentalising
the important figures of history or dragging them down to the
level of private, psychological trivia. Thus Scott humanises his
historical heroes, while avoiding what Hegel calls the psychology
of the valet, namely the detailed analysis of small, human peculi-

arities which have nothing to do with the historical mission of the person concerned.

However, this manner of composition certainly does not mean that Scott's historical figures are not individualised down to their smallest human peculiarities. They are never mere representatives of historical movements, ideas, etc. Scott's great art consists precisely in individualising his historical heroes in such a way that certain, purely individual traits of character, quite peculiar to them, are brought into a very complex, very live relationship with the age in which they live, with the movement which they represent and endeavour to lead to victory. Scott represents simultaneously the historical necessity of this particular individual personality and the individual role which he plays in history. What results from this peculiar relationship is not merely whether the struggle will end in victory or defeat, but also the special, historical character of the victory or defeat, its special historical *valeur*, its class timbre.

One of the greatest feats of portrayal in world literature, for instance, is the way Mary Stuart concentrates all the features which from the outset condemn to failure her *coup d'état* and flight. The shadow of these qualities may already be felt in the composition and conduct of her supporters, who are preparing the *coup*, long before she herself is shown to the readers. Her own conduct adds consciousness to this feeling, and the defeat itself is only the fulfilment of an expectation which has been fostered for a long time. With equal mastery, but with quite different technical means, Scott depicts the superiority and victorious diplomacy of the French King, Louis XI. At the beginning the contrast, social and human, between the King and his retinue, still mostly feudal-chivalrous in sentiment, only appears in a few small preliminary skirmishes. Then for the entire middle action of the novel the King vanishes from the scene. He has cunningly saddled the correct, chivalrous hero, Quentin Durward, with a dangerous, indeed insoluble, task. And only at the end does he reappear in what is, outwardly, a completely desperate plight as a prisoner in the camp of the feudal-chivalrous, adventuresome, and politically stupid Duke of Burgundy, where purely by use of reason and cunning he extracts such advantages as to leave the reader in no doubt that, despite the draw with which the novel ends, the principle for which he stands has triumphed. These complex and yet straightforward interactions between the representatives of different classes, between the "above" and "below" of society create that incomparably truthful, historical atmosphere which in every novel of Scott reawakens a period; and which reawakens not only its historical-social content, but its human and emotional qualities, its particular redolence and ring.

This truthfulness of historical atmosphere which we are able to relive in Scott rests on the popular character of his art. This popular character met with growing incomprehension during the literary and cultural decadence. Taine asserts quite erroneously that Scott's art propagated feudal attitudes. This false theory was taken over whole by vulgar sociology and further extended, the sole difference being that Scott was now conceived as the poet, not of the feudal world, but of the English merchants and colonisers of contemporary English imperialism. Such "theories" of the historical novel – devised in order to erect a Chinese wall between the classical past and the present and so to deny the Socialist character of our present-day culture *à la* Trotsky – see in Scott nothing but the bard of the colonising merchants.

The precise opposite is true. And this was clearly recognised by Scott's immediate contemporaries and important successors. George Sand quite rightly said of him: "He is the poet of the peasant, soldier, outlaw and artisan." For, as we have seen, Scott portrays the great transformations of history as transformations of popular life. He always starts by showing how important historical changes affect everyday life, the effect of material and psychological changes upon people who react immediately and violently to them, without understanding their causes. Only by working up from this basis, does he portray the complicated ideological, political, and moral movements to which such changes inevitably give rise. The popular character of Scott's art, therefore, does not consist in an exclusive portrayal of the oppressed and exploited classes. That would be a narrow interpretation. Like every great popular writer, Scott aims at portraying the totality of national life in its complex interaction between "above" and "below"; his vigorous popular character is expressed in the fact that "below" is seen as the material basis and artistic explanation for what happens "above".

In *Ivanhoe* Scott portrays the central problem of medieval England, the opposition between the Saxons and Normans, in this way. He makes it very clear that this opposition is above all one between Saxon serfs and Norman feudal lords. But, in a true historical manner, he goes further than this opposition. He knows that a section of the Saxon nobility, though materially restricted and robbed of its political power, is still in possession of its aristocratic privileges and that this provides the ideological and political centre of the Saxons' national resistance to the Normans. However, as a great portrayer of historical, national life Scott sees and shows with eminent plasticity how important sections of the Saxon nobility sink into apathy and inertia, how others again are only waiting for the opportunity to strike a compromise with the more moderate sections of the Norman nobility whose representative is Richard *Coeur de Lion*. Thus, when Belinsky quite rightly says that Ivanhoe, the hero of this novel and likewise an aristocratic adherent of this compromise, is overshadowed by the minor characters, this formal problem of the historical novel has a very clear historical-political and popular content. For although one of the figures who overshadows Ivanhoe is his father, the brave and ascetic Saxon nobleman, Cedric, the most important of these figures are the latter's serfs, Gurth and Wamba, and above all the leader of the armed resistance to Norman rule, the legendary popular hero, Robin Hood. The interaction between "above" and "below", the sum of which constitutes the totality of popular life, is thus manifested in the fact that, while on the whole the historical tendencies "above" receive a more distinct and generalised expression, we find the true heroism with which the historical antagonisms are fought out, with few exceptions, "below".

The picture of popular life is drawn in just the same way in the other novels. Admittedly, in *Waverley* Vich Ian Vohr is the tragic hero, who for his loyalty to the Stuarts ends on the gallows. Yet we do not find the real, humanly stirring, unproblematic heroism in this – when all is said – ambiguous adventurer figure, but among his supporters in the Scottish clan. One of the greatest portrayals of simple, wordless heroism is the proposal of Evan Dhu, Vich Ian Vohr's fellow clansman, at the trial where they are both condemned to death: Evan Dhu whom the court would willingly

I

pardon, suggests that he and a few other members of the clan should be executed in return for the release of their chief.

In touches such as these Scott's combination of popular spirit and historical authenticity emerges very clearly. Historical authenticity means for him the quality of the inner life, the morality, heroism, capacity for sacrifice, steadfastness, etc., peculiar to a given age. This is the important, imperishable and – for the history of literature – epoch-making thing about Scott's historical authenticity and not the much-discussed, so-called "local colour" of the descriptions which is only one among many ancillary, artistic devices and could never on its own reawaken the spirit of an age. Both the great human qualities as well as the vices and limitations of Scott's heroes spring from a clearly embodied historical basis of existence. It is neither by analysis, nor by psychological explanation of its ideas that Scott familiarises by a broad portrayal of its being, by showing how thoughts, feelings, modes of behaviour grow up out of this basis.

This is always shown in a masterly way in the course of some interesting happening. Thus Waverley becomes acquainted with the clansmen for the first time through a transaction between the clan and a Scottish landowner on the occasion of a cattle theft. They are still as unintelligible for him as they are for the reader. He then spends a considerable time among the clan, getting to know thoroughly the everyday life of the clansmen, their habits, joys, and sorrows. When the clan then goes to war, and Waverley with it, both he and the reader are already familiar with the peculiar being and consciousness of these people still living in a gentile order. When in the first battle against the royal troops, Waverley wishes to save a wounded English soldier from his own estate, the clansmen first of all protest against this assistance to an enemy. Only when they realise that the wounded Englishman belongs to Waverley's "clan" do they help and honour Waverley as a provident chieftain. The breathtaking effect of Evan Dhu's heroism is only possible upon the basis of this broad display of the material and moral character of clan life, its being and behaviour. And one experiences other kinds of past heroism in Scott in a very similar way, for example the heroism of the Puritans, etc.

Scott's great artistic aim, in portraying the historical crises of popular life, is to show the *human greatness* which is liberated in its important representatives by a disturbance of this all-embracing kind. There is no doubt that, consciously or unconsciously, it was the experience of the French Revolution which awoke this tendency in literature. It is already present, though very sporadically, in the period which directly prepared the Revolution, most significantly in Goethe's figure of Klärchen in *Egmont*. But this heroism, though occasioned by the Netherlands revolution, is nevertheless immediately called to life by Klärchen's love for Egmont. After the French Revolution Goethe himself finds a still more purely human expression for this tendency in his figure of Dorothea. Simple, strong, determined and heroic qualities spring to life in her as a result of the events of the French Revolution and the fate which her immediate environment suffers through these events. Goethe's great epic art shows itself in the way he draws Dorothea's heroism. It appears in complete accord with her simple and straightforward character: a quality which has always lain dormant in her as a potentiality and which is called to life by the great events of the time. Yet this heroism is not something which entails an irrevocable change in her life and psychological constitution. When the objective necessity for her heroic behaviour is over, Dorothea returns to everyday life.

Whether Scott knew these works of Goethe at all or to any extent is immaterial. The point is that, historically, he continues and extends this tendency of Goethe. His novels abound in such stories; everywhere we find this sudden blaze of great yet simple heroism among artless, seemingly average children of the people. Scott's extension of Goethe's tendency lies primarily in the fact that he brings out, much more strongly than Goethe, the historical character of this heroism, the peculiar historical quality of the human grandeur which it expresses. Goethe draws the general outlines of popular movements, of both the Netherlands and French Revolution, with extraordinary faithfulness to life. Nevertheless, while the minor characters in *Egmont* exhibit very definite contemporary historical features, while Klärchen, too, in every reaction provoked by her idyllic love for Egmont remains the child of her class and people, her heroic upsurge lacks a definite and emphatic historical character. It is true-to-life and authentic, for it shows human greatness within given historical circumstances, it follows organically from Klärchen's psychology, but its peculiar quality is not characterised historically. The same applies to the characterisation of Dorothea. In neither case does the poet use specifically social-historical features when it comes to portraying the actual heroic upsurge. Such features are given prominence before in both cases (and, in the case of Dorothea, afterwards too). Yet they serve merely as a framework for the heroism itself and give it no historical colouring.

It is different in Scott. One sees this tendency at its clearest in *The Heart of Midlothian*. Here Scott has created his greatest female character in the figure of the Puritan peasant girl, Jeanie Deans. Events face the daughter of a radical soldier of Cromwell's army with a terrible dilemma. Her sister is charged with infanticide; according to the inhuman laws of the time, proof that she has kept her pregnancy secret is sufficient to condemn her to death. She was compelled to keep this secrecy, but was not responsible for the infanticide. Now Jeanie could save her sister by perjuring herself. But despite intense love for her sister, despite unending sympathy for her fate, her Puritan conscience triumphs and, accordingly, she declares the truth. Her sister is condemned to death. And so then the peasant girl, uneducated, penniless, and unfamiliar with the world, walks to London in order to secure her sister's pardon from the King. The story of these inner battles and of this struggle to save her sister show the rich humanity and simple heroism of a really great human being. Yet Scott's picture of his heroine never for a moment obscures her narrow Puritan and Scottish peasant traits, indeed it is they which again and again form the specific character of the naïve and grand heroism of this popular figure.

Having successfully carried through her aim, Jeanie Deans returns to everyday life, and never again does she experience a similar upsurge in her life to betray the presence of such strengths. Scott draws this final stage in rather too broad and philistine a detail, while Goethe who aims at beauty of line and classical perfection, contents himself with indicating that Dorothea's heroic life is over and that she, too, must now recede into simple everyday life.

Both instances involve a formal epic requirement. But in both instances this formal requirement expresses a profound human and historical truth. The important thing for these great writers is to lay bare those vast, heroic, human potentialities which are always latently present in the people and which, on each big occasion, with every deep disturbance of the social or even the more personal life, emerge "suddenly", with colossal force, to the surface. The greatness of the crisis periods of humanity rests to a large extent on the fact that such hidden forces are always dormant in the people, and that they require only the occasion for them to appear on the surface. The epic requirement for such figures to recede after the accomplishment of their mission underlines just how general this phenomenon is. Neither Goethe, in the case of Dorothea, nor Scott, in the case of Jeanie Deans, wished to present an exceptional human being, an outstanding talent, who rises from the people to become the leader of a popular movement (Scott draws figures of this kind in Robin Hood and Rob Roy). On the contrary, they wished to show that the possibilities for this human upsurge and heroism are widespread among the popular masses, that endless numbers of people live out their lives quietly, without this upsurge, because no opportunity has come their way to evoke such an exertion of powers. Revolutions are thus the great periods of mankind because in and through them such rapid upward movements in human capacities become widespread.

Through this manner of human-historical portrayal Scott makes history live. As has been shown, he presents history as a series of great crises. His presentation of historical development, above all that of England and France, is of an uninterrupted series of such revolutionary crises. Thus if Scott's main tendency in all his novels – and which forms of them in a sense a kind of cycle – is to represent and defend progress, then this progress is for him always a process full of contradictions, the driving force and material basis of which is the living contradiction between conflicting historical forces, the antagonisms of classes and nations.

Scott affirms this progress. He is a patriot, he is proud of the development of his people. This is vital for the creation of a real historical novel, i.e. one which brings the past close to us and allows us to experience its real and true being. Without a felt relationship to the present, a portrayal of history is impossible. But this relationship, in the case of really great historical art, does not consist in alluding to contemporary events, a practice

which Pushkin cruelly ridiculed in the work of Scott's incompe-
tent imitators, but in bringing the past to life as the prehistory of
the present, in giving poetic life to those historical, social and
human forces which, in the course of a long evolution, have made
our present-day life what it is and as we experience it. Hegel
remarks: "The historical is only then ours . . . when we can regard
the present in general as a consequence of those events in whose
chain the characters or deeds represented constitute an essential
link. . . . For art does not exist for a small, closed circle of the
privilegedly cultured few, but for the nation as a whole. What
holds good for the work of art in general, however, also has its
application for the outer side of the historical reality represented.
It, too, must be made clear and accessible to us without extensive
learning so that we, who belong to our own time and nation, may
find ourselves at home therein, and not be obliged to halt before
it, as before some alien and unintelligible world."

Scott's patriotism forms the premise of this living connexion
with the past. And only vulgar sociologists can see in this
patriotism a glorification of the exploiting merchants. Goethe had
an infinitely deeper and truer understanding of Scott's relationship
to English history. In a conversation with Eckermann he speaks
of Scott's *Rob Roy*, in which the central figure, interestingly
enough, happens to be both a hero of the Scottish people and a
peculiar compound of rebel, cattle thief and smuggler – hence a
significant example of Scott's "social equivalent". Goethe says of
this novel: "Here, naturally everything is on the grand scale:
material, content, characters, treatment. . . . But one sees what
English history is and what it means when such a heritage falls to
the lot of a capable poet." Goethe thus clearly senses what it is
that constitutes Scott's pride in English history: on the one hand,
naturally, the gradual maturing of national strength and greatness,
the continuity of which Scott wishes to illustrate in his "middle
way": but on the other, and inseparable from this, the crises of this
growth, the extremes whose struggles produce this "middle way"
as their end-result and which could never be removed from the
picture of national greatness without robbing it precisely of all its
greatness, wealth and substance.

Scott sees and portrays the complex and intricate path which led
to England's national greatness and to the formation of the

national character. As a sober, conservative petty aristocrat, he naturally affirms the result, and the necessity of this result is the ground on which he stands. But Scott's artistic world-view by no means stops here. Scott sees the endless field of ruin, wrecked existences, wrecked or wasted heroic, human endeavour, broken social formations, etc., which were the necessary preconditons of the end-result.

Undoubtedly, there is a certain contradiction here between Scott's directly political views and his artistic world picture. He too, like so many great realists, such as Balzac or Tolstoy, became a great realist despite his own political and social views. In Scott, too, one can establish Engels's "triumph of realism" over his personal, political, and social views. Sir Walter Scott, the Scottish petty aristocrat, automatically affirms this development with a sober rationality. Scott, the writer, on the other hand, embodies the sentiment of the Roman poet, Lucan: "Victrix causa diis placuit, sed victa Catoni" (the victorious cause pleased the gods, but the vanquished pleased Cato).

It would be wrong, however, to interpret this contrast all too rigidly, without interconnexions: namely, to see in the sober affirmation of English reality, of the "middle way" of English development something purely negative, something which could only have hindered the unfolding of Scott's great historical art. On the contrary, we must see that this great historical art arose precisely out of the interaction, out of the dialectical interpenetration of both these sides of Scott's personality. It is precisely because of his character that Scott did not become a Romantic, a glorifier or elegist of past ages. And it was for this reason that he was able to portray objectively the ruination of past social formations, despite all his human sympathy for, and artistic sensitivity, to the splendid, heroic qualities which they contained. Objectively, in a large historical and artistic sense: he saw at one and the same time their outstanding qualities and the historical necessity of their decline.

This objectivity, however, only enhances the true poetry of the past. We have seen that the official representatives of earlier ruling classes by no means play the leading role in Scott's picture of history, quite contrary to the misrepresentations of later critics. Among the aristocratic figures of his novels – if one leaves out the

correct "middle-of-the-road heroes", who can only very condi-
tionally be called positive heroes – there are very few positively
drawn figures. On the contrary, Scott very often shows in a
humorous, satirical or tragic manner the weakness, the human and
moral degeneration of the upper strata. Admittedly the Pretender
in *Waverley*, Mary Stuart in *The Abbot*, even the Prince of Wales in
The Fair Maid of Perth exhibit humanly attractive and winning
features, but the chief tendency in their portrayal is to show their
inability to fulfil their historic missions. In such cases Scott
achieves his poetry by conveying to us the objectively historical,
social reasons for this personal inability via the atmosphere of the
whole, without pedantic analysis. Further, in a whole number of
figures, Scott draws the repellently brutal sides of aristocratic rule
(e.g. the Knight Templar in *Waverley*,[2] etc.) as well as the already
comic incapacity of the court nobility, increasingly severed from
national life, to cope with the problems of their age. The few
positive figures are made positive mostly by simple fulfilment of
duty and gentlemanliness. Only a few great champions of historical progress, such as Louis XI in particular, are allowed
historical monumentality.

In most cases where aristocratic figures play a positive role,
whether completely positive or problematic, this rests upon their
connexion with the people, which of course usually takes the
form of a living or, at least, not yet extinct patriarchal relationship
(e.g. in the case of the Duke of Argyle in *The Heart of Midlothian*).
The real life in Scott's historical reality is formed by the life of the
people themselves. As an English petty aristocrat with strong ties
both in tradition and individual habits of life with the bourgeoisie,
Scott has a deep sympathy for the defiant self-assurance of the
medieval English-Scots burgher and the independent, free
peasant. In the character of Henry Gow in particular (*The Fair
Maid of Perth*), he gives a fine picture of this medieval burgher
courage and self-confidence. Henry Gow as a fighter is at least the
equal of every knight, but he proudly declines the knighthood
offered to him by the Earl of Douglas; burgher he is and free
burgher he will live and die.

In Scott's life-work we find marvellous scenes and characters
from the life of the serfs and the free peasants, from the fortunes

[2] This is probably a mistake and *Ivanhoe* is intended. *Ed.*

of society's outlaws, the smugglers, robbers, professional soldiers, deserters, and so on. Yet it is in his unforgettable portrayal of the survivals of gentile society, of the Scottish clans where the poetry of his portrayal of past life chiefly lies. Here in material and subject-matter alone, there is present such a powerful element of the heroic period of mankind, that Scott's novels at their height do indeed approach the old epics. Scott is a giant discoverer and awakener of this long vanished past. It is true that the eighteenth century already loved and enjoyed the poetry of primitive life. And in the wave of enthusiasm for Homer, in Homer's ousting of Virgil as the model, there is undoubtedly a dawning awareness of this infant period of mankind. Important thinkers such as Ferguson even saw the relationship between the Homeric heroes and the American Indians. Nevertheless this predilection remained abstract and moralising in quality. Scott was the first actually to bring this period to life, by introducing us into the everyday life of the clans, by portraying upon this real basis both the exceptional and unequalled human greatness of this primitive order as well as the inner necessity of its tragic downfall.

In this way, by bringing to life those objective poetic principles which really underlie the poetry of popular life and history, Scott became the great poet of past ages, the really popular portrayer of history. Heine clearly understood this quality and saw, too, that the strength of Scott's writing lay precisely in this presentation of popular life, in the fact that the official big events and great historical figures were not given a central place. He says: "Walter Scott's novels sometimes reproduce the spirit of English history much more faithfully than Hume." The important historians and philosophers of history of this period, Thierry and Hegel, aspire to a similar interpretation of history. But with them it goes no further than a demand, a theoretical pronouncement of this necessity. For in the field of theory and historiography only historical materialism is capable of intellectually unearthing this basis of history, of showing what the childhood of mankind was really like. But what in Morgan, Marx, and Engels was worked out and proved with theoretical and historical clarity, lives, moves and has its being poetically in the best historical novels of Scott. For this reason Heine very rightly stresses this side of Scott, his popular side: "Strange whim of the people! They demand their history from the hand of the poet and not from the hand of the historian. They demand not a faithful report of bare facts, but those facts dissolved back into the original poetry whence they came."

We repeat: this poetry is objectively bound up with the necessary downfall of gentile society. We experience in the various novels of Scott the individual stages of this downfall in all its historical concreteness and differentiation. Scott did not – in the pedantic sense of Gustav Freytag's *Ahnen* (*Our Forefathers*) – wish to make a coherent cycle of his novels. But in regard to the fate of the clans this great historical connexion, the inexorable necessity of their tragedy emerges into colossal relief – if only because their fortunes always spring from a living interaction with the social-historical world around them. They are never presented independently or in isolation, but always in the context of a general crisis of Scottish or English-Scottish popular life. The chain of these crises extends from the first great struggles between the rising Scottish middle class and the nobility, from Royalty's attempt to use these struggles in strengthening central power (*The Fair Maid of Perth* – end of the fourteenth century) to the last attempts of the Stuarts to turn back the clock of history, to restore outdated Absolutism in an already far advanced capitalist England (*Rob Roy* – end of the eighteenth century).

The clans are, of historical necessity, always the exploited, the cheated, the deceived. Their very heroic qualities which stem from the primitiveness of their social being, make them the toy of the humanly far inferior representatives of the ruling powers of the given stage of civilisation. What Engels shows scientifically, namely how civilisation achieves things beyond the powers of the old gentile society, this Scott portrays. In particular, he portrays the contrast in the human sphere, which Engels stresses in his analysis of this inevitable collapse of gentile society in face of civilisation: "But it achieved them by setting in motion the lowest instincts and passions in man and developing them at the expense of all his other abilities."

As soon as absolute monarchy appears as a force within the class struggles of feudalism, it ruthlessly exploits the unimportant feud[s] of the clans, turning them into mutual massacres. The mutual extermination of all the able-bodied men of two clans which forms the action of the first of the above-named novels is admittedly a crude and exceptional case of this and only Scott's great art is able to extract from it the typical. But Scott can do this only because, on a spontaneous, more isolated and episodic scale, the inability of the clans to defend their common interests against nobility or bourgeoisie and the dissipation of all their energies in the local insularity of such petty struggles are an inevitable result of the basis of clan life. The bodyguard of the French king, Louis XI, already consists of members of the old clans who have been more or less forcibly scattered and thrown on to their own resources (*Quentin Durward*). And the parties in the later civil wars, Parliament as well as the Stuarts, are already ruthlessly and extensively exploiting the courageous, devoted clan warriors as cannon fodder for political ends totally foreign to the clans (*A Legend of Montrose, Waverley, Rob Roy*).

With the suppression of the uprising of 1745 – which is depicted in *Waverley* – the real downfall of gentile society in Scotland begins, says Engels. Several decades later (in *Rob Roy*) we see the clans already in a state of complete economic dissolution. One character in this novel, the shrewd merchant and bailiff of Glasgow, Jarvie, clearly sees that it has become a matter of economic necessity for the clans to wage their desperate and hopeless battles on behalf of the Stuarts. They are no longer able to maintain themselves on the basis of their primitive economy. They possess a surplus population, permanently armed and well seasoned who cannot be put to any normal use, who must resort to plunder and pillage, and for whom an uprising of this kind is the only way out of a hopeless situation. Thus we have here already an element of dissolution, the beginnings of class-uprooting which were as yet absent from the clan picture of *Waverley*.

Once more we must admire here Scott's extraordinarily realistic presentation of history, his ability to translate these new elements of economic and social change into human fates, into an altered psychology. His genuine popular feeling shows itself here in two ways. On the one hand he brings out these declassed features with implacable realism, particularly in the romantically adventurous behaviour of Rob Roy himself, who thereby differs very sharply, historically, from the primitive simplicity of the clan leaders of earlier periods. On the other he portrays this downfall of the clans with all the real popular heroism which attends it.

Despite the declassing tendencies Rob Roy also concentrates in himself the magnificent human qualities of the old clan heroes. The downfall of gentile society in Scott is a heroic tragedy, not a wretched decline.

Scott then becomes a great poet of history because he has a deeper, more genuine and differentiated sense of historical necessity than any writer before him. Historical necessity in his novels is of the most severe, implacable kind. Yet this necessity is no otherworldly fate divorced from men; it is the complex interaction of concrete historical circumstances in their process of transformation, in their interaction with the concrete human beings, who have grown up in these circumstances, have been very variously influenced by them, and who act in an individual way according to their personal passions. Thus, in Scott's portrayal, historical necessity is always a resultant, never a presupposition; it is the tragic atmosphere of a period and not the object of the writer's reflections.

This does not mean, of course, that Scott's characters do not reflect upon their aims and tasks. However, these are the reflexions of people acting in concrete circumstances. And the atmosphere of historical necessity arises out of the very subtly portrayed dialectic between the effectiveness and impotence of a correct insight in concrete historical circumstances. In *A Legend of Montrose* Scott portrays a Scottish episode in the great English Revolution. Both the Parliamentary army and the Royalists attempt to win over the warlike clans to themselves. Their instruments are the two great chieftains, Argyle and Montrose. Now it is extremely interesting that there is a small chieftain involved in this situation, who realises quite clearly that to join either King or Parliament means his own inevitable downfall. His insight, however, is rendered impotent from the outset by the clan's adherence to the great leaders. The war between Argyle and Montrose begins.

This same inner necessity, however, which here favoured Montrose's plan, sets narrow clan limits to its realisation. Montrose has defeated his opponent and would now like to join battle with the English enemies of the King; an army column with fresh forces might even change the course of the war in England. This, however, is objectively impossible. Only a Scottish clan war can be fought with an army of clan members. Montrose's followers will go through fire and water for him; yet in their conviction that the real enemy is not Parliament, but the hostile group of clans led by Argyle, they will yield neither to persuasion nor authority, however unlimited Montrose's power while he moves within the bounds of clan ideology. And one of the subtle and grand historical features in Scott's characterisation is that he does not permit a merely external resolution of this opposition. Montrose is indeed an aristocrat, a convinced Royalist, an army commander of distinguished abilities, a man of great political ambition, yet at heart he is also a clan chieftain. The clansmen's way of thinking also affects him inwardly; necessity, outer and inner, makes him give up his great plans and squander his energies in a petty clan war against Argyle.

In portraying how historical necessity asserts itself in this way through the passionate actions of individuals, but often against their individual psychology, in showing how this necessity has its roots in the real social and economic basis of popular life Scott manifests his *historical faithfulness*. Measured against this authentic reproduction of the real components of historical necessity, it matters little whether individual details, individual facts are historically correct or not. Of course, Scott is particularly strong and authentic in respect of these details too. But never in the antiquarian or exotic sense of later writers. Detail for Scott is only a means for achieving the historical faithfulness here described, for making concretely clear the historical necessity of a concrete situation. This historical faithfulness in Scott is the authenticity of the historical psychology of his characters, the genuine *hic et nunc* (here and now) of their inner motives and behaviour.

Scott preserves this historical faithfulness in the human-oral conception of his characters. The most conflicting and divergent reactions to particular events always occur in his successful novels within the objective dialectical framework of a particular historical crisis. In this sense he never creates eccentric figures, figures who fall psychologically outside the atmosphere of the age. This would merit a detailed analysis on the basis of some outstanding examples. We shall only mention briefly Jeanie Deans's sister, Effie. Apparently she stands in the sharpest psychological and moral contrast to her father and sister. But Scott portrays with great subtlety how this contrast arose precisely out of opposition to the basic peasant-Puritan character of the family, how a number of circumstances in her upbringing provided the opportunities for this exceptional development and how, nevertheless, she retained many psychological traits which, even during her tragic crisis and later social rise, preserved what was common to the society and time in which she and her family lived. This manner of portrayal shows that Scott, in sharp contrast to the post-1848 development of the historical novel, *never modernises* the psychology of his characters.

This modernising is, of course, not a new "achievement" of the post-1848 historical novel. On the contrary. It is the false inheritance which Scott himself overcame. And the struggle between genuine historical psychology and psychological modernisation forms the central problem on which minds divided in Scott's time, too. In the following we shall be dealing with this problem at length. Let it merely be said here that while the pseudo-historical novels of the seventeenth and eighteenth centuries simply equated naïvely the world of feeling of the past with that of the present, there is with Chateaubriand and German Romanticism a different, more dangerous trend of modernisation. For the German Romantics, in particular, place extreme emphasis upon the historical faithfulness of every detail. They discover the picturesque charm of the Middle Ages and reproduce it with "nazarene" accuracy: everything, from medieval Catholicism to antique furniture is reproduced with craftsmanlike precision, which often becomes mere decorative pedantry. The human beings, however, who act in this picturesque world, have the psychology of a tormented Romantic or a freshly converted apologist of the Holy Alliance.

This decorative caricature of historical faithfulness was firmly rejected in Germany by the great champions of progress in literature and culture, Goethe and Hegel. The historical novel of Scott is the living counterpart of this at once false historicism and inartistic modernisation. But does faithfulness to the past mean a chronicle-like, naturalistic reproduction of the language, mode of thought and feeling of the past? Of course not. And Scott's great German contemporaries, Goethe and Hegel, stated this problem with great theoretical clarity. Goethe brings up this question in a discussion of Manzoni's historical tragedy, *Adelchi*. He writes: "We pronounce in his defence what may seem paradoxical: that all poetry in fact moves in the element of anachronism. Whatever in the past we evoke, in order to recite it after our own fashion to our contemporaries, we must grant a higher culture to the ancient happening than it in fact had. . . . The *Iliad* and the *Odyssey*, all the great tragedians and all that has remained of true poetry lives and breathes only in anachronisms. To all conditions one lends the modern spirit, for only in this way can we see and, indeed, bear to see them. . . ."

How far these statements of Goethe directly influenced Hegel's aesthetics, we do not know. At any rate, Hegel in an aesthetic-conceptual generalisation of the problem speaks already of *necessary anachronism* in art. But what he has to say regarding the concretisation and historical dialectic of the problem goes, of course, considerably further than Goethe; he states theoretically those principles which determine Scott's historical practice. Hegel discusses necessary anachronism in the following way: "The inner substance of what is represented remains the same, but the developed culture in representing and unfolding the substantial necessitates a change in the expression and form of the latter."

This formulation sounds quite similar to Goethe's, but is really an extension. For Hegel already interprets the relation of present to past in a more consciously historical way than Goethe. Goethe is concerned chiefly with the breakthrough of universal human and humanist principles from the concrete basis of history. He wishes to remould the historical basis so as to allow for this break-through while preserving historical truth in its essentials. (We refer here to our earlier analysis of the portrayal of Dorothea and Klärchen.) Hegel, on the other hand, interprets this relation to the present historically. He maintains that "necessary anachronism" can emerge organically from historical material, if the past portrayed is clearly recognised and experienced by contemporary writers as the *necessary prehistory* of the present. Then the only kind of heightening required – in modes of expression, consciousness, etc. – is such that will clarify and underline this relationship. And then the remoulding of events, customs, etc., in the past would simply come to this: the writer would allow those tendencies which were alive and active in the past and which in historical reality have led up to the present (but whose later significance contemporaries naturally could not see) to emerge with that emphasis which they possess in objective, historical terms for the product of this past, namely, the present.

The ideas of Hegel sketch the aesthetic limits of historical subject-matter. He goes on for instance to contrast the necessary anachronism of the Homeric poems and the Greek tragedians with the medieval chivalric-feudal treatment of the *Nibelungenlied*. "This recasting takes a very different form when attitudes and ideas of a *later* development of religious and moral consciousness are transposed to an age or nation whose entire outlook *contradicts* such modern ideas." Modernisation, therefore, arises of aesthetic and historical necessity, whenever this living connexion between past and present is absent or only forcibly created.

There is, of course, an enormous historical difference, which is aesthetically reflected too, between the naïve unconsciousness and unconcern with which the poet of the *Nibelungenlied* refashioned the sagas of gentile times according to feudal-Christian ideas and the extravagant apologetics with which the reactionary Romantics transported the principles of Legitimism into the Middle Ages, turning them into a social idyll for decadent *déclassé* heroes.

Scott put Goethe's and Hegel's "necessary anachronism" into practice while we may be sure he had no knowledge of their reflexions. All the more significant, therefore, is the fact that the important progressive poet and thinker of this period should agree with Scott's creative principles. Particularly so, when one considers that he was quite conscious about them artistically, though he gave them no philosophical foundation. In the Dedicatory Epistle to *Ivanhoe* he writes on this question: "It is true that I neither can nor do pretend to the observation of complete accuracy, even in matters of outward costume, much less in the more important points of language and manners. But the same motive which prevents my writing the dialogue of the piece in Anglo-Saxon or in Norman French, and which prohibits my sending forth to the public this essay printed with the types of Caxton or Wynken de Worde, prevents my attempting to confine myself within the limits of the period in which my story is laid. It is necessary for exciting interest of any kind that the subject assumed should be, as it were, *translated* (my italics G.L.) into the manners, as well as the language, of the age we live in . . .

"It is true that this licence is confined . . . within legitimate bounds . . . the author . . . must introduce nothing inconsistent with the manners of the age."

Scott's artistic faithfulness to history is an extension and application to history of the creative principles of the great English realist writers of the eighteenth century. And not only in the sense of a broadening of theme, an assimilation of historical material to the great tradition of realism, but in the sense of portraying men and events historically. What, for instance, was only latent in Fielding, becomes with Scott the driving spirit of literary portrayal. Scott's "necessary anachronism" consists, therefore, simply in allowing his characters to express feelings and thoughts about real, historical relationships in a much clearer way than the actual men and women of the time could have done. But the content of these feelings and thoughts, their relation to their real object is always historically and socially correct. The extent to which this expression of thought and feeling outstrips the consciousness of the age is no more than is absolutely necessary for elucidating the given historical relationship. At the same time Scott gives this expression the timbre, colour, cadence of the time, the class and so on. In this balance lies Scott's great poetic sensitivity.

K

Walter Bagehot

THE WAVERLEY NOVELS[1]

It is not commonly on the generation which was contemporary with the production of great works of art that they exercise their most magical influence. Nor is it on the distant people whom we call posterity. Contemporaries bring to new books formed minds and stiffened creeds; posterity, if it regard them at all, looks at them as old subjects, worn-out topics, and hears a disputation on their merits with languid impartiality, like aged judges in a court of appeal. Even standard authors exercise but slender influence on the susceptible minds of a rising generation; they are become "papa's books"; the walls of the library are adorned with their regular volumes; but no hand touches them. Their fame is itself half an obstacle to their popularity; a delicate fancy shrinks from employing so great a celebrity as the companion of an idle hour. The generation which is really most influenced by a work of genius is commonly that which is still young when the first controversy respecting its merits arises; with the eagerness of youth they read and re-read; their vanity is not unwilling to adjudicate: in the process their imagination is formed; the creations of the author range themselves in the memory; they become part of the substance of the very mind. The works of Sir Walter Scott can hardly be said to have gone through this exact process. Their immediate popularity was unbounded. No one – a few most captious critics apart – ever questioned their peculiar power. Still, they are subject to a transition which is in principle the same. At the time of their publication mature contemporaries read them

[1] First published in *National Review*, VI (April 1858) pp. 444–71. Later published in *Literary Studies*, vol. II, London (Longmans Green) 1879, pp. 146–83 and in *Collected Works*, ed. M. St John Stevas. London (*The Economist*) 1965, pp. 45–75.

with delight. Superficial the reading of grown men in some sort must ever be; it is only once in a lifetime that we can know the passionate reading of youth; men soon lose its eager learning power. But from peculiarities in their structure, which we shall try to indicate, the novels of Scott suffered less than almost any book of equal excellence from this inevitable superficiality of perusal. Their plain, and, so to say, cheerful merits suit the occupied man of genial middle life. Their appreciation was to an unusual degree coincident with their popularity. The next generation, hearing the praises of their fathers in their earliest reading time, seized with avidity on the volumes; and there is much in very many of them which is admirably fitted for the delight of boyhood. A third generation has now risen into at least the commencement of literary life, which is quite removed from the unbounded enthusiasm with which the Scotch novels were originally received, and does not always share the still more eager partiality of those who, in the opening of their minds, first received the tradition of their excellence. New books have arisen to compete with these; new interests distract us from them. The time, therefore, is not perhaps unfavourable for a slight criticism of these celebrated fictions; and their continual republication, without any criticism for many years, seems almost to demand it.

There are two kinds of fiction which, though in common literature they may run very much into one another, are yet in reality distinguishable and separate. One of these, which we may call the *ubiquitous*, aims at describing the whole of human life in all its spheres, in all its aspects, with all its varied interests, aims, and objects. It searches through the whole life of man; his practical pursuits, his speculative attempts, his romantic youth, and his domestic age. It gives an entire feature[2] of all these; or if there be any lineaments which it forbears to depict, they are only such as the inevitable repression of a regulated society excludes from the admitted province of literary art. Of this kind are the novels of Cervantes and Le Sage, and, to a certain extent, of Smollett or Fielding. In our own time, Mr Dickens is an author whom nature intended to write to a certain extent with this aim. He

[2] In his edition of Bagehot Mr Norman St John Stevas has suggested reading "picture" instead of "feature", which appears in the text of the article in the *National Review*. *Ed.*

should have given us *not* disjointed novels, with a vague attempt at a romantic plot, but sketches of diversified scenes, and the obvious life of varied mankind. The literary fates, however, if such beings there are, allotted otherwise. By a very terrible example of the way in which in this world great interests are postponed to little ones, the genius of authors is habitually sacrificed to the tastes of readers. In this age, the great readers of fiction are young people. The "addiction" of these is to romance; and accordingly a kind of novel has become so familiar to us as almost to engross the name, which deals solely with the passion of love; and if it uses other parts of human life for the occasions of its art, it does so only cursorily and occasionally, and with a view of throwing into a stronger or more delicate light those sentimental parts of earthly affairs which are the special objects of delineation. All prolonged delineation of other parts of human life is considered "dry", stupid, and distracts the mind of the youthful generation from the "fantasies" which peculiarly charm it. Mr Olmsted has a story of some deputation of the Indians, at which the American orator harangued the barbarian audience about the "great spirit", and "the land of their fathers", in the style of Mr Cooper's novels; during a moment's pause in the great stream, an old Indian asked the deputation, "Why does your chief speak thus to us? we did not wish great instruction or fine words; we desire brandy and tobacco." No critic in a time of competition will speak uncourteously of any reader of either sex: but it is indisputable that the old kind of novel, full of "great instruction" and varied pictures, does not afford to some young gentlemen and some young ladies either the peculiar stimulus or the peculiar solace which they desire.

The Waverley Novels were published at a time when the causes that thus limit the sphere of fiction were coming into operation, but when they had not yet become so omnipotent as they are now. Accordingly, these novels everywhere bear marks of a state of transition. They are not devoted with anything like the present exclusiveness to the sentimental part of human life. They describe great events, singular characters, strange accidents, strange states of society; they dwell with a peculiar interest, and as if for their own sake, on antiquarian details relating to a past society. Singular customs, social practices, even political institutions which existed once in Scotland, and even elsewhere, during the Middle Ages, are explained with a careful minuteness. At the same time the sentimental element assumes a great deal of prominence. The book is in fact, as well as in theory, a narrative of the feelings and fortunes of the hero and heroine. An attempt, more or less successful, has been made to insert an interesting love-story in each novel. Sir Walter was quite aware that the best delineation of the oddest characters, or the most quaint societies, or the strangest incidents, would not in general satisfy his readers. He has invariably attempted an account of youthful, sometimes of decidedly juvenile, feelings and actions. The difference between Sir Walter's novels and the specially romantic fictions of the present day is, that in the former the love-story is always, or nearly always, connected with some great event, or the fortunes of some great historical character or the peculiar movements and incidents of some strange state of society; and that the author did not suppose or expect that his readers would be so absorbed in the sentimental aspect of human life as to be unable or unwilling to be interested in, or to attend to, any other. There is always a *locus in quo*, if the expression may be pardoned, in the Waverley Novels. The hero and heroine walk among the trees of the forest according to rule, but we are expected to take an interest in the forest as well as in them.

No novel, therefore, of Sir Walter Scott's can be considered to come exactly within the class which we have called the ubiquitous. None of them in any material degree attempts to deal with human affairs in all their spheres – to delineate as a whole the life of man. The canvas has a large background, in some cases too large either for artistic effect or the common reader's interest: but there are always real boundaries – Sir Walter had no *thesis* to maintain. Scarcely any writer will set himself to delineate the whole of human life, unless he has a doctrine concerning human life to put forth and inculcate. The effort is *doctrinaire*. Scott's imagination was strictly conservative. He could understand (with a few exceptions) any considerable movement of human life and action, and could always describe with easy freshness everything which he did understand: but he was not obliged by stress of fanaticism to maintain a dogma concerning them, or to show their peculiar relation to the general sphere of life. He described vigorously and boldly the peculiar scene and society which in every novel he had selected as the theatre of romantic action. Partly from their fidelity to nature, and partly from a consistency in the artist's mode of representation, these pictures group themselves from the several novels in the imagination, and an habitual reader comes to think of and understand what is meant by "Scott's world": but the writer had no such distinct object before him. No one novel was designed to be a delineation of the world as Scott viewed it. We have vivid and fragmentary histories; it is for the slow critic of after-times to piece together their teaching.

From this intermediate position of the Waverley Novels, or at any rate in exact accordance with its requirements, is the special characteristic for which they are most remarkable. We may call this in a brief phrase their *romantic sense*; and perhaps we cannot better illustrate it than by a quotation from the novel to which the series owes its most usual name. It occurs in the description of the court-ball which Charles Edward is described as giving at Holyrood House the night before his march southward on his strange adventure. The striking interest of the scene before him, and the peculiar position of his own sentimental career, are described as influencing the mind of the hero.

"Under the influence of these mixed sensations, and cheered at times by a smile of intelligence and approbation from the Prince as he passed the group, Waverley exerted his powers of fancy, animation and eloquence, and attracted the general admiration of the company. The conversation gradually assumed the tone best qualified for the display of his talents and acquisitions. The gaiety of the evening was exalted in character, rather than checked, by the approaching dangers of the morrow. All nerves were strung for the future, and prepared to enjoy the present. This mood of mind is highly favourable for the exercise of the powers of imagination, for poetry, and for that eloquence which is allied to poetry."

Neither "eloquence" nor "poetry" are the exact words with which it would be appropriate to describe the fresh style of the Waverley Novels: but the imagination of their author was stimulated by a fancied mixture of sentiment and fact, very much as he describes Waverley's to have been by a real experience of the two at once. The second volume of *Waverley* is one of the most striking illustrations of this peculiarity. The character of Charles

Edward, his adventurous undertaking, his ancestral rights, the mixed selfishness and enthusiasm of the Highland chiefs, the fidelity of their hereditary followers, their striking and strange array, the contrast with the Baron of Bradwardine and the Lowland gentry; the collision of the motley and half-appointed host with the formed and finished English society, its passage by the Cumberland mountains and the blue lake of Ullswater – are unceasingly and without effort present to the mind of the writer, and incite with their historical interest the susceptibility of his imagination. But at the same time the mental struggle, or rather transition, in the mind of Waverley – for his mind was of the faint order which scarcely struggles – is never for an instant lost sight of. In the very midst of the inroad and the conflict, the acquiescent placidity with which the hero exchanges the service of the imperious for the appreciation of the "nice" heroine is kept before us, and the imagination of Scott wandered without effort from the great scene of martial affairs to the natural but rather unheroic sentiments of a young gentleman not very difficult to please. There is no trace of effort in the transition, as is so common in the inferior works of later copyists. Many historical novelists, especially those who with care and pains have "read up" their detail, are often evidently in a strait how to pass from their history to their sentiment. The fancy of Sir Walter could not help connecting the two. If he had given us the English side of the race to Derby, he would have described the Bank of England paying in sixpences, and also the loves of the cashier.

It is not unremarkable in connexion with this, the special characteristic of the "Scotch novels", that their author began his literary life by collecting the old ballads of his native country. Ballad poetry is, in comparison at least with many other kinds of poetry, a sensible thing. It describes not only romantic events, but historical ones, incidents in which there is a form and body and consistence – events which have a result. Such a poem as "Chevy Chace", we need not explain, has its prosaic side. The latest historian of Greece has nowhere been more successful than in his attempt to derive from Homer, the greatest of ballad poets, a thorough and consistent account of the political working of the Homeric state of society. The early natural imagination of men seizes firmly on all which interests the minds and hearts of natural men. We find in its delineations the council as well as the marriage, the harsh conflict as well as the deep love-affair. Scott's own poetry is essentially a modernised edition of the traditional poems which his early youth was occupied in collecting. The *Lady of the Lake* is a sort of *boudoir* ballad, yet it contains its element of common sense and broad delineation. The exact position of Lowlander and Highlander would not be more aptly described in a set treatise than in the well-known lines:

> Saxon, from yonder mountain high,
> I mark'd thee send delighted eye,
> Far to the south and east, where lay,
> Extended in succession gay,
> Deep waving fields and pastures green,
> With gentle slopes and groves between:
> These fertile plains, that softn'd vale,
> Were once the birthright of the Gael;
> The stranger came with iron hand,
> And from our fathers rent the land.
> Where dwell we now? See, rudely swell
> Crag over crag, and fell o'er fell.
> Ask we this savage hill we tread
> For fattened steer or household bread;
> As we for flocks those shingles dry,
> And well the mountain might reply –
> "To you, as to your sires of yore,
> Belong the target and claymore!
> I give you shelter in my breast,
> Your own good blades must win the rest."
> Pent in this fortress of the North,
> Think'st thou we will not sally forth,
> To spoil the spoiler as we may,
> And from the robber rend the prey?
> Ay, by my soul! While on yon plain
> The Saxon rears one shock of grain,
> While of ten thousand herds there strays
> But one along yon river's maze,
> The Gael, of plain and river heir,
> Shall with strong hand redeem his share.[3]

[3] *L.L.*, stanza 7.

We need not search the same poem for specimens of the romantic element, for the whole poem is full of them. The incident in which Ellen discovers who Fitz-James really is, is perhaps excessively romantic. At any rate the lines –

> To him each lady's look was lent;
> On him each courtier's eye was bent;
> Midst furs and silks and jewels sheen,
> He stood in simple Lincoln green,
> The centre of the glittering ring:
> And Snowdoun's knight is Scotland's king –[4]

may be cited as very sufficient example of the sort of sentimental incident which is separable from extreme feeling. When Scott, according to his own half-jesting but half-serious expression, was "beaten out of poetry" by Byron, he began to express in more pliable prose the same combination which his verse had been used to convey. As might have been expected, the sense became in the novels more free, vigorous, and flowing, because it is less cramped by the vehicle in which it is conveyed. The range of character which can be adequately delineated in narrative verse is much narrower than that which can be described in the combination of narrative with dramatic prose; and perhaps even the sentiment of the novels is manlier and freer; a delicate unreality hovers over the *Lady of the Lake*.

The sensible element, if we may so express it, of the Waverley Novels appears in various forms. One of the most striking is in the delineation of great political events and influential political institutions. We are not by any means about to contend that Scott is to be taken as an infallible or an impartial authority for the parts of history which he delineates. On the contrary, we believe all the world now agrees that there are many deductions to be made from, many exceptions to be taken to, the accuracy of his delineations. Still, whatever period or incident we take, we shall always find in the error a great, in one or two cases perhaps an extreme mixture of the mental element which we term common sense. The strongest *un*sensible feeling in Scott was perhaps his Jacobitism, which crept out even in small incidents and recurring prejudice

[4] *Op. cit.*, stanza 26.

throughout the whole of his active career, and was, so to say, the
emotional aspect of his habitual Toryism. Yet no one can have
given a more sensible delineation, we might say a more states-
manlike analysis, of the various causes which led to the momentary
success, and to the speedy ruin, of the enterprise of Charles
Edward. Mr Lockhart says that, notwithstanding Scott's
imaginative readiness to exalt Scotland at the expense of England,
no man would have been more willing to join in emphatic
opposition to an anti-English party, if any such had presented
itself with a practical object. Similarly his Jacobitism, though not
without moments of real influence, passed away when his mind
was directed to broad masses of fact and general conclusions of
political reasoning. A similar observation may be made as to
Scott's Toryism; although it is certain that there was an enthusiastic and, in the malicious sense, poetical element in Scott's
Toryism, yet it quite as indisputably partook largely of two other
elements, which are in common repute prosaic. He shared
abundantly in the love of administration and organisation,
common to all men of great active powers. He liked to contem-
plate method at work and order in action. Everybody hates to
hear that the Duke of Wellington asked "how the king's government was to be carried on". No amount of warning wisdom will
bear so fearful a repetition. Still, he *did* say it, and Scott had a
sympathising foresight of the oracle before it was spoken. One
element of his conservatism is his sympathy with the administrative
arrangement, which is confused by the objections of a Whiggish
opposition, and is liable to be altogether destroyed by uprisings
of the populace. His biographer, while pointing out the strong
contrast between Scott and the argumentative and parliamentary
statesmen of his age, avows his opinion that in other times, and
with sufficient opportunities, Scott's ability in managing men would
have enabled him to "play the part of Cecil or of Gondomar". We
may see how much an insensible enthusiasm for such abilities
breaks out, not only in the description of hereditary monarchs,
where the sentiment might be ascribed to a different origin, but
also in the delineation of upstart rulers who could have no
hereditary sanctity in the eyes of any Tory. Roland Græme, in *The
Abbot*, is well described as losing in the presence of the Regent
Murray the natural impertinence of his disposition. "He might

have braved with indifference the presence of an earl merely distinguished by his belt and coronet; but he felt overawed in that of the eminent soldier and statesman, the wielder of a nation's power, and the leader of her armies." It is easy to perceive that the author shares the feeling of his hero by the evident pleasure with which he dwells on the Regent's demeanour: "He then turned slowly round towards Roland Græme, and the marks of gaiety, real or assumed, disappeared from his countenance as completely as the passing bubbles leave the dark mirror of a still profound lake into which a traveller has cast a stone; in the course of a minute his noble features had assumed their natural expression of a deep and even melancholy gravity", etc. In real life, Scott used to say that he never remembered feeling abashed in any one's presence except the Duke of Wellington's. Like that of the hero of his novel, his imagination was very susceptible to the influence of great achievement and prolonged success in wide-spreading affairs.

The view which Scott seems to have taken of democracy indicates exactly the same sort of application of a plain sense to the visible parts of the subject. His imagination was singularly penetrated with the strange varieties and motley composition of human life. The extraordinary multitude and striking contrast of the characters in his novels show this at once. And even more strikingly is the same habit of mind indicated by a tendency never to omit an opportunity of describing those varied crowds and assemblages which concentrate for a moment into a unity the scattered and unlike varieties of mankind. Thus, but a page or two before the passage which we alluded to in *The Abbot*, we find the following:

It was indeed no common sight to Roland, the vestibule of a palace, traversed by its various groups, – some radiant with gaiety – some pensive, and apparently weighed down by affairs concerning the state, or concerning themselves. Here the hoary statesman, with his cautious yet commanding look, his furred cloak and sable pantoufles; there the soldier in buff and steel, his long sword jarring against the pavement, and his whiskered upper lip and frowning brow looking an habitual defiance of danger which perhaps was not always made good; there again passed my lord's serving-man, high of heart and bloody of hand, humble to his master and his master's equals, insolent to all others. To these might be added the poor suitor, with his anxious look and depressed mien – the officer, full of his brief authority, elbowing his betters, and possibly his benefactors, out of the road – the proud priest, who sought a better benefice – the proud baron, who sought a grant of church lands – the robber chief, who came to solicit a pardon for the injuries he had inflicted on his neighbours – the plundered franklin, who came to seek vengeance for that which he had himself received. Besides, there was the mustering and disposition of guards and soldiers – the despatching of messengers, and the receiving them – the trampling and neighing of horses without the gate – the flashing of arms, and rustling of plumes, and jingling of spurs within it. In short, it was that gay and splendid confusion, in which the eye of youth sees all that is brave and brilliant, and that of experience much that is doubtful, deceitful, false, and hollow – hopes that will never be gratified – promises which will never be fulfilled – pride in the disguise of humility – and insolence in that of frank and generous bounty.[5]

As in the imagination of Shakespeare, so in that of Scott, the principal form and object were the structure – that is a hard word – the undulation and diversified composition of human society; the picture of this stood in the centre, and everything else was accessory and secondary to it. The old "rows of books", in which Scott so peculiarly delighted, were made to contribute their element to this varied imagination of humanity. From old family histories, odd memoirs, old law-trials, his fancy elicited new traits to add to the motley assemblage. His objection to democracy – an objection of which we can only appreciate the emphatic force when we remember that his youth was contemporary with the first French Revolution and the controversy as to the uniform and stereotyped rights of man – was, that it would sweep away this entire picture, level prince and peasant in a common *égalité*, substitute a scientific rigidity for the irregular and picturesque growth of

[5] *Ab.* Ch. 18.

centuries, replace an abounding and genial life by a symmetrical but lifeless mechanism. All the descriptions of society in the novels – whether of feudal society, of modern Scotch society, or of English society – are largely coloured by this feeling. It peeps out everywhere, and liberal critics have endeavoured to show that it was a narrow Toryism: but in reality it is a subtle compound of the natural instinct of the artist with the plain sagacity of the man of the world.

It would be tedious to show how clearly the same sagacity appears in his delineation of the various great events and movements in society which are described in the Scotch novels. There is scarcely one of them which does not bear it on its surface. Objections may, as we shall show, be urged to the delineation which Scott has given of the Puritan resistance and rebellions, yet scarcely any one will say there is not a worldly sense in it. On the contrary, the very objection is, that it is too worldly, and far too exclusively sensible.

The same thoroughly well-grounded sagacity and comprehensive appreciation of human life is shown in the treatment of what we may call *anomalous* characters. In general, monstrosity is no topic for art. Every one has known in real life characters which if, apart from much experience, he had found described in books, he would have thought unnatural and impossible. Scott, however, abounds in such characters. Meg Merrilies, Edie Ochiltree, Ratcliffe, are more or less of that description. That of Meg Merrilies especially is as distorted and eccentric as anything can be. Her appearance is described as making Mannering "start"; and well it might:

> She was full six feet high, wore a man's greatcoat over the rest of her dress, had in her hand a goodly sloethorn cudgel, and in all points of equipment except the petticoats seemed rather masculine than feminine. Her dark elf-locks shot out like the snakes of the Gorgon between an old-fashioned bonnet called a bongrace, heightening the singular effect of her strong and weather-beaten features, which they partly shadowed, while her eye had a wild roll that indicated something like real or affected insanity.[6]

[6] *G.M.*, Ch. 3.

Her career in the tale corresponds with the strangeness of her exterior. "Harlot, thief, witch, and gipsy", as she describes herself, the hero is preserved by her virtues; half-crazed as she is described to be, he owes his safety on more than one occasion to her skill in stratagem and ability in managing those with whom she is connected, and who are most likely to be familiar with her weakness and to detect her craft. Yet on hardly any occasion is the natural reader conscious of this strangeness. Something is of course attributable to the skill of the artist; for no other power of mind could produce the effect, unless it were aided by the unconscious tact of detailed expression. But the fundamental explanation of this remarkable success is the distinctness with which Scott saw how such a character as Meg Merrilies arose and was produced out of the peculiar circumstances of gipsy life in the localities in which he has placed his scene. He has exhibited this to his readers not by lengthy or elaborate description, but by chosen incidents, short comments, and touches of which he scarcely foresaw the effect. This is the only way in which the fundamental objection to making eccentricity the subject of artistic treatment can be obviated. Monstrosity ceases to be such when we discern the laws of nature which evolve it: when a real science explains its phenomena, we find that it is in strict accordance with what we call the natural type, but that some rare adjunct or uncommon casualty has interfered and distorted a nature, which is really the same, into a phenomenon which is altogether different. Just so with eccentricity in human character; it becomes a topic of literary art only when its identity with the ordinary principles of human nature is exhibited in the midst of, and as it were, by means of the superficial unlikeness. Such a skill, however, requires an easy careless familiarity with usual human life and common human conduct. A writer must have a sympathy with health before he can show us how, and where, and to what extent, that which is unhealthy deviates from it; and it is this consistent acquaintance with regular life which makes the irregular characters of Scott so happy a contrast to the uneasy distortions of less sagacious novelists.

A good deal of the same criticism may be applied to the delineation which Scott has given us of the *poor*. In truth, poverty is an anomaly to rich people. It is very difficult to make out why people who want dinner do not ring the bell. One half of the world, according to the saying, do not know how the other half lives. Accordingly, nothing is so rare in fiction as a good delineation of the poor. Though perpetually with us in reality, we rarely meet them in our reading. The requirements of the case present an unusual difficulty to artistic delineation. A good deal of the character of the poor is an unfit topic for continuous art, and yet we wish to have in our books a lifelike exhibition of the whole of that character. Mean manners and mean vices are unfit for prolonged delineation; the every-day pressure of narrow necessities is too petty a pain and too anxious a reality to be dwelt upon. We can bear the mere description of *The Parish Register* –

> But this poor farce has neither truth nor art,
> To please the fancy or to touch the heart;
> Dark but not awful, dismal but yet mean,
> With anxious bustle moves the cumbrous scene;
> Presents no objects tender or profound,
> But spreads its cold unmeaning gloom around; –[7]

but who could bear to have a long narrative of fortunes "dismal but yet mean", with characters "dark but not awful", and no objects "tender or profound"? Mr Dickens has in various parts of his writings been led by a sort of pre-Raphaelite *cultus* of reality into an error of this species. His poor people have taken to their poverty very thoroughly; they are poor talkers and poor livers, and in all ways poor people to read about. A whole array of writers have fallen into an opposite mistake. Wishing to preserve their delineations clear from the defects of meanness and vulgarity, they have attributed to the poor a fancied happiness and Arcadian simplicity. The conventional shepherd of ancient times was scarcely displeasing: that which is by everything except express avowal removed from the sphere of reality does not annoy us by its deviations from reality: but the fictitious poor of sentimental novelists are brought almost into contact with real life, half claim to be copies of what actually exists at our very doors, are introduced in close proximity to characters moving in a higher rank, over whom no such ideal charm is diffused, and who are painted

[7] Crabbe, *The Parish Register*, pt. III.

with as much truth as the writer's ability enables him to give. Accordingly, the contrast is evident and displeasing: the harsh outlines of poverty will not bear the artificial rose-tint; they are seen through it, like high cheek-bones through the delicate colours of artificial youth; we turn away with some disgust from the false elegance and undeceiving art; we prefer the rough poor of nature to the petted poor of the refining describer. Scott has most felicitously avoided both these errors. His poor people are never coarse and never vulgar; their lineaments have the rude traits which a life of conflict will inevitably leave on the minds and manners of those who are to lead it; their notions have the narrowness which is inseparable from a contracted experience; their knowledge is not more extended than their restricted means of attaining it would render possible. Almost alone among novelists, Scott has given a thorough, minute, life-like description of poor persons, which is at the same time genial and pleasing. The reason seems to be, that the firm sagacity of his genius comprehended the industrial aspect of poor people's life thoroughly and comprehensively, his experience brought it before him easily and naturally, and his artist's mind and genial disposition enabled him to dwell on those features which would be most pleasing to the world in general. In fact, his own mind of itself and by its own nature, dwelt on those very peculiarities. He could not remove his firm and instructed genius into the domain of Arcadian unreality, but he was equally unable to dwell principally, peculiarly, or consecutively, on those petty, vulgar, mean details in which such a writer as Crabbe lives and breathes. Hazlitt said that Crabbe described a poor man's cottage like a man who came to distrain for rent; he catalogued every trivial piece of furniture, defects and cracks and all. Scott describes it as a cheerful but most sensible landlord would describe a cottage on his property; he has a pleasure in it. No detail, or few details, in the life of the inmates escape his experienced and interested eye: but he dwells on those which do not displease him. He sympathises with their rough industry and plain joys and sorrows. He does not fatigue himself or excite their wondering smile by theoretical plans of impossible relief. He makes the best of the life which is given, and by a sanguine sympathy makes it still better. A hard life many characters in Scott seem to lead; but he appreciates, and makes his reader appreciate, the full value of natural feelings, plain thoughts, and applied sagacity.

His ideas of political economy are equally characteristic of his strong sense and genial mind. He was always sneering at Adam Smith, and telling many legends of that philosopher's absence of mind and inaptitude for the ordinary conduct of life. A contact with the Edinburgh logicians had, doubtless, not augmented his faith in the formal deductions of abstract economy; nevertheless, with the facts before him, he could give a very plain and satisfactory exposition of the genial consequences of old abuses, the distinct necessity for stern reform and the delicate humanity requisite for introducing that reform temperately and with feeling:

Even so the Laird of Ellangowan ruthlessly commenced his magisterial reform, at the expense of various established and superannuated pickers and stealers, who had been his neighbours for half a century. He wrought his miracles like a second Duke Humphrey; and by the influence of the beadle's rod, caused the lame to walk, the blind to see, and the palsied to labour. He detected poachers, black-fishers, orchardbreakers, and pigeon-shooters; had the applause of the bench for his reward, and the public credit of an active magistrate.

All this good had its ratable proportion of evil. Even an admitted nuisance, of ancient standing, should not be abated without some caution. The zeal of our worthy friend now involved in great distress sundry personages whose idle and mendicant habits his own *lachesse* had contributed to foster until these habits had become irreclaimable, or whose real incapacity for exertion rendered them fit objects, in their own phrase, for the charity of all well-disposed Christians. "The long-remembered beggar", who for twenty years had made his regular rounds within the neighbourhood, received rather as an humble friend than as an object of charity, was sent to the neighbouring workhouse. The decrepit dame, who travelled round the parish upon a hand-barrow, circulating from house to house like a bad shilling, which every one is in haste to pass to his neighbour – she, who used to call for her bearers as loud, or louder, than a traveller demands posthorses, even she shared the same disastrous fate. The "daft

L

Jock", who, half knave, half idiot, had been the sport of each succeeding race of village children for a good part of a century, was remitted to the county bridewell, where, secluded from free air and sunshine, the only advantages he was capable of enjoying, he pined and died in the course of six months. The old sailor, who had so long rejoiced the smoky rafters of every kitchen in the country by singing *Captain Ward* and *Bold Admiral Benbow*, was banished from the country for no better reason than that he was supposed to speak with a strong Irish accent. Even the annual rounds of the pedlar were abolished by the Justice, in his hasty zeal for the administration of rural police.

These things did not pass without notice and censure. We are not made of wood or stone, and the things which connect themselves with our hearts and habits cannot, like bark or lichen, be rent away without our missing them. The farmer's dame lacked her usual share of intelligence, perhaps also the self-applause which she had felt while distributing the *awmous* (alms), in shape of a *gowpen* (handful) of oatmeal to the medicant who brought the news. The cottage felt inconvenience from interruption of the petty trade carried on by the itinerant dealers. The children lacked their supply of sugar-plums and toys; the young women wanted pins, ribbons, combs, and ballads; and the old could no longer barter their eggs for salt, snuff, and tobacco. All these circumstances brought the busy Laird of Ellangowan into discredit, which was the more general on account of his former popularity. Even his lineage was brought up in judgment against him. They thought "naething of what the like of Greenside, or Burnville, or Viewforth might do, that were strangers in the country; but Ellangowan! that had been a name amang them since the mirk Monanday, and lang before – *him* to be grinding the puir at that rate! – They ca'd his grandfather the Wicked Laird; but though he was wiles fractious aneuch, when he got into roving company and had ta'en the drap drink, he would have scorned to gang on at this gate. Na, na, the muckle chumlay in the Auld Place reeked like a killogie in his time, and there were as mony puir folk riving at the banes in the court and about the door, as there were gentles in the ha'. And the leddy, on ilka Christmas night as it came round, gae twelve siller pennies to ilka puir body about, in honour of the twelve apostles like. They were fond to ca' it papistrie; but I think our great folk might take a lesson frae the papists whiles. They gie another sort o' help to puir folk than just dinging down a saxpence in the brod on the Sabbath, and kilting, and scourging, and drumming them a' the sax days o' the week besides."[8]

Many other indications of the same healthy and natural sense, which gives so much of their characteristic charm to the Scotch novels, might be pointed out, if it were necessary to weary our readers by dwelling longer on a point we have already laboured so much. One more, however, demands notice because of its importance, and perhaps also because, from its somewhat less obvious character, it might otherwise escape without notice. There has been frequent controversy as to the penal code, if we may so call it, of fiction; that is, as to the apportionment of reward and punishment respectively to the good and evil personages therein delineated; and the practice of authors has been as various as the legislation of critics. One school abandons all thought on the matter, and declares that in the real life we see around us, good people often fail, and wicked people continually prosper; and would deduce the precept, that it is unwise in an art which should hold the "mirror up to nature", not to copy the uncertain and irregular distribution of its sanctions. Another school, with an exactness which savours at times of pedantry, apportions the success and the failure, the pain and the pleasure, of fictitious life to the moral qualities of those who are living in it – does not think at all, or but little, of every other quality in those characters, and does not at all care whether the penalty and reward are evolved in natural sequence from the circumstances and characters of the tale, or are owing to some monstrous accident far removed from all relation of cause or consequence to those facts and people. Both these classes of writers produce works which jar on the natural sense of common readers, and are at issue with the analytic criticism of the best critics. One school leaves an impression of an

[8] *G.M.*, Ch. 6.

uncared-for world, in which there is no right and no wrong; the other, of a sort of Governesses' Institution of a world, where all praise and all blame, all good and all pain, are made to turn on special graces and petty offences, pesteringly spoken of and teasingly watched for. The manner of Scott is thoroughly different; you can scarcely lay down any novel of his without a strong feeling that the world in which the fiction has been laid, and in which your imagination has been moving, is one subject to *laws* of retribution which, though not apparent on a superficial glance, are yet in steady and consistent operation, and will be quite sure to work their due effect, if time is only given to them. Sagacious men know that this is in its best aspect the condition of life. Certain of the ungodly may, notwithstanding the Psalmist, flourish even through life like a green bay-tree; for providence, in external appearance (far differently from the real truth of things, as we may one day see it), works by a scheme of averages. Most people who ought to succeed, do succeed; most people who do fail, ought to fail. But there is no exact adjustment of "mark" to merit; the competitive examination system appears to have an origin more recent than the creation of the world– "on the whole", "speaking generally", "looking at life as a whole", are the words in which we must describe the providential adjustment of visible good and evil to visible goodness and badness. And when we look more closely, we see that these general results are the consequences of certain principles which work half unseen, and which are effectual in the main, though thwarted here and there. It is this comprehensive though inexact distribution of good and evil which is suited to the novelist, and it is exactly this which Scott instinctively adopted. Taking a firm and genial view of the common facts of life – seeing it as an experienced observer and tried man of action – he could not help giving the representation of it which is insensibly borne in on the minds of such persons. He delineates it as a world moving according to laws which are always producing their effect, never *have* produced it; sometimes fall short a little; are always nearly successful. Good sense produces its effect as well as good intention; ability is valuable as well as virtue. It is this peculiarity which gives to his works, more than anything else, the life-likeness which distinguishes them; the average of the copy is struck on the same scale as that of reality;

an unexplained uncommented-on adjustment works in the one, just as a hidden imperceptible principle of apportionment operates in the other.

The romantic susceptibility of Scott's imagination is as obvious in his novels as his matter-of-fact sagacity. We can find much of it in the place in which we should naturally look first for it – his treatment of his heroines. We are no indiscrimate admirers of these young ladies, and shall shortly try to show how much they are inferior as imaginative creations to similar creations of the very highest artists. But the mode in which the writer speaks of them everywhere indicates an imagination continually under the illusion which we term romance. A gentle tone of manly admiration pervades the whole delineation of their words and actions. If we look carefully at the narratives of some remarkable female novelists – it would be invidious to give the instances by name – we shall be struck at once with the absence of this; they do not half like their heroines. It would be satirical to say that they were jealous of them: but it is certain that they analyse the mode in which their charms produce their effects, and the *minutiae* of their operation, much in the same way in which a slightly jealous lady examines the claims of the heroines of society. The same writers have invented the atrocious species of *plain* heroines. Possibly none of the frauds which are now so much the topic of common remark are so irritating as that to which the purchaser of a novel is a victim on finding that he has only to peruse a narrative of the conduct and sentiments of an ugly lady. "Two-and-sixpence to know the heart which was high cheek-bones!" Was there ever such an imposition? Scott would have recoiled from such conception. Even Jeanie Deans, though no heroine like Flora MacIvor, is described as "comely", and capable of looking almost pretty when required, and she has a compensating set-off in her sister, who is beautiful as well as unwise. Speaking generally, as is the necessity of criticism, Scott makes his heroines, at least by profession, attractive, and dwells on their attractiveness, though not with the wild ecstasy of insane youth, yet with the tempered and mellow admiration common to genial men in this world. Perhaps at times we are rather displeased at his explicitness, and disposed to hang back and carp at the admirable qualities displayed to us. But this is only a stronger evidence of the peculiarity which we speak of – of the unconscious sentiments inseparable from Scott's imagination.

The same romantic tinge undeniably shows itself in Scott's pictures of the past. Many exceptions have been taken to the detail of medieval life as it is described to us in *Ivanhoe*: but one merit will always remain to it, and will be enough to secure to it immense popularity. It describes the Middle Ages as we should have wished them to have been. We do not mean that the delineation satisfies those accomplished admirers of the old Church system who fancy that they have found among the prelates and barons of the fourteenth century a close approximation of the theocracy which they would recommend for our adoption. On the contrary, the theological merits of the Middle Ages are not prominent in Scott's delineation. "Dogma" was not in his way: a cheerful man of the world is not anxious for a precise definition of peculiar doctrines. The charm of *Ivanhoe* is addressed to a simpler sort of imagination – to that kind of boyish fancy which idolises medieval society as the "fighting time". Every boy has heard of tournaments, and has a firm persuasion that in an age of tournaments life was thoroughly well understood. A martial society, where men fought hand to hand on good horses with large lances, in peace for pleasure, and in war for business, seems the very ideal of perfection to a bold and simply fanciful boy. *Ivanhoe* spreads before him the full landscape of such a realm, with Richard Cœur-de-Lion, a black horse, and the passage of arms at Ashby. Of course he admires it, and thinks there was never such a writer, and will nevermore be such a world. And a mature critic will share his admiration, at least to the extent of admitting that nowhere else have the elements of a martial romance been so gorgeously accumulated without becoming oppressive; their fanciful charm been so powerfully delineated, and yet so constantly relieved by touches of vigorous sagacity. One single fact shows how great the romantic illusion is. The pressure of painful necessity is scarcely so great in this novel as in novels of the same writer in which the scene is laid in modern times. Much may be said in favour of the medieval system as contradistinguished from existing society; much has been said. But no one can maintain that general comfort was as much diffused as it is now. A certain ease[9] pervades

[9] Mr St John Stevas reads "case". *Ed.*

the structure of later society. Our houses may not last so long, are not so picturesque, will leave no such ruins behind them: but they are warmed with hot water, have no draughts, and contain sofas instead of rushes. A slight daily unconscious luxury is hardly ever wanting to the dwellings in civilisation; like the gentle air of a genial climate, it is a perpetual minute enjoyment. The absence of this marks a rude barbaric time. We may avail ourselves of rough pleasures, stirring amusement, exciting actions, strange rumours: but life is hard and harsh. The cold air of the keen North may brace and invigorate, but it cannot soothe us. All sensible people know that the Middle Ages must have been very uncomfortable; there was a difficulty about "good food"; almost insuperable obstacles to the cultivation of nice detail and small enjoyment. No one knew the abstract facts on which this conclusion rests better than Scott; but his delineation gives no general idea of the result. A thoughtless reader rises with the impression that the Middle Ages had the same elements of happiness which we have at present, and that they had fighting besides. We do not assert that this tenet is explicitly taught; on the contrary, many facts are explained, and many customs elucidated, from which a discriminating and deducing reader would infer the meanness of poverty and the harshness of barbarism. But these less imposing traits escape the rapid, and still more the boyish reader. His general impression is one of romance; and though, when roused, Scott was quite able to take a distinct view of the opposing facts, he liked his own mind to rest for the most part in the same pleasing illusion.

The same sort of historical romance is shown likewise in Scott's picture of remarkable historical characters. His Richard I is the traditional Richard, with traits heightened and ennobled in perfect conformity to the spirit of tradition. Some illustration of the same quality might be drawn from his delineations of the Puritan rebellions and the Cavalier enthusiasm. We might show that he ever dwells on the traits and incidents most attractive to a genial and spirited imagination. But the most remarkable instance of the power which romantic illusion exercised over him is his delineation of Mary Queen of Scots. He refused at one time of his life to write a biography of that princess "because his opinion was contrary to his feeling". He evidently considered her guilt to be clearly established, and thought, with a distinguished lawyer, that he should "direct a jury to find her guilty": but his fancy, like that of most of his countrymen, took a peculiar and special interest in the beautiful lady who, at any rate, had suffered so much and so fatally at the hands of a queen of England. He could not bring himself to dwell with nice accuracy on the evidence which substantiates her criminality, or on the still clearer indications of that unsound and over-crafty judgment, which was the fatal inheritance of the Stuart family, and which, in spite of advantages that scarcely any other family in the world has enjoyed, has made their name an historical byword for misfortune. The picture in the *Abbot*, one of the best historical pictures which Scott has given us, is principally the picture of the queen as the fond tradition of his countrymen exhibited her. Her entire innocence, it is true, is never alleged: but the enthusiasm of her followers is dwelt on with approving sympathy; their confidence is set forth at large; her influence over them is skilfully delineated; the fascination of charms chastened by misfortune is delicately indicated. We see a complete picture of the beautiful queen, of the suffering and sorrowful but yet not insensible woman. Scott could not, however, as a close study will show us, quite conceal the unfavourable nature of his fundamental opinion. In one remarkable passage the struggle of the judgment is even conspicuous, and in others the sagacity of the practised lawyer – the thread of the attorney, as he used to call it, in his nature – qualifies and modifies the sentiment hereditary in his countrymen and congenial to himself.

This romantic imagination is a habit or power (as we may choose to call it) of mind which is almost essential to the highest success in the historical novel. The aim, at any rate the effect, of this class of works seems to be to deepen and confirm the received view of historical personages. A great and acute writer may, from an accurate study of original documents, discover that those impressions are erroneous, and by a process of elaborate argument substitute others which he deems more accurate. But this can only be effected by writing a regular history. The essence of the achievement is the proof. If Mr Froude had put forward his view of Henry the Eighth's character in a professed novel, he would have been laughed at. It is only by a rigid adherence to attested facts and authentic documents, that a view so original could obtain even a hearing. We start back with a little anger from a representation which is avowedly imaginative, and which contradicts our impressions. We do not like to have our opinions disturbed by reasoning: but it is impertinent to attempt to disturb them by fancies. A writer of the historical novel is bound by the popular conception of his subject; and commonly it will be found that this popular impression is to some extent a romantic one. An element of exaggeration clings to the popular judgment: great vices are made greater, great virtues greater also; interesting incidents are made more interesting, soft legends more soft. The novelist who disregards this tendency will do so at the peril of his popularity. His business is to make attraction more attractive, and not to impair the pleasant pictures of ready-made romance by an attempt at grim reality.

We may therefore sum up the indications of this characteristic excellence of Scott's novels by saying, that more than any novelist he has given us fresh pictures of practical human society, with its cares and troubles, its excitements and its pleasures; that he has delineated more distinctly than any one else the framework in which this society inheres, and by the boundaries of which it is shaped and limited; that he has made more clear the way in which strange and eccentric characters grow out of that ordinary and usual system of life; that he has extended his view over several periods of society, and given an animated description of the external appearance of each, and a firm representation of its social institutions; that he has shown very graphically what we may call the worldly laws of moral government; and that over all these he has spread the glow of sentiment natural to a manly mind, and an atmosphere of generosity congenial to a cheerful one. It is from the collective effect of these causes, and from the union of sense and sentiment which is the principle of them all, that Scott derives the peculiar healthiness which distinguishes him. There are no such books as his for the sick-room, or for freshening the painful intervals of a morbid mind. Mere sense is dull, mere sentiment unsubstantial; a sensation of genial healthiness is only given by what combines the solidity of the one and the brightening charm of the other.

Some guide to Scott's defects, or to the limitations of his genius, if we would employ a less ungenial and perhaps more correct expression, is to be discovered, as usual, from the consideration of his characteristic excellence. As it is his merit to give bold and animated pictures of this world, it is his defect to give but insufficient representations of qualities which this world does not exceedingly prize, of such as do not thrust themselves very forward in it, of such as are in some sense above it. We may illustrate this in several ways.

One of the parts of human nature which is systematically omitted in Scott is the searching and abstract intellect. This did not lie in his way. No man had a stronger sagacity, better adapted for the guidance of common men and the conduct of common transactions. Few could hope to form a more correct opinion on things and subjects which were brought before him in actual life; no man had a more useful intellect. But on the other hand, as will be generally observed to be the case, no one was less inclined to that probing and seeking and anxious inquiry into things in general which is the necessity of some minds, and a sort of intellectual famine in their nature. He had no call to investigate the theory of the universe, and he would not have been able to comprehend those who did. Such a mind as Shelley's would have been entirely removed from his comprehension. He had no call to mix "awful talk and asking looks" with his love of the visible scene. He could not have addressed the universe:

> I have watched
> Thy shadow, and the darkness of thy steps,
> And my heart ever gazes on the depth
> Of thy deep mysteries. I have made my bed
> In charnels and on coffins, where black death
> Keeps records of the trophies won from thee,
> Hoping to still these obstinate questionings
> Of thee and thine, by forcing some lone ghost,
> Thy messenger, to render up the tale
> Of what we are.[10]

Such thoughts would have been to him "thinking without an object", "abstracted speculations", "cobwebs of the unintelligible brain". Above all minds his had the Baconian propensity to work upon "stuff". At first sight, it would not seem that this was a

[10] Shelley, "The Spirit of Solitude", ll. 20–29.

defect likely to be very hurtful to the works of a novelist. The labours of the searching and introspective intellect, however needful, absorbing, and in some degree delicious, to the seeker himself, are not in general very delightful to those who are not seeking. Genial men in middle life are commonly intolerant of that philosophising which their prototype in old times classed side by side with the lisping of youth. The theological novel, which was a few years ago so popular, and which is likely to have a recurring influence in times when men's belief is unsettled, and persons who cannot or will not read large treatises have thoughts in their minds and inquiries in their hearts, suggests to those who are accustomed to it the absence elsewhere of what is necessarily one of its most distinctive and prominent subjects. The desire to attain belief, which has become one of the most familiar sentiments of heroes and heroines, would have seemed utterly incongruous to the plain sagacity of Scott, and also to his old-fashioned art. Creeds are *data* in his novels: people have different creeds, but each keeps his own. Some persons will think that this is not altogether amiss; nor do we particularly wish to take up the defence of the dogmatic novel. Nevertheless, it will strike those who are accustomed to the youthful generation of a cultivated time, that the passion of intellectual inquiry is one of the strongest impulses in many of them, and one of those which give the predominant colouring to the conversation and exterior mind of many more. And a novelist will not exercise the most potent influence over those subject to that passion, if he entirely omit the delineation of it. Scott's works have only one merit in this relation: they are an excellent rest to those who have felt this passion, and have had something too much of it.

The same indisposition to the abstract exercises of the intellect shows itself in the reflective portions of Scott's novels, and perhaps contributes to their popularity with that immense majority of the world who strongly share in that same indisposition: it prevents, however, their having the most powerful intellectual influence on those who have at any time of their lives voluntarily submitted themselves to this acute and refining discipline. The reflections of a practised thinker have a peculiar charm, like the last touches of the accomplished artist. The cunning exactitude of the professional hand leaves a trace in the very language. A nice discrimination of thought makes men solicitous of the most apt expressions to diffuse their thoughts. Both words and meaning gain a metallic brilliancy, like the glittering precision of the pure Attic air. Scott's is a healthy and genial world of reflexion, but it wants the charm of delicate exactitude.

The same limitation of Scott's genius shows itself in a very different portion of art – in his delineation of his heroines. The same blunt sagacity of imagination which fitted him to excel in the rough description of obvious life, rather unfitted him for delineating the less substantial essence of the female character. The nice *minutiae* of society, by means of which female novelists have been so successful in delineating their own sex, were rather too small for his robust and powerful mind. Perhaps, too, a certain unworldliness of *imagination* is necessary to enable men to comprehend or delineate that essence: unworldliness of *life* is no doubt not requisite; rather, perhaps, worldliness is necessary to the acquisition of a sufficient experience. But an absorption of the practical world does not seem favourable to a comprehension of anything which does not precisely belong to it. Its interests are too engrossing; its excitements too keen; it modifies the fancy, and in the change unfits it for everything else. Something too, in Scott's character and history made it more difficult for him to give a representation of women than of men. Goethe used to say that his idea of woman was not drawn from his experience, but that it came to him before experience, and that he explained his experience by a reference to it. And though this is a German, and not very happy, form of expression, yet it appears to indicate a very important distinction. Some efforts of the imagination are made so early in life, just as it were at the dawn of the conscious faculties, that we are never able to fancy ourselves as destitute of them. They are part of the mental constitution with which, so to speak, we awoke to existence. These are always far more firm, vivid, and definite than any other images of our fancy, and we apply them, half unconsciously, to any facts and sentiments and actions which may occur to us later in life, whether arising from within or thrust upon us from the outward world. Goethe doubtless meant that the idea of the female character was to him one of these first elements of imagination; not a thing puzzled out, or which he

remembered having conceived, but a part of the primitive conceptions which, being coeval with his memory, seemed inseparable from his consciousness. The descriptions of women
likely to be given by this sort of imagination will probably be the
best descriptions. A mind which would arrive at this idea of the
female character by this process, and so early, would be one
obviously of more than usual susceptibility. The early imagination
does not commonly take this direction; it thinks most of horses
and lances, tournaments and knights; only a mind with an unusual
and instinctive tendency to this kind of thought, would be borne
thither so early or so effectually. And even independently of this
probable peculiarity of the individual, the primitive imagination in
general is likely to be the most accurate which men can form; not,
of course, of the external manifestations and detailed manners, but
of the inner sentiment and characteristic feeling of women. The
early imagination conceives what it does conceive very justly;
fresh from the facts, stirred by the new aspects of things, un-
dimmed by the daily passage of constantly forgotten images, not
misled by the irregular analogies of a dislocated life – the early
mind sees what it does see with a spirit and an intentness never
given to it again. A mind like Goethe's, of very strong imagination,
aroused at the earliest age – not of course by passions, but by an
unusual strength in that undefined longing which is the prelude to
our passions – will form the best idea of the inmost female nature
which masculine nature can form. The difference[11] is evident in
the characters of women formed by Goethe's imagination or
Shakespeare's, and those formed by such an imagination as that of
Scott. The latter seems so external. We have traits, features,
manners; we know the heroine as she appeared in the street; in
some degree we know how she talked, but we never know how
she felt – least of all what she was: we always feel there is a world
behind, unanalysed, unrepresented, which we cannot attain to.
Such a character as Margaret in *Faust* is known to us to the very
soul; so is Imogen; so is Ophelia. Edith Bellenden, Flora MacIvor
Miss Wardour, are young ladies who, we are told, were good-
looking, and well-dressed (according to the old fashion), and
sensible: but we feel we know but very little of them, and they do

[11] Mr Norman St John Stevas has substituted "difference" in his text for
"trace" which appeared in the *National Review* text of 1858. *Ed.*

not haunt our imaginations. The failure of Scott in this line of art is more conspicuous, because he had not in any remarkable degree the later experience of female detail, with which some minds have endeavoured to supply the want of the early essential imagination, and which Goethe possessed in addition to it. It was rather late, according to his biographer, before Scott set up for a "a squire of dames"; he was a "lame young man, very enthusiastic about ballad poetry"; he was deeply in love with a young lady, supposed to be imaginatively represented by Flora MacIvor, but he was unsuccessful. It would be over-ingenious to argue, from his failing in a single love-affair, that he had no peculiar interest in young ladies in general: but the whole description of his youth shows that young ladies exercised over him a rather more divided influence than is usual. Other pursuits intervened, much more than is common with persons of the imaginative temperament, and he never led the life of flirtation from which Goethe believed that he derived so much instruction. Scott's heroines, therefore, are, not unnaturally, faulty, since from a want of the very peculiar instinctive imagination he could not give us the essence of women, and from the habits of his life he could not delineate to us their detailed life with the appreciative accuracy of habitual experience. Jeanie Deans is probably the best of his heroines, and she is so because she is the least of a heroine. The plain matter-of-fact element in the peasant-girl's life and circumstances suited a robust imagination. There is little in the part of her character that is very finely described which is characteristically feminine. She is not a masculine, but she is an epicene heroine. Her love-affair with Butler, a single remarkable scene excepted, is rather commonplace than otherwise.

A similar criticism might be applied to Scott's heroes. Everyone feels how commonplace they are – Waverley excepted, whose very vacillation gives him a sort of character. They have little personality. They are all of the same type; excellent young men – rather strong – able to ride and climb and jump. They are always said to be sensible, and bear out the character by being not unwilling sometimes to talk platitudes. But we know nothing of their inner life. They are said to be in love: but we have no special account of their individual sentiments. People show their character in their love more than in anything else. These young gentlemen all love in the same way – in the vague commonplace way of this world. We have no sketch or dramatic expression of the life within. Their souls are quite unknown to us. If there is an exception, it is Edgar Ravenswood. But if we look closely, we may observe that the notion which we obtain of his character, unusually broad as it is, is not a notion of him in his capacity of hero, but in his capacity of distressed peer. His proud poverty gives a distinctness which otherwise his lineaments would not have. We think little of his love; we think much of his narrow circumstances and compressed haughtiness.

The same exterior delineation of character shows itself in its treatment of men's religious nature. A novelist is scarcely, in the notion of ordinary readers, bound to deal with this at all; if he does, it will be one of his great difficulties to indicate it graphically, yet without dwelling on it. Men who purchase a novel do not wish a stone or a sermon. All lengthened reflexions must be omitted – the whole armoury of pulpit eloquence. But no delineation of human nature can be considered complete which omits to deal with man in relation to the questions which occupy him as man, with his convictions as to the theory of the universe and his own destiny; the human heart throbs on few subjects with a passion so intense, so peculiar, and so typical. From an artistic view, it is a blunder to omit an element which is so characteristic of human life, which contributes so much to its animation, and which is so picturesque. A reader of a more simple mind, little apt to indulge in such criticism, feels "a want of depth", as he would speak, in delineations from which so large an element of his own most passionate and deepest nature is omitted. It can hardly be said that there is an omission of the religious nature in Scott. But at the same time there is no adequate delineation of it. If we refer to the facts of his life, and the view of his character which we collect from thence, we shall find that his religion was of a qualified and double sort. He was a genial man of the world, and had the easy faith in the kindly *Dieu des bons gens* which is natural to such a person; and he had also a half-poetic principle of superstition in his nature, inclining him to believe in ghosts, legends, fairies, and elfs, which did not affect his daily life or possibly his superficial belief, but was nevertheless very constantly present to his fancy, and [which] affected, as is the constitution of human nature, by that frequency, the undefined,[12] half-expressed, inexpressible feelings which are at the root of that belief. Superstition was a kind of Jacobitism in his religion; as a sort of absurd reliance on the hereditary principle modified insensibly his leanings in the practical world, so a belief in the existence of unevidenced, and often absurd, supernatural beings, qualified his commonest speculations on the higher world. Both these elements may be thought to enter into the highest religion; there is a principle of cheerfulness which will justify in its measure a genial enjoyment, and also a principle of fear which those who think only of that enjoyment will deem superstition, and which will really become superstition in the over-anxious and credulous acceptor of it. But in a true religion these two elements will be combined. The character of God images itself very imperfectly in any human soul, but in the highest it imagines itself as a whole; it leaves an abiding impression which will justify anxiety and allow of happiness. The highest aim of the religious novelist would be to show how this operates in human character; to exhibit in their curious modification our religious love, and also our religious fear. In the novels of Scott the two elements appear in a state of separation, as they did in his own mind. We have the superstition of the peasantry in the *Antiquary*, in *Guy Mannering*, everywhere almost; we have likewise a pervading tone of genial easy reflexion characteristic of the man of the world who produced, and agreeable to the people of the world who read, these works. But we have no picture of the two in combination. We are scarcely led to think on the subject at all, so much do other subjects distract our interest: but if we do think, we are puzzled at the contrast. We do not know which is true, the uneasy belief of superstition, or the easy satisfaction of the world; we waver between the two, and have no suggestion even hinted to us of the possibility of a reconciliation. The character of the Puritans certainly did not in general embody such a reconciliation, but it might have been made by a sympathising artist the vehicle for a delineation of a struggle after it. The two elements of love and fear ranked side

[12] Mr Norman St John Stevas adds "which" (this does not appear in the *National Review* text) and alters "in defined" to "undefined". I have followed him in these points but I have not thought it necessary to alter the original text's "by" to "through" as he does. *Ed.*

by side in their minds with an intensity which is rare even in minds that feel only one of them. The delineation of Scott is amusing, but superficial. He caught the ludicrous traits which tempt the mirthful imagination, but no other side of the character pleased him. The man of the world was displeased with their obstinate interfering zeal; their intensity of faith was an opposition force in the old Scotch polity, of which he liked to fancy the harmonious working. They were superstitious enough: but nobody likes other people's superstitions. Scott's were of a wholly different kind. He made no difficulty as to the observance of Christmas Day, and would have eaten potatoes without the faintest scruple, although their name does not occur in Scripture. Doubtless also his residence in the land of Puritanism did not incline him to give anything except a satirical representation of that belief. You must not expect from a dissenter a faithful appreciation of the creed from which he dissents. You cannot be impartial on the religion of the place in which you live; you may believe it, or you may dislike it; it crosses your path in too many forms for you to be able to look at it with equanimity. Scott had rather a rigid form of Puritanism forced upon him in his infancy; it is asking too much to expect him to be partial to it. The aspect of religion which Scott delineates best is that which appears in griefs, especially in the grief of strong characters. His strong *natural* nature felt the power of death. He has given us many pictures of rude and simple men subdued, if only for a moment, into devotion by its presence.

On the whole, and speaking roughly, these defects in the delineation which Scott has given us of human life are but two. He omits to give us a delineation of the soul. We have mind, manners, animation, but it is the stir of this world. We miss the consecrating power; and we miss it not only in its own peculiar sphere, which, from the difficulty of introducing the deepest elements into a novel, would have been scarcely matter for a harsh criticism, but in the place in which a novelist might most be expected to delineate it. There are perhaps such things as the love-affairs of immortal beings, but no one would learn it from Scott. His heroes and heroines are well dressed for this world, but not for another; there is nothing even in their love which is suitable for immortality. As has been noticed, Scott also omits any delineation of the abstract unworldly intellect. This too might not

M

have been so severe a reproach, considering its undramatic, unanimated nature, if it had stood alone: but taken in connexion with the omission which we have just spoken of, it is most important. As the union of sense and romance makes the world of Scott so characteristically agreeable – a fascinating picture of this world in the light in which we like best to dwell on[13] it; so the deficiency in the attenuated, striving intellect, as well as in the supernatural soul, gives to the "world" of Scott the cumbrousness and temporality, in short, the materialism, which is characteristic of the world.

We have dwelt so much on what we think are the characteristic features of Scott's imaginative representations that we have left ourselves no room to criticise the two most natural points of criticism in a novelist – plot and style. This is not, however, so important in Scott's case as it would commonly be. He used to say, "It was of no use having a plot; you could not keep to it." He modified and changed his thread of story from day to day – sometimes even from bookselling reasons, and on the suggestion of others. An elaborate work of narrative art could not be produced in this way, everyone will concede; the highest imagination, able to look far over the work, is necessary for that task. But the plots produced, so to say, by the pen of the writer as he passes over the events are likely to have a freshness and a suitableness to those events which is not possessed by the inferior writers who make up a mechanical plot before they commence. The procedure of the highest genius doubtless is scarcely a procedure: the view of the whole story comes at once upon its imagination like the delicate end and the distinct beginning of some long vista. But all minds do not possess the highest mode of conception; and among lower modes, it is doubtless better to possess the vigorous fancy which creates each separate scene in succession as it goes, than the pedantic intellect which designs everything long before it is wanted. There is a play in unconscious creation which no voluntary elaboration and preconceived fitting of distinct ideas can ever hope to produce. If the whole cannot be created by one bounding effort, it is better that each part should be created separately and in detail.

[13] Mr Norman St John Stevas's reading is followed here. The *National Review* text has "in" for "on". *Ed.*

The style of Scott would deserve the highest praise if M. Thiers could establish his theory of narrative language. He maintains that a historian's language approaches perfection in proportion as it aptly communicates what is meant to be narrated without drawing any attention to itself. Scott's style fulfills this condition. Nobody rises from his works without a most vivid idea of what is related, and no one is able to quote a single phrase in which it has been narrated. We are inclined, however, to differ from the great French historian, and to oppose to him a theory derived from a very different writer. Coleridge used to maintain that all good poetry was untranslatable into words of the same language without injury to the sense: the meaning was, in his view, to be so inseparably intertwined even with the shades of the language, that the change of a single expression would make a difference in the accompanying feeling, if not in the bare signification: consequently, all good poetry must be remembered exactly – to change a word is to modify the essence. Rigidly this theory can only be applied to a few kinds of poetry, or special passages in which the imagination is exerting itself to the utmost, and collecting from the whole range of associated language the very expressions which it requires. The highest excitation of feeling is necessary to this peculiar felicity of choice. In calmer moments the mind has either a less choice, or less acuteness of selective power. Accordingly, in prose it would be absurd to expect any such nicety. Still, on great occasions in imaginative fiction, there should be passages in which the words seem to cleave to the matter. The excitement is as great as in poetry. The words should become part of the sense. They should attract our attention, as this is necessary to impress them on the memory; but they should not in so doing distract attention from the meaning conveyed. On the contrary, it is their inseparability from their meaning which gives them their charm and their power. In truth, Scott's language, like his sense, was such as became a bold sagacious man of the world. He used the first sufficient words which came uppermost, and seems hardly to have been sensible, even in the works of others, of that exquisite accuracy and inexplicable appropriateness of which we have been speaking.

To analyse in detail the faults and merits of even a few of the greatest of the Waverley Novels would be impossible in the space at our command on the present occasion. We have only attempted a general account of a few main characteristics. Every critic must, however, regret to have to leave topics so tempting to remark as many of Scott's stories, and a yet greater number of his characters.

Robin Mayhead

SCOTT AND THE IDEA OF JUSTICE

In a way most pre-twentieth-century novels are about justice being done, literally or ironically. Leaving aside for the time being the nineteenth-century stereotype of the worsted villain and the richly rewarded though originally tribulation-ridden hero and heroine, or such examples of the ironically inevitable as the sentences that fate passes on the characters of Hardy, we can discern a justice-theme of one sort or another in works like *Pride and Prejudice* or *Middlemarch*. The former is very much a matter of Elizabeth and Darcy coming to "do justice" to each other; and in the latter there are two kinds of justice-theme – the descent of Nemesis on Bulstrode, and the superbly subtle case of the Lydgates. Here the reader finds it just short of possible to be as hard on Rosamond and as sympathetic towards her husband as he would like to be; and Lydgate's demise as an authority on the upper-class disease of gout, together with Rosamond's smug gratification at having been granted her "reward", presents us with levels of irony in the probing of what is just or unjust that go infinitely deeper than the execution of Tess Durbeyfield. Even *Wuthering Heights*, in its notoriously odd way, depends on firm traditional notions of justice or injustice in human behaviour.

Such things, of course, can be embraced in various ways within the "poetic justice" category. They are a natural outcome of the nineteenth-century novelist's kind of moral outlook. Dickens, for instance, is full of them. Yet to mention him is to realise that the critical pinpointing of justice-themes has a pretty limited use. Take the case of *Bleak House*. For all the impressive beastliness of the Court of Chancery, for all the swelling (and often effective) rhetoric directed against the evils of injustice, one can hardly say at

167

the end of the book that its theme *is* "justice". Far more does it seem to give a comprehensive vision of human evil, of which the subtleties of legal cruelty are for Dickens simply a concentrated and dramatically powerful embodiment. I imagine that few readers would claim that an "idea of justice" emerged from the rich amalgam of Krook, Chadband, Turveydrop, and Smallweed, even though, as in the case of Krook's unlovely departure from this world, considerations of "poetic justice" are obviously in place.

The disengagement of justice-themes from the texture of a novel then, though it may be an illuminating game, can also be a wild-goose-chase if one is looking for what the novel most centrally means. But there are novels in which justice appears very specifically at the nerve-centre of the whole organisation, and it is not surprising that Sir Walter Scott's legal home background and training should have made him the author of some of the most interesting.

I

One novel in which justice obviously bulks large is *The Heart of Midlothian*. Whilst the nature of justice probably cannot be claimed to be *the* theme, the one unifying principle of the book's structure,[1] it is of very great importance in the overall scheme. Though it reaches its central climax in the conclusion of Effie Deans's trial, the "debate on the nature of Justice in general is pursued right through the book", to quote one of the few modern critics to take Scott at all seriously.[2]

This debate is associated with a whole "series of cultural oppositions",[3] and is a powerful presence in the conflicts of conscience undergone by the principal characters. In a large sequential way it is carried on in the manner in which Scott plays off different notions of justice against one another in the events leading up to the "execution" of Porteous: but the following very typical

[1] I do not today hold the extreme view put forward in my essay, "*The Heart of Midlothian*: Scott as Artist" in *Essays in Criticism*, VI (1956) pp. 266–77.

[2] Thomas Crawford in *Scott*, Writers and Critics. Edinburgh (Oliver & Boyd) 1965, p. 88.

[3] *Op. cit.*, p. 88.

passage of dialogue between Davie Deans and Bartoline Saddletree is of equal significance for Scott's inquiry:

Encouraged by these symptoms of acquiescence, Saddletree, who, as an amateur of the law, had a supreme deference
for all constituted authorities, again recurred to his other
topic of interest, the murder, namely, of Porteous, and pro-
nounced severe censure on the parties concerned.
"These are kittle times – kittle times, Mr. Deans, when the
people take the power of life and death out of the hands of the
rightful magistrate into their ain rough grip. I am of
opinion, and so I believe will Mr. Crossmyloof and the privy
council, that this rising in effeir of war, to take away the life of
a reprieved man, will prove little better than perduellion."
"If I hadna that on my mind whilk is ill to bear, Mr.
Saddletree," said Deans, "I wad make bold to dispute that
point wi' you."
"How could you dispute what's plain law, man?" said
Saddletree, somewhat contemptuously; "there's no a callant
that e'er carried a pock wi' a process in't, but will tell you that
perduellion is the warst and maist virulent kind of treason,
being an open convocating of the king's lieges against his
authority, mair especially in arms, and by touk of drum, to
baith whilk accessories my een and lugs bore witness, and
muckle warse than lese-majesty, or the concealment of a
treasonable purpose. It winna bear a dispute, neighbour."
"But it will, though," retorted Douce Davie Deans; "I tell
ye it will bear a dispute. I never like your cauld, legal, formal
doctrines, neighbour Saddletree. I haud unco little by the
Parliament House, since the awfu' downfall of the hopes of
honest folk that followed the Revolution."
"But what wad ye hae had, Mr. Deans?" said Saddletree,
impatiently; "didna ye get baith liberty and conscience made
fast, and settled by tailzie on you and your heirs for ever?"
"Mr. Saddletree," retorted Deans, "I ken ye are one of
those that are wise after the manner of this world, and that ye
haud your part, and cast in your portion, wi' the lang-heads
and lang-gowns, and keep with the smart witty-pated lawyers
of this our land. Weary on the dark and dolefu' cast that they

hae gien this unhappy kingdom, when their black hands of defection were clasped in the red hands of our sworn murtherers; when those who had numbered the towers of our Zion, and marked the bulwarks of Reformation, saw their hope turn into a snare, and their rejoicing into weeping."

"I canna understand this, neighbour," answered Saddletree. "I am an honest Presbyterian of the Kirk of Scotland, and stand by her and the General Assembly, and the due administration of justice by the fifteen Lords o' Session, and the five Lord's o' Justiciary."

"Out upon ye, Mr. Saddletree!" exclaimed David, who, in an opportunity of giving his testimony on the offences and backslidings of the land, forgot for a moment his own domestic calamity – "out upon your General Assembly, and the back of my hand to your Court o' Session! – What is the tane but a waefu' bunch o' cauldrife professors and ministers, that sate bien and warm when the persecuted remnant were warstling wi' hunger, and cauld, and fear of death, and danger of fire and sword, upon wet brae-sides, peat-haggs, and flow-mosses, and that now creep out of their holes, like bluebottle flees in a blink of sunshine, to take the pu'pits and places of better folk – of them that witnessed, and testified, and fought, and endured pit, prison-house, and transportation beyond seas? A bonny bike there's o' them! And for your Court o' Session . . ."[4]

Now, it is easy enough to write off Saddletree as merely a pompous idiot, and Deans as a bombastic and narrow-minded religious enthusiast. The former's unquestioning reverence for "all constituted authorities" looks pretty unintelligent; the latter's purple patch about "'black hands of defection . . . clasped in the red hands of our sworn murtherers'" is luridly strained to the verge of absurdity. But a little thought soon shows that the two men cannot be quite so simply "placed" as that. Ridiculous though Saddletree's would-be authoritative recital of terms like "perduellion", "lese-majesty", and "concealment of a treasonable purpose" may be, there is a deal of common sense on his side. Can we dismiss, for example, his impatient query "'didna ye get baith liberty and conscience made fast, and settled by tailzie on you and your heirs for ever?'" The reference to "tailzie" is typical of the amateur lawyer, yet it is hard not to take Saddletree's protest as a reasonable reaction to Deans's gloomy fulminations against Parliament and Union.

At the same time, this kind of rationality, the rationality of "'those that are wise after the manner of this world'", may itself be open to question. The world, after all, is a place in which people live, and Saddletree's preoccupation with abstract justice is in danger of losing sight of this. Even if we find the rant of the fiery old Covenanter rather hard to take, we realise that his world is very definitely a *peopled* world, for all that the only kind of human being he would like to find in it is the type of "'the persecuted remnant'". His objection to Saddletree's "'cauld, legal, formal doctrines'" has more to it than one might initially suppose. It reminds us, for instance, of the plight of poor Effie Deans herself, "guilty" of "'a murder of the law's inferring or construction ... this species of murther being one of its ain creation'",[5] and thus brings the passage of dialogue into relation with the very heart of the book.

Perhaps the best instance of the way in which the reader's response to the two men is qualified comes in the last part of their exchange of words. On the one hand there is the solid worldly prudence of Saddletree's faith in the "'due administration of justice'", given a touch of absurdity by his pedantic concern to show that he knows how many Lords of Session and Lords of Justiciary there are; on the other hand there is a glint of amusement in Scott's eye as he speaks of Deans "giving his testimony on the offences and backslidings of the land", yet Davie's vision of the sheer physical miseries of "'the persecuted remnant'" comes across to us with an effect of perfectly genuine human pathos.

2

That passage from a novel which has admittedly had more of its due of critical attention than others in the Waverley series, compactly illustrates certain basic qualities in the mind and art of

[5] Saddletree in Ch. 5.

Scott. There is a judicious blend of sympathy and irony; the reader's assent is directed now here, now there, through the deft placing of key phrases in the utterances of the two speakers. On the scale of a whole novel much the same kind of thing goes on in *Old Mortality*, where Henry Morton the rational and humane is placed between the extremes of Burley and Claverhouse. In that design, Morton occupies a position which might be said to approximate to that which Scott would like his reader to take up between the much less frightening excesses of Saddletree and Douce Davie. Now, *Old Mortality* has its own very real impressiveness, irrespective of whether or not it is historically "fair" to either Puritan or Government: but it may be suggested that the high degree of explicitness with which the rational central position is defined makes its art distinctly cruder, and thus less convincing, than that of our passage from *The Heart of Midlothian*. Scott could hardly have treated the issues raised in that passage with the same sort of explicitness, indeed, for they are issues that make his sane, civilised, eminently humane self uncomfortable, at times insecure, even at times somewhat scared.

Thomas Crawford[6] does well to remind us that Scott is not just a survival from the eighteenth century. We can accept the Augustan element in his make-up as outstandingly important: but at the same time we should beware of overstressing it in our anxiety to rescue him from the turbid waters of second-rate Romanticism. Consider Bartoline Saddletree again. To claim him as an ironical self-portrait of the author would be as critically absurd as Saddletree is legalistically absurd. Having said that, however, and having made allowance for the fact that Scott is exploiting amateur legal pedantry (and he would have come across plenty of it in real life) for humorous effect, just as he revels in the archaeological claptrap of Sir Arthur Wardour in *The Antiquary*, can we not see some sort of link between Saddletree and the Sheriff-Deputy of Selkirkshire?

Davie Deans would assuredly have seen it; for what he objects to most of all in his interlocutor is his worldliness, and Scott was nothing if not worldly. Yet the passage as a whole indicates that he just could not rest smugly content with worldly common sense. Why, otherwise, should he have given it so laughable a

6 Crawford, pp. 8–9.

spokesman? It is not simply that the author has a "heart" that goes out to the wretched Covenanters of whose doctrines his reason disapproves; their refuge in the "'wet brae-sides, peat-haggs and flow-mosses'" evokes a side of existence that makes Saddletree's "'due administration of justice'" seem formal and abstract indeed.

Whether or not we say that this is the "Romantic" breaking out in the man who is in many ways so profoundly anti-Romantic, whether or not we see here the supremacy of Sandyknowe over Edinburgh, does not seem to matter particularly. It is more rewarding to think of it not so much in terms of movements or influences, but rather in terms of that humane mind which, while finding so much to cherish in the monuments of civilisation, sometimes turned upon them an alarmed scrutiny – not in a bout of revolutionary bravado, but in the spirit, paradoxically, of that very humanity which made him place upon them the value that he did. And the monument that worries him the most is the one that he knew best – the law.

3

So far the word "justice" has been used deliberately without precise definition: justice thought of in connexion with legal statutes, "poetic justice", and the justice that people do or do not do to one another have all been jumbled together. But this variety of meaning can aid discussion of two novels in which Scott's probings and queries on the subject of legal justice are associated with an ancillary concern with justice of other kinds. The idea of what is just or unjust in a diversity of circumstances, and a pre-occupation with the limits within which justice as embodied in the law may be trusted, act together as a structural principle.

Guy Mannering, the simpler and less disturbing of these works, is of course very obviously a novel about "justice being done" in the familiar nineteenth-century sense. Gilbert Glossin and Dirk Hatteraick meet the due fate of villains, and the book trium-phantly winds up with the fulfilment of the prophecy that

> Bertram's right and Bertram's might,
> Shall meet on Ellangowan height.[7]

[7] *G.M.*, Ch. 41.

But this "poetic justice" aspect of the book is structurally linked
with considerations of justice in other shapes. Godfrey Bertram,
for example, declaims bitterly to Mannering on the "injustice" of
his not being made a justice of the peace. When, however, his
nomination at last comes, Bertram turns out to be, in the eyes of
many, an "unjust" justice, for he "was no sooner possessed of the
judicial authority which he had so much longed for, than he began
to exercise it with more severity than mercy, and totally belied all
the opinions which had hitherto been formed of his inert good
nature".[8] The chief sufferers from his judicial rigour are the gipsy
settlers of Ellangowan, descended from a race which had contrived to prosper in spite of a law "which rendered the character of
gipsy equal, in the judicial balance, to that of common and habitual
thief, and prescribed his punishment accordingly".[9] If Bertram is
"unjust" enough to drive these gipsies from his land, it is not,
however, from any personal animosity toward them, but rather
because he has been accused (ironically to the reader) of a kind of
flagrantly hypocritical injustice in respect of the proper law and
order of the neighbourhood. An opponent in county politics has
objected that "while he affected a great zeal for the public police,
and seemed ambitious of the fame of an active magistrate, he
fostered a tribe of the greatest rogues in the country, and permitted
them to harbour within a mile of the house of Ellangowan".[10]

To their eviction the devotion of Meg Merrilies to the house of
Ellangowan lends a ghastly irony, for to her Bertram is the very
type of the unquestionably reliable hereditary aristocrat, "'a real
gentleman for sae mony hundred years, and never hunds puir fowk
aff your grund as if they were mad tykes'".[11] Yet notwithstanding
her subsequent bitterness, Meg is appalled by the news that the
estate has been sold after Bertram's death, and almost incredulous
that it should have fallen into the hands of Gilbert Glossin:

> "Sell'd!" echoed the gipsy, with something like a scream;
> "and wha durst buy Ellangowan that was not of Bertram's
> blude? and wha could tell whether the bonny knave-bairn
> may not come back to claim his ain? wha durst buy the estate
> and the castle of Ellangowan?"

[8] *Op. cit.*, Ch. 6.   [9] *Op. cit.*, Ch. 7.   [10] *Ibid.*
[11] *Op. cit.*, Ch. 3.

"Troth, gudewife, just ane o' thae writer chields that buys a' thing; they ca' him Glossin, I think."

"Glossin! Gibbie Glossin! that I have carried in my creels a hundred times, for his mother wasna muckle better than mysell – he to presume to buy the barony of Ellangowan! Gude be wi' us; it is an awfu' warld! I wished him ill; but no sic a downfa' as a' that neither. Wae's me! wae's me to think o't!"[12]

Not only does Meg feel that social justice has been shockingly out-raged; she goes on to speak of a justice in the very elements inter-vening to correct this state of affairs: "'It will be seen and heard of – earth and sea will not hold their peace langer!'" No wonder, then, that she gives the astonished Brown the purse of treasure with the words "'Many's the awmous your house has gi'en Meg and hers; and she has lived to pay it back in a small degree'"[13] For her there is a justice of human sentiment and traditional loyalty that is able to forgive what she has regarded as a human injustice committed in the name of the law by one whom weakness made vulnerable to the taunts of parochial antagonism. And it is of great significance that this woman, whose mysterious comings and goings, quite apart from the reputation of her race, make her a figure decidedly outside the law, should be one of the two characters mainly responsible for seeing that "justice is done" at the end of the novel.

The other character, of course, is Mr Counsellor Pleydell. This gentleman needs to be rather carefully discussed if the design of *Guy Mannering* is to be properly understood. An obvious answer to the question "What part does Mr. Pleydell take in the organization of the book?" might seem to be "Apart from his straight con-tribution to the working out of the plot, he is the opposite of Glossin – the honest lawyer in antithesis to the roguish one". Now one sees that this is true in a very broad way, but attention to Scott's text makes such a view hard to accept without some qualification. Consider the following piece of dialogue from the ending of Chapter LVI:

"And now," said Pleydell, "make out warrants for

[12] *Op. cit.*, Ch. 22.
[13] *Op. cit.*, Ch. 28.

commitment for Hatteraick and Glossin until liberated in
due course of law. Yet," he said, "I am sorry for Glossin."

"Now, I think," said Mannering, "that he's incomparably
the least deserving of pity of the two. The other's a bold
fellow, though as hard as flint."

"Very natural, Colonel," said the Advocate, "that you
should be interested in the ruffian and I in the knave, that's
all professional taste; but I can tell you Glossin would have
been a pretty lawyer had he not had such a turn for the
roguish part of the profession."

What Mr Pleydell's rejoinder amounts to is an admission that
each of us, while agreeing with one another in principle on the
justice meted out to villains "in due course of law", will nevertheless hold his own view of the precise extent to which their sentences are deserved, and that such opinions may be based upon
considerations or prejudices that have nothing to do with crime
and punishment. That in itself has little originality, to be sure,
though it does link up with this novel's constant preoccupation
with the differences which may arise between what seems humanly
just and what is just or otherwise according to the law. But the
real interest of the passage comes out in Mr Pleydell's sly remark
(hardly a flattering one!) that it is "natural" for Mannering to feel
more sympathy for the "ruffian". Observe that he here addresses
Mannering as "Colonel", and although he does this often enough
in other parts of the book, his subsequent allusion to "professional
taste" makes it plain that this subtle-witted man really does mean
that a soldier is more likely than not to have a sense of fellow-
feeling for a bold scoundrel. Yet he is far from indulging in a
mere facile gibe at the military profession, for he immediately
turns the joke against himself by saying that it is just as "natural"
for the lawyer to side with the "knave". Thus the upright lawyer
in Mr Pleydell condemns Glossin for his offences against act and
statute, whilst at the same time that very lawyer as professional
man cannot resist a certain decidedly non-legal admiration for the
unscrupulous creature's acumen.

I am not suggesting that Mr Pleydell under different circumstances might have been a Glossin, except in so far as it is always
possible to say that A, given certain circumstances, could have

turned out to be a B. What I do want to point out is that Pleydell, to a much greater extent than the other "good" legal figure in the novel, Mr Mac-Morlan, is very definitely *the professional man* – to his finger-tips, indeed. Like Mac-Morlan he is eminently humane; witness his words about Lucy Bertram when Mannering first meets him in the droll surroundings of the Edinburgh tavern.[14] But there is something of the cynic in his make-up too, even if we allow for an element of conscious exaggeration. When he jokingly tells Mannering "'I always speak truth of a Saturday night'", and the Colonel adds "'And sometimes through the week, I should suppose'", Mr Pleydell replies

> "Why, yes; as far as my vocation will permit. I am as Hamlet says, indifferent honest, when my clients and their solicitors do not make me the medium of conveying their double-distilled lies to the bench. But *oportet vivere*! it is a sad thing."[15]

And although in Chapter LVI he defends the law against Mannering's hint that the roguishness of Glossin might have been to his vocational advantage rather than the reverse, he admits that it cannot be regarded as a wonder-working medicine, effective no matter who administers it: "'Law's like laudanum; it's much more easy to use it as a quack does than to learn to apply it like a physician.'"

Meg Merrilies and Mr Pleydell, the "extra-legal" vagrant and the skilled advocate, the wanderer in wet and wilderness and the sophisticated urban gentleman, dominate the structure of *Guy Mannering*. In their different ways they lead the reader constantly to examine and re-examine his notions and preconceptions regarding justice of both the rationally "legal" kind and the emotionally "human" type. Together they make a frame for and affect our reaction to such varied things as the crooked dealings of Gilbert Glossin, Mannering's haunting sense of having been unjust to his wife and to Brown in India, his friend Mervyn's would-be consolatory advice on the justice of defending one's reputation, Dandie Dinmont's obsession with seeing that "justice is done" in what seems a ludicrously unimportant case, and Sir Robert Hazlewood's "sliding scale" conception of justice, in which the

[14] *Op. cit.*, Ch. 36.   [15] *Op. cit.*, Ch. 37.

magnitude of the offence varies according to the social rank of the person against whom it is committed.

4

Its justice theme (or themes) can be shown to give *Guy Mannering* an architectural solidity and a density of interest lacking in the kind of nineteenth-century stereotype mentioned at the beginning of this essay. Though outwardly more diffuse, it is in reality far more concentrated than such a late example of the stereotype as J. Meade Falkner's excellent *Moonfleet*, with which it has certain things in common. Nevertheless, it has more of the quality of a romantic adventure-story than that curious novel *Redgauntlet*. To put it another way: while both books contain a wealth of varied incident and setting, *Guy Mannering* is the more straightforwardly enjoyable on a simple level. Even when due attention is given to the justice theme, the book has still a frank directness of appeal, whereas *Redgauntlet* leaves the reader with uncertainties, suspended judgments, and (despite some magnificent comedy) a rather bitter taste in the mouth.

To say this is in no way to criticise the work adversely, but rather to call attention to its distinctive quality. An attempt at defining that quality might begin by recalling two climactic episodes in *Guy Mannering*, both connected with the assertion of "Bertram's right". In Chapter XLI Glossin comes upon Brown, now metamorphosed into young Bertram, standing by "a large old oak-tree, the only one on the esplanade, and which, having been used for executions by the barons of Ellangowan, was called the Justice Tree". The symbolism is doubtless effective enough, but over-obvious and too dependent on what Scott himself describes as a "remarkable" coincidence. It resembles some of the less happy ironic effects of Hardy. *Redgauntlet*, however, uses symbolism in a subtle and original way. Consider the deadly Solway tide, to which Darsie Latimer nearly falls victim on two occasions. On the simplest level the Solway is the dividing line between Scotland, where Darsie is safe, and the England upon whose soil he has been warned not to set foot – the treacherous tide being thus a symbolic reminder of the dangers awaiting him on the English shore. But there is more to it than that. The tide rushes up the estuary with lethal speed, yet Redgauntlet himself, though abundantly aware of its perils, seems quite at home with it. And it is no accident that this should be so, for both Redgauntlet and the tide pursue their courses with a common impetuosity and ruthlessness once they have begun. Both sweep everything before them. Redgauntlet has no more respect for the law (though he may use it when it suits his purpose) than has the great onrush of water.

The second incident from *Guy Mannering* that seems *à propos* comes in Chapter LIV, when Meg Merrilies, having gone with Hatteraick into the cavern, utters the appointed words "*'Because the Hour's come, and the Man'*" which are the signal for Bertram and Dinmont to spring upon the ruffian. Hatteraick discharges his pistol at her when he sees that he has been betrayed, and she falls with the words "'I kenn'd it would be this way'". Here we have a bringing together of two kinds of justice. Meg's signal heralds the final triumph of "Bertram's right", and the words she speaks as she falls show her acceptance of this kind of death as being inevitable and "right" according to the fatalistic idea of justice in which she believes. Unlike the "Justice Tree" incident, this strikes me as being one of the book's most telling strokes, simple though it is.

Justice, in the legal sense, is not a matter of concern to Redgauntlet the man; the only kind of secular justice that has any meaning for him is the justice, as he sees it, of the Stewart cause. And although he speaks of the days "'When Scotland was herself, and had her own King and Legislature'", it is obvious to the reader that even the law of independent Scotland would have meant little to him. For he is as much a fatalist as Meg Merrilies herself. If he does not believe in law, it is because he does not believe in freedom. In Chapter VIII, from which the words just quoted are taken, Darsie, who is in his uncle's hands, claims "'the privilege of acting for myself'", and declares "'constraint shall not deprive me of an Englishman's best privilege'". Redgauntlet makes short work of what he calls "'the true cant of the day'":

> "The privilege of free action belongs to no mortal; we are tied down by the fetters of duty, our mortal path is limited by the regulations of honour, our most indifferent actions are

N

> but meshes of the web of destiny by which we are all sur-
> rounded. . . . Yes, young man, in doing and suffering we play
> but the part allotted by Destiny, the manager of this strange
> drama, stand bound to act no more than is prescribed, to say
> no more than is set down for us; and yet we mouth about
> free-will, and freedom of thought and action, as if Richard
> must not die, or Richmond conquer, exactly where the
> author has decreed it shall be so!"[16]

"The day", as the book's sub-title reminds us, is the eighteenth
century. Certainly nothing could be more distant from eighteenth-
century rationality than such an outburst. For not only does it
deny the reality of free-will; it also jumbles together duty, honour,
and destiny in a wild confusion. Redgauntlet is no lunatic, but his
words give the impression of a total disregard for reason and
distinction parallel to his contempt for the justice of the law.

If Redgauntlet's outburst bespeaks a belief in justice meted out
by Destiny, as inexorable as the justice to which Shakespeare
brings Richard III, this exchange between nephew and uncle has
an effect completely opposite to that of the cavern passage from
Guy Mannering. There, fate and the law were thought of as working hand in hand; here the two notions of justice are starkly
separated, as the Solway tide separates the shores of England and
Scotland. And that great careering flood is as inexorable as the
justice Redgauntlet believes in.

For every reader there are particular impressions, moods,
scenes, and so on, that remain hauntingly in the memory when a
novel is closed. In the case of *Redgauntlet*, whatever else the
individual reader may retain with special vividness, there must
surely be two things that stand out as seeming to characterise the
peculiar flavour of this book: an impression of law and order (and
the justice associated with them) breaking down, and the poignant
scene (one of fiction's most splendidly deliberate anticlimaxes) in
which Charles Edward's "supporters" virtually disown him.

The impression of judicial breakdown arises most powerfully
from the extraordinary imprisonment to which Darsie is subjected,
a restraint at which a bona fide if fatuous magistrate connives.
But it is also associated with a whole series of characters who are,

16 R., Ch. 8.

in one way or another, "outside the law". In this sort of world, we are made to feel, it is not surprising that Darsie's protest that his detention is illegal and "'highly punishable by the laws which protect the liberties of the subject'"[17] should be uttered in vain. There is, for example, Nanty Ewart, that amiable drunk, "who, by his own account, had been a pirate, and who was at present, in all probability, an outlaw as well as a contraband trader";[18] there is that pseudo-pious humbug Thomas Trumbull, who appears superficially to be very much *within* the law, but whose speciality, apart from smuggling, seems to be the dissemination of obscene literature; there is even "the notorious little Benjie", a promising case of youthful delinquency; there is, for that matter, Wandering Willie – not, to be sure, characteristically engaged in strikingly illicit activities, but living, as his name indicates, a life that is essentially a law unto itself. Finally there is the Cavalier, Prince Charles Edward, together with those who seek to advance his cause.

Directly opposed to everything those characters stand for in the organisation of the novel, is legal Edinburgh, with the pedantic and punctilious Mr Fairford at its centre as far as the story is concerned. Whatever his virtues, Saunders Fairford is no Counsellor Pleydell. In him legal professionalism, though eminently honest and dogged, is totally unadorned with the graces of urbanity. And indeed the law in this novel, though Alan Fairford applies himself to it with a tolerably good grace and with considerable promise, hardly shines out as a beacon of civilised enlightenment. It is significant that the case in which Alan at first makes so good an impression should be the preposterous Peter Peebles affair. Peebles is certainly an exquisitely funny creation, but Alan's professional plea for him as "'a victim to protracted justice, and to that hope delayed which sickens the heart'"[19] awakens in the reader (as distinct from the Bench) only a very little sympathy, so rapacious a waster is this creature. And even the severely limited pity the reader may once have felt is quite swept away by the lies Peebles tells when he is in pursuit of Alan later in the book. Peebles, in fact, affords a good example of the kind of suspended judgment which is so typical of this novel. We find ourselves uncertain whether he really is a sad victim of the law's delay, in

[17] *Op. cit.*, Ch. 5.   [18] *Op. cit.*, Ch. 14.   [19] *Op. cit.*, Ch. 1.

which case his disreputable behaviour has some measure of excuse, or whether he is so fundamentally disreputable a person that his failure to get a judgment in his favour is actually richly deserved. "Evidence", one way or another, is offered from time to time, but we can never be quite sure what to think, and conclude that the fairest thing is simply to pronounce him crazy and leave it at that. In any case his association in the book with courts and legal figures serves to surround the law with a certain atmosphere of seediness and futility.

A thoroughgoing analysis of *Redgauntlet* would have to take into account a good many instances of the uncertain or suspended judgment. (What precisely, for example, are we to think about Joshua Geddes and his fish-traps, from the point of view of either strict legality or plain human fairness? Is the attack on them actually "unjust", or is it a case of equivocal "justice", like the elder Bertram's eviction of the gipsies from Ellangowan? With what degree of sympathy or the reverse are we to regard Maxwell of Summertrees, in Chapter xi?). But all these are subordinate to and a preparation for the extraordinary climax of the book. Many readers will have found it extremely upsetting, perhaps because they have a sense of having been "cheated". The narrative has built up a deal of mystery and suspense, events seem to be sweeping their way to a grand explosion of violence, and what happens? There are, it is true, the violent deaths of Nanty Ewart and Cristal Nixon, which respectively awaken compassion and satisfy a very straightforward desire for "poetic justice"; but, as far as the Prince and Redgauntlet are concerned, the story just fizzles out.

In fact this ending is thoroughly in keeping with the tone of the book. Almost everywhere we turn there is breakdown: the frightening atmosphere of lawlessness, which is, as has been pointed out, so often apparent, and also examples of breakdown in the "government" of the single individual. Both Nanty Ewart and Peter Peebles are to different degrees human wrecks. Thomas Trumbull is a moral wreck, and well on the way to being a physical one to boot. Charles Edward himself is presented as a man in premature physical decay, whose private morals will not bear the closest inspection. Events often carry with them similar implications. The hearing of the Peebles case breaks down when

Alan learns of his friend's peril and hurries off. The peaceful, ordered life of the Geddes couple is shattered by violence. Even the weird tale told by Wandering Willie, in which the frontier between reality and fantasy is broken down with a vengeance, is seen by the teller as having had sadly disruptive consequences for his own life.

The Jacobite conspiracy likewise breaks down. In one sense, of course, this may be taken as a plain instance of "justice being done". The whole enterprise is a desperate affair, calculated to plunge the country into useless bloodshed. Its failure to reach the stage of armed uprising, through internal breakdown, is thus from government's point of view an entirely "just" conclusion. It may be urged, indeed, that the Prince and Redgauntlet are accorded considerably more than justice when General Campbell allows them to depart unharmed.

But the thoughtful reader will find it impossible to rest content with so simple a view. He may or may not feel that it is a good thing the conspiracy has caved in; he is certain to feel uncomfortable about the *way* in which it has expired.

If we consider both the actual scene before the Prince in the improvised presence chamber, and the discussion which precedes it, we find it extraordinarily hard to pass definite judgments. The conspirators are in so appallingly difficult and complex a position, that although we may feel admiration for some or contempt for others from time to time, we cannot persist in definite judgment for long – except in the case of Redgauntlet himself, who retains our qualified admiration for his single-minded devotion, supremely dangerous though we know him to be.

There are certainly moments at which we feel that the Prince's "champions" are guilty of shocking injustice towards him in backing out of the enterprise with apparently so much alacrity. But awkward counter-considerations present themselves. Charles Edward, after all, is guilty of injustice toward *them* (even Redgauntlet sees this), in persisting in a politically dangerous infatuation. There is consequently considerable "justice" in Sir Richard Glendale's declaration that he will see the Prince safely to his departing ship and defend him against any possible attack on the way to it, but that once the sails are spread he will take immediate measures for his own protection, surrendering himself if necessary to a Justice of Peace, and giving security that he will thenceforward "'live quiet, and submit to the ruling powers'".[20] It is a sad, a pitiful state of affairs, and although we may be glad that civil strife has not actually broken out, we take away from the book a nagging sense that true justice has somehow *not* been done – though what "true justice" may be taken to mean we are far from sure, for the whole organisation of the novel has success-fully undermined simple notions of justice in any guise.

5

Scott is not an "intellectual". He is not interested in ideas in and for themselves, but rather in the emotional consequences to which ideas give rise. And in any case he is a popular novelist, with a public to cater for, whether we deplore this or not. Nothing by way of a cogent, systematised, philosophically satisfying "idea of justice" emerges from these two books.

Yet, in *Guy Mannering* and *Redgauntlet*, a host of differing views of what justice may be held to mean in widely various contexts are held up to be inspected for what they are worth. There are the solid achievements of legal justice; equally there are the dangerous things that can be done with it by the unscrupulous, and the frightening occasions when it seems to be powerless, at the mercy of forces stronger than itself. And there are all the varieties of social and personal justice and injustice, beside which the justice of the law must always be seen if it is truly to be regarded as a monument of civilisation. Finally, the justice themes give the two books a structural coherence, a satisfying richness and solidity, that should make us value Scott more in the twentieth century than most readers have been inclined to do. It is well to remind ourselves of what Flaubert once said about *The Pickwick Papers*: "Some parts are magnificent, but what a defective structure! All English writers are like that. Walter Scott apart, they lack com-position." We do not need to go all the way with Flaubert to see what he means.

[20] *Op. cit.*, Ch. 22.

Donald Cameron

THE WEB OF DESTINY:
THE STRUCTURE OF
THE BRIDE OF LAMMERMOOR

Almost alone among Scott's novels, *The Bride of Lammermoor* has
been widely admired for its structure and its economy.[1] It holds a
number of his dominant preoccupations in an unusual balance
which is never upset in any important way. The nature of this
harmony has never been fully discussed, but the key to it is Scott's
brilliant use of the supernatural as a device to suggest certain
qualities of the historical context, to express the secret desires of
the characters, and to control the pace of the narrative.

The solid base of *The Bride of Lammermoor* is, not surprisingly,
historical and social. The major conflict between the Presbyterian
Lord Keeper and the Tory, Episcopalian Master of Ravenswood
is carefully connected to the religious and political situation in
early eighteenth-century Scotland, and the importance of the
national theme is always clear.[2] In post-union Scotland, the
crown is remote; opportunists and moral decay are constantly
uncovered. The rapid pen-portrait of the new peer Lord

[1] Pelham Edgar, *The Art of the Novel.* New York (Macmillan) 1933, p. 83;
E. A. Baker, *History of the English Novel*, 10 vols., 1924–39, VI, p. 168;
Colburn's *New Monthly*, V (1882), p. 77, quoted by J. T. Hillhouse, *The
Waverley Novels and their Critics*, Minneapolis, 1936, p. 65; Una Pope-Hen-
nessy, *Sir Walter Scott*, London (Home & Van Thal) 1948, p. 88; J. L.
Adolphus, *Letters to Richard Heber*, London, 1821, p. 15; Leslie Stephen,
Hours in a Library, New York, 1875, p. 79.

[2] On religion, see K. Bos, *Religious Creeds . . . in Sir Walter Scott's Works. . . .*
Amsterdam (H. J. Paris) 1932, p. 159; on the political and social situation, see
R. C. Gordon, "*The Bride of Lammermoor*: A Novel of Tory Pessimism",
in *Nineteenth Century Fiction*, XII (1957) pp. 110–24.

Bittlebrains, for instance, is acid.[3] In Scott's novels, such periods
of turbulence and social disintegration foster the supernatural[4] –
reasonably enough, given Scott's general attitude that phenomena
such as witchcraft are commonly tools which the unscrupulous
use to gain their own sordid ends.

Throughout, the novel insists upon the infection of all levels of
society. A tragic time produces no Edie Ochiltrees and Dandie
Dinmonts; instead it produces, at its best, the fate-haunted gravity
of old Alice, and at its worst the sexton Mortsheugh, and the three
old hags. Even such fleetingly-glimpsed characters as Lord
Turntippet and Lady Blenkensop are consumed by selfishness.
So are the villagers of Wolf's Hope, caught in the agonies of
historical change as feudalism crumbles.

From this basis in social life the supernaturalism takes its rise.
The supernatural in Scott is almost invariably associated with a
Scottish peasant superstition and derives much of its power from
its origin as the best explanation of various unusual occurrences
available to good untutored minds. "I think," Scott wrote as
early as 1801, "the Marvellous in poetry is ill-timed and disgusting
when not managed with moderation & ingrafted upon some
circumstance of popular tradition or belief which sometimes can
give even to the improbable an air of something like probability."[5]
In his review of Hoffmann's novels, "On the Supernatural in
Fictitious Composition", he claimed that such traditions usually
possess an insight and a firmness of thought that can be missed
when the supernatural is purely a product of the individual
writer's imagination.[6]

Writing anonymously of *Old Mortality*, he connects this strong
vein of supernaturalism to his national concerns:

[3] Quotations from the Waverley Novels are taken from the Dryburgh
Edition, 25 vols. London (A. C. Black) 1892–94.
[4] C. O. Parsons, *Witchcraft and Demonology in Scott's Fiction*. Edinburgh
(Oliver & Boyd) 1964, pp. 282–3.
[5] *The Letters of Sir Walter Scott*, eds. H. J. C. Grierson, *et. al.*, 12 vols.
London (Constable) 1932–7, I, p. 121.
[6] *Foreign Quarterly Review*, 1 (1927) p. 67. Hence M. C. Boatright finds that
"Scott's success in the use of demonology is proportional to the closeness
with which he adhered to the traditions of his region". "Demonology in the
Novels of Sir Walter Scott", *University of Texas Bulletin, Studies in English* No.
14 (1934) p. 83.

The traditions and manners of the Scotch were so blended with superstitious practices and fears, that the author of these novels seems to have deemed it incumbent on him, to transfer many more such incidents to his novels, than seem either probable or natural to an English reader. It may be some apology that his story would have lost the national cast, which it was chiefly his object to preserve, had this been otherwise.[7]

Scott reports that the last Scottish witch was burned in 1722, just under fifty years before his own birth; in 1827, he says, there still linger considerable traces of belief in witchcraft in Scotland. These traces led him to conclude that "the belief in witchcraft is only asleep, and might in remote corners be again awakened to deeds of blood".[8] Witchcraft, because an historical reality, he considered a legitimate subject for fiction – a revealing way of deciding what is legitimate.[9]

In his criticism he points out the effectiveness of showing the terror that allegedly supernatural events produce in the characters of the story. His favourite example is in *Tom Jones*:[10] the ghost in *Hamlet* does not frighten Partridge at all, but the terror of Garrick's Hamlet does. A folk-oriented version of this "fear-by-association" effect underlies several of Scott's stories in which belief in the supernatural is deeply ingrained in the minor characters; the depth and passion of their belief makes it to some extent infective. If a woman talks as old Ailsie Gourlay does, something is surely going to come of it. Possibly she is only a "half-crazed being who believes herself an ally of condemned spirits, and desires to be so", but he thought such a creature "a sublime subject".[11] "The use of these superstitious peasants enables Scott to present belief and its effects without either sharing it or asking his readers to. The supernatural can be taken seriously if not literally.

Questions of social and historical fact raise the matter of Scott's sources, which he gives very fully in the Introduction and Notes

---

[7] *Quarterly Review*, XVI (1817) p. 435.

[8] *Letters on Demonology and Witchcraft*, 1830. Intro. Henry Morley, 1885, p. 272.

[9] *Letters*, v, p. 398.   [10] Book XVI, Ch. 5.

[11] *Journal*, ed. J. G. Tait, 1 vol. Edinburgh (Oliver & Boyd) 1950, p. 376.

to the collected edition. Aside from a change of scene and a few minor alterations such as changing the death of the bridegroom in the legend to that of the lover, the novel follows its sources closely – more closely, in fact, than most of the Waverley Novels. The one major alteration is the addition of the brooding omens and the supernatural atmosphere, particularly the prophecy of Thomas the Rhymer. Coleman O. Parsons sees the problem of the added supernaturalism as the crucial problem in the novel's composition:

> The narrative, if shorn of the supernatural, would have been trite and would certainly have lost much of its gloomy intensity; yet motivation which directly depended on witch-craft and diabolical retribution was grotesque. . . . His solution was to allow the tragedy to unfold on two planes of consciousness, the realistic-romantic and the superstitious. The central figures move in the former plane, but sometimes descend to the latter, where – in the last third of the novel – they meet a band of weird women which acts as chorus to the catastrophe of the main action.[12]

Some of Scott's most powerful supernatural effects come from a connexion with history. His use of omen and prophecy is particularly striking: a spectre or a soothsayer, or even a tradition, tells an individual that to proceed along his current path will be disastrous, but the character is imprisoned by the actions he has already carried out and by his own nature. The catastrophe inevitably follows. A harmony and tension develop in the story between the portents of disaster and the historically-moulded psychological forces which determine the behaviour of the characters. The sharpening contrast between the apparent prosperity and the genuine doom which is approaching is one of the means Scott uses to gain a steady increase of suspense. This pattern shapes the three narratives in which the supernatural is one of the chief determinants of the structure – the two fine stories in *The Chronicles of the Canongate* called *The Two Drovers* and *The Highland Widow*, and *The Bride of Lammermoor*. The same pattern plays a part in the much less successful *A Legend of Montrose*, and

[12] C. O. Parsons, "The Dalrymple Legend in *The Bride of Lammermoor*", *Review of English Studies*, XIX (1943) p. 58.

in the Bodach Glas passages of *Waverley*; a mirror-image of it foreshadows the abduction of Harry Bertram and the happy conclusion of *Guy Mannering*.

Obviously historical determinism lies very near the heart of this pattern. The supernatural here resembles an inspired guess about the future, based on a sudden intuitive understanding of the lines of force in another's life, a heightened and deepened form of the parent's warning to the child: "If you go on doing that kind of thing you'll kill yourself." In the social sphere, an analogy to these private intuitions is afforded by the close relation between Scott's sense of history and what is very nearly the same thing, his sense of fate.

Scott's sense of fate is the product of a modern's general view of human life, the view that the events of life may be under the general guidance of a deity but on the whole are to be understood in natural terms. He has no strong feeling of God's immediate supervision of human events, and he is bound by the fact that he is writing a novel, a modern, more or less realistic account of events in which causation is not embodied in any specially developed symbolism such as the gods represent in Greek drama. The most Scott can do is adapt a part of the realistic environment (such as the landscape, or the three old women) to symbolic uses. For both Scott and the Greeks, though, one's character and circumstances are one's destiny, whatever the conventions used in exposing them. John Erskine describes "the definition of fate that Scott would subscribe to" as "the knowledge the gods have of us".[13]

Overlapping with this is the historical sense, the awareness of the intimate and detailed relation of historical effects to historical causes. Scott's sense of fate includes historical determinism as a limiting factor rather than as a universal explanation of events. His comments here are not entirely harmonious, but over a human lifetime few men's comments can be. He has a strong feeling for pessimistic fatalism; as Rob Roy puts it, "every wight has his weird, and we maun a' dee when our day comes".[14] He also displays a good deal of sunshine and optimism, particularly in the

[13] "The Waverley Novels", *The Delight of Great Books*. London (Eveleigh, Nash & Grayson) 1928, p. 195.
[14] R.R., Ch. 34.

novels, and his pessimism sometimes appears to be romantic literary posturing. On occasion he specifically denies an all-embracing determinism such as that of Jasper Dryfesdale in *The Abbot*, for instance, and in *The Pirate* he remarks:

> The freedom of the will is permitted to us in the occurrences of ordinary life, as in our moral conduct; and in the former as well as the latter case is often the means of misguiding those who possess it.[15]

The irony of that last clause, its unusual sardonic quality, suggests that for Scott, free will is real but limited by the historical situation. With all the wit and all the will and all the vigour there are things men cannot do. No one, not even Charles Edward, could have brought the Jacobites success. Even Rob Roy cannot keep the heroic age alive. The greatest expression of this sense of fate and free will is the chained and defiant Redgauntlet, fighting hopelessly and faithfully for a cause that he knows to be lost. When Darsie Latimer protests at the loss of his freedom, Redgauntlet makes the finest statement of the case for determinism that appears anywhere in the Waverley Novels. The nub of the passage is that

> The privilege of free action belongs to no mortal: we are tied down by the fetters of duty, our moral path is limited by the regulations of honour, our most indifferent actions are but meshes in the web of destiny by which we are all surrounded.

And again, "Nothing . . . is the work of chance, nothing is the consequence of free will. . . ."[16] But the voice of Redgauntlet is not the voice of *Redgauntlet*. Darsie spins part of the web of his destiny for himself.

Scott knew that the action of omens and prophecies in the mind gives them much of their power, and the conjunction of the supernatural with the subtler workings of the mind is the most remarkable feature of his use of supernatural phenomena. Scott is not usually considered a psychological novelist, but he had a sophisticated apprehension of the adaptability of the mind, the untrustworthiness and yet the general truth of its reports of the world. Consider dreams, which he uses repeatedly as structural

[15] *P.*, Ch. 13.   [16] *R.*, Ch. 8.

units. In *Old Mortality* Morton, unaware of Burley's recent part in the assassination of Archbishop Sharp, has put him to bed in the barn; Morton retires himself and has a nightmare, "a blended vision of horror" involving both Burley and Edith Bellenden, "weeping, and with dishevelled hair, and appearing to call on him for comfort and assistance which he had it not in his power to render".[17] Morton then goes out to awaken Burley, and finds him still sleeping, but also dreaming:

> A ray of light streamed on his uncurtained couch, and showed to Morton the working of his harsh features, which seemed agitated by some strong internal cause of disturbance. He had not undressed. Both his arms were above the bed-cover, the right hand strongly clenched, and occasionally making that abortive attempt to strike which usually attends dreams of violence; the left was extended, and agitated from time to time by a movement as if repulsing someone. The perspiration stood on his brow "like bubbles in a late disturbed stream", and these marks of emotion were accompanied with broken words which escaped from him at intervals – "Thou art taken, Judas – thou art taken. Cling not to my knees – cling not to my knees; hew him down! A priest! Ay, a priest of Baal, to be bound and slain, even at the brook Kishon. Firearms will not prevail against him. Strike – thrust with the cold iron – put him out of pain – put him out of pain, were it but for the sake of his grey hairs."[18]

In a passage in the *Letters on Demonology and Witchcraft*, Scott discusses with great fascination the mechanisms by which dreams are manufactured:

> . . . it may be remarked, that any sudden noise which the slumberer hears, without being actually awakened by it – any casual touch of his person occurring in the same manner – becomes instantly adopted in his dream, and accommodated to the tenor of the current train of thought whatever that may happen to be; and nothing is more remarkable than the rapidity with which imagination supplies a complete explanation of the interruption, according to the previous train of

[17] *O.M.*, Ch. 6.   [18] *Ibid.*

ideas expressed in the dream, even when scarce a moment of time is allowed for that purpose. In dreaming, for example, of a duel, the external sound becomes, in the twinkling of an eye, the discharge of the combatants' pistols. . . . In short, an explanatory system is adopted during sleep with such extreme rapidity, that supposing the intruding alarm to have been the first call of some person to awaken the slumberer, the explanation, though requiring some process of argument or deduction, is usually formed and perfect before the second effort of the speaker has restored the dreamer to the waking world and its realities.

This instant adaptation of the dream is a feature Scott uses repeatedly in his imaginative writing.[19]

Scott's sense of the elusiveness of mental processes is by no means limited to admittedly unconscious states such as sleep. Our waking minds, especially under stress, can equally readily mislead us – can mislead us, for instance, into believing literally in the supernatural. In such cases,

who shall doubt that imagination, favoured by circumstances, has power to summon up to the organ of sight, spectres which only exist in the mind of those by whom their apparition seems to be witnessed?

Apparitions such as these, awake or asleep, will usually seem genuine instances of the supernatural:

And if any event, such as the death of the person dreamt of, chances to take place, so as to correspond with the nature and the time of the apparition, the coincidence, though one which must be frequent, since our dreams usually refer to the accomplishment of that which haunts our minds when awake, and often presage the most probable events, seems perfect, and the chain of circumstances touching the evidence may not unreasonably be considered as complete.[20]

Perhaps the most striking example of Scott's use in connexion

[19] *Letters on Demonology and Witchcraft*, pp. 28–9; J. L. Adolphus, *Letters to Richard Heber, Esq.* (2nd edn) London 1821, pp. 233–9.
[20] *Letters on Demonology and Witchcraft*, p. 13.

with the supernatural of concepts closely resembling the unconscious is an anecdote in his review of John Galt's *The Omen*.
Remarkably parallel to Wandering Willie's Tale, this anecdote is
particularly provocative in that Scott here offers an astute explanation in natural terms of events that seem verifiably supernatural. A
man who can find no evidence for his belief that his dead father
has paid a certain debt is summoned to the law courts in London
over the matter. On the eve of his journey, however, his father
appears to him in a dream and tells him to consult a particular
attorney whom the father uncharacteristically had happened to use
on this occasion; if the attorney has forgotten the incident, the
son can help his recollection by reminding him of the double
Portugal piece with which he was paid, and for which there had
been some trouble finding change.

> The vision was correct in all points. The slumbering memory
> of the ex-attorney was roused by the recollection of the
> doubloon – the writings were recovered – and the dreamer
> freed from the prosecution brought against him.
> This remarkable story we have every reason to believe
> accurate matter of fact, at least in its general bearings.[21]

Now, Scott asks, how are we to account for this? Genuinely
supernatural? All Christians must believe that theoretically
possible, but it is most unlikely. Accident? Again, possible, but
extremely improbable. No, Scott argues, probably the mind,
working without conscious direction, here makes the same kind of
intuitive leap that accounted for prophecies:

> Every one is sensible, that among the stuff which dreams are
> made of, we can recognise broken and disjointed remnants of
> forgotten realities which dwell imperfectly on the memory.
> We are of opinion, therefore, that in this and similar cases, the
> sleeping imagination is actually weaving its web out of the
> broken realities of actual facts. The mind, at some early
> period, had been, according to the story, impressed with a
> strong belief that the debt had actually been paid, which
> belief must have arisen from some early convictions on the

[21] Review (1824) of Galt's *The Omen, Miscellaneous Prose Works*, 28 vols,
1834–61, XVIII, p. 351.

subject, of which the ground-work was decayed. But in the course of the watches of the night, Fancy, in her own time and manner, dresses up the faded materials of early recollection. The idea of the father once introduced, naturally recalls to memory what the dreamer, at some forgotten period, had actually heard from his parent; and by this clue he arrives at the truth of a fact, as he might have done at the result of a calculation, though without comprehending the mode by which he arrived at the truth.[22]

This is extremely acute, and ought by itself to demand a re-examination of the supernatural passages in the novels. Such a re-reading reveals that the supernatural in Scott often serves as a way of dealing with aspects of experience for which Scott's broadly rationalist eighteenth-century approach to fiction had no adequate symbolic language. In a Scott story, for instance, the devil is always interior, a symbol of the forces of evil in the self. It is in these terms that M. C. Boatright interprets the scene in which Morton approaches Burley in his cavern retreat[23] when Burley is still – a nice touch – fighting his conscience over the assassination of Sharp.[24] Parsons makes the same point: Scott's diabolism is "passional, not supernatural". So is witchcraft: "Considered as a moral state, not as a system of perverse power, witchcraft can hardly be said not to exist."[25]

Scott knew that prophecies tend to be self-fulfilling, and that even the knowledge of a supernatural phenomenon's natural causes may not alleviate the distress it produces, just as the knowledge that a disease is psychosomatic in origin does not cure it and does not alter the fact that it is a genuine physical disease. To take the last point first: in the Letters on Demonology and Witchcraft Scott tells the story of a prominent Scottish lawyer who developed the hallucination that a large cat was following him everywhere. After some weeks, the cat gave place to a gentleman-usher, who preceded the lawyer wherever he went; this was eventually superseded by a skeleton. The lawyer knew that these creatures were imaginary, but that did not eliminate them, and he concluded that

[22] *Miscellaneous Prose Works*, XVIII, pp. 352-3.
[23] *O.M.*, Ch. 43.   [24] M. C. Boatright, pp. 79-80.
[25] C. O. Parsons, *Witchcraft and Demonology in Scott's Fiction*, pp. 195, 161.

this haunting would ultimately kill him – which it did. Perhaps the knowledge that one is oppressed by forces within oneself is the worst kind of haunting.

The idea of the self-fulfilling prophecy occurs a number of times in Scott. The *Letters on Demonology and Witchcraft* describe

> that visionary summons which the natives of the Hebrides acknowledged as one sure sight of approaching fate. The voice of some absent, or probably some deceased, relative was, in such cases, heard as repeating the party's name. Sometimes the aerial summoner intimated his own death, and at others it was no uncommon circumstance that the person who fancied himself so called, died in consequence; – for the same reason that the negro pines to death who is laid under the ban of an Obi woman. . . .[26]

Reviewing *The Omen*, Scott was again arrested by the potency of prophecy:

> He would be a stout sceptic who would choose, like the hero of our tale, to tack his wedding to the conclusion of a funeral, or even to place the representation of a death's-head on a marriage-ring; and yet the marriage might be a happy one in either case, were there not the risk that the evil omen might work its own accomplishment by its effect on the minds of the parties.[27]

Early in *A Legend of Montrose* Menteith comments on Allan M'Aulay's prophetic gifts:

> "I think that he persuades himself that the predictions which are in reality the result of judgment and reflection are super- natural impressions on his mind, just as fanatics conceive the workings of their own imagination to be divine inspiration."[28]

The seer himself may be misled, then, by his own mind; Scott's later comment implies that Allan's visions are the result of a sort of mental civil war:

[26] *Letters on Demonology and Witchcraft*, pp. 40–1. The lawyer's hallucination, pp. 29–34.
[27] *Miscellaneous Prose Works*, XVIII, pp. 348–9.
[28] *A Legend of Montrose*, Ch. 5.

o

> The incredulous held that all this was idle dreaming, and that Allan's supposed vision was but a consequence of the private suggestions of his own passion, which, having long seen in Menteith a rival more beloved than himself, struggled with his better nature, and impressed upon him, as it were involuntarily, the idea of killing his competitor.[29]

It is the triumph of the subconscious.

Prophecy, Scott thought, still drew belief long after other forms of the supernatural had been entirely discredited,[30] perhaps because it was self-fulfilling, an interior rather than an external phenomenon. No doubt the same psychological characteristic also accounts for the fact that prophecy alone of all supernaturalism makes an important contribution to his fiction. The old archer Gilbert Greenleaf, in *Castle Dangerous*, even suggests an analogy between the way prophecy may operate upon the mind of the individual and the way in which such portents, operating like rumours, may affect a society. The remark is provocative, since the catastrophic conclusion of *The Bride of Lammermoor* depends on a variety of events controlled by several people. Greenleaf says,

> "I have observed that these mouldering parchments, when or by whomsoever composed, have so far a certain coincidence with the truth, that when such predictions which they contain are spread abroad in the country, and create rumours of plots, conspiracies, and bloody wars, they are very apt to cause the very mischances which they would be thought only to predict."[31]

Both the structure and the achievement of *The Bride of Lammermoor* are much clearer against the general background of Scott's interest in the supernatural and the quality of his understanding of it. In its structure each of two main lines of action, as Parsons said, corresponds to a level of reality. One of these lines is the supernatural, the succession of omens and prophecies which involves the world of hags and sextons, peasant superstitions, lower-class hatreds, and loyalties for the great folk. This area of the novel is associated with cankered old age delighting in the

[29] *Op. cit.*, Ch. 23.   [30] *Miscellaneous Prose Works*, XVIII, pp. 337–8.
[31] *B.L.*, Ch. 18.

disasters that kill the young: one notes that the three old cummers think with pleasure of the lovers in terms of winding-sheets and dead-deal; they have an almost voluptuous physical awareness of them. Age as experience allies itself with prophecy. These old people understand, above all, limitation: such a love can only culminate in catastrophe.

The Master, the more active of the lovers, is often associated with the old, with the values of the past, through Caleb and the old housekeeper and through his links with tradition. However, he actually moves at most points on the second level, the level of optimism, prosperity, possibility, the young generation which defies tradition and overcomes fate. In social terms, of course, men like Ashton and the Master have a kind of independence denied the peasants. (The title "the Master" is relevant, though in the context it is ironic.) This second level of reality is on the whole the Whig level, dominated by ideas of progress and reason, and Sir William Ashton is its most important representative, the prosperous man of the world whose prospects appear to be limited only by his energies, who ignores traditions and does not understand at all what they mean to others. He cannot even tell the Master what has happened to the old Ravenswood family relics.

The second, optimistic line of action moves forward towards apparently certain prosperity, the death of the past, the union of the Ashtons and the Ravenswoods under the benign aegis of Sir William. Against this optimistic line runs the other, however, submerged and subjugated but showing itself periodically in portents, omens and the mutterings of peasants; eventually the forces represented by these signs erupt and shatter the apparently inevitable prosperous future. The tragic note is struck at the outset, and there is never any real doubt about the outcome.

Yet from the start the novel moves in some surprising directions. Ashton, for instance, turns out to be not a malignant fiend, but an ordinary enough tricky politician. Even more important, circumstances of politics lead both Ashton and the Marquis of A— to support the possibility of a marriage between Lucy and Edgar. In acquiescing, however, Edgar feels bitterly that he is selling out, abandoning the things he really stands for. Some of his remarks to Lucy reflect very badly on her family and his taste (and, in another way, on his manners); he seems to blame those qualities in her which he most loves for having made him play false to the traditions, the proud ancestry, that he ultimately values more than life itself. Or does he? The doubt plagues him. Other doubts arise: old Alice suggests that his love for Lucy may mask a desire to hurt the Ashtons through her, and the violence of his response suggests that there is more truth in this than he wishes to admit. Seeing this, she abruptly drops the topic.

E. M. Forster's criticism of the novel's structure, that the Lord Keeper is really a misleading excrescence rather than the central figure Scott indicates,[32] is now readily countered; the disastrous finale is foreshadowed throughout, but on a supernatural plane, and how could any tragic tension develop were there no possibility felt that the events could culminate happily? It is true that Ashton does not cause the disaster, but any survey of the possible alternative strategies reveals that we do not object, because the substance of the evil omens is redeemed by the conclusion; the only misconception was that Ashton rather than Lady Ashton would be responsible. Even so, Sir William's weakness and emasculation have a negative effect; he cannot and does not make his own wishes for Lucy prevail over his wife's. However, the amicability of his character is one of the novel's surprises, and it is the essence of this kind of story that the foreshadowed conclusion should seem ever more improbable until it actually occurs; such surprises make this effect possible. And without the connivance of Sir William, would Edgar ever have come close enough to be attached to Lucy?

Even Caleb Balderstone, who plays an unjustifiably large role, occasionally helps the love affair along, though he disapproves of it. Caleb is connected to a descant of hysterical laughter that runs through the novel; for instance, one of his frauds, produced when Lucy and her father have unexpectedly come to dinner, is so bizarre that the Ashtons and the Master alike explode in laughter, to Caleb's chagrin.[33] This has an odd effect. On the one hand, it is so natural and attractive that it is perfectly convincing; on the other hand it relieves (but thereby nearly recognises) tensions which have been unacknowledged. The scene seems to undercut

[32] *Aspects of the Novel.* New York, n.d., pp. 33-4.
[33] *B.L.,* Ch. 11.

the symbolic significance of the thunderstorm; simultaneously it brings the doom suggested by the thunder a great deal closer, for after this strangely intimate scene the Master can no longer be remote; he has been obliged to establish a personal relationship with the Ashtons which leads directly to his attachment to Lucy.

The final irony of the structure is that it brings the Master to his death through the operation of the forces for which he himself essentially stands; what seals his doom is his attempt to overcome these representatives of the dead hand of the past. The character, the self-concept and the divided mind of this most complex of Scott's heroes reveal within him a division analogous to the contrapuntal movement of prosperity and doom in the novel as a whole. For the Master sees himself as a tragic and heroic figure, the last doomed representative of a noble house, the fated and ruined heir of a vendetta. Such a self-concept is displayed in his vengeful speech after his father's funeral, and also in his intention to confront Ashton and then leave Scotland for the Continent in company with Bucklaw and Craigengelt. (Interestingly, Craigengelt suggests that the Master does not know his own mind: he does not intend to kill Ashton, but in the event he probably will.) "There is ill luck," Ravenswood says, "in whatever belongs to me."[34]

Nor is he simply responding to his situation: he willingly plays this role, as his speech shows, as his dress shows (the black plume on his hat "partly concealed his features"), as his feeling for drama shows ("Request nothing of ME, my lord! I am the Master of Ravenswood").[35] He has needs that are deeply satisfied by such a romantic self-concept. The role is undoubtedly appealing. It elevates Ravenswood: he will never grow old, the grandeur of his emotions and his destiny is above the common lot. ("Pride" is a word closely associated with him, and the desire for revenge to which it gives rise is referred to by Bucklaw as "the snake" or "the viper" within Ravenswood.) The Master can feel he matters to the gods, he is a focus of the action of history, a true man in a dissolute time. In his Life of Bage, Scott revealed a shrewd awareness of the potency of such role-playing in certain types of men.

[34] Op. cit., Ch. 7.　　[35] Op. cit., Ch. 5.

Some philosophers there were, who, as instructors in morality showed a laudable example to their followers; and we will not invidiously enquire how far these were supported in their self-denial, either by vanity, or the desire of preserving consistency, or the importance annexed to the founder of a sect. . . .[36]

Yet Ravenswood is at bottom self-destructive: he will die rather than submit to the inevitable process of becoming a man like other men, subject to the petty erosions of daily life, obliged to consult the needs and desires of others. Part of Ravenswood's mind, realising the dangers of his romantic egocentrism, leads him to attempt to save himself by involvement in such a human obligation as his relation with Lucy.

This relation is very curious – "love" is an imprecise way of describing it. There seems no particular reason for Ravenswood to fall in love with Lucy (though *her* motives are given some attention) and Scott several times specifically points out that Ravenswood is not conscious of the growth of his love until he is obliged to confront it in its full blossom. Indeed, Edgar's attachment to Lucy takes place on a clearly subconscious level:

There already existed in his bosom two contradictory passions – a desire to revenge the death of his father, strangely qualified by admiration of his enemy's daughter. Against the former feeling he had struggled, until it seemed to him upon the wane; against the latter he used no means of resistance, for he did not suspect its existence.[37]

Consequently even the declaration of love comes upon him by surprise. Moreover, he distrusts the quality of Lucy's affection, and he fears from the outset that she may break her troth:[38] he has been told she does not have the qualities of heart and mind to sustain a deep affection over a long time.[39] In the betrothal scene he has just left old Alice, with her harrowing questions:

"Are you prepared to sit lowest at the board which was once your father's own, unwillingly, as a connexion and ally of his

---

[36] *The Lives of the Novelists* (1821–24), intro., G. Saintsbury. London (J. M. Dent, Everyman edn.) 1910, p. 288.

[37] *B.L.*, Ch. 8.   [38] *Op. cit.*, Chs., 20, 24.   [39] *Op. cit.*, Chs., 5, 19.

proud successor? Are you ready to live on his bounty, to follow him in the bye-paths of intrigue and chicane, which none can better point out to you; to gnaw the bones of his prey when he has devoured the substance? Can you say as Sir William Ashton says, think as he thinks, vote as he votes, and call your father's murderer your worshipful father-in-law and revered patron?"[40]

It is almost evident to Ravenswood himself that a happy outcome of his love for Lucy could not be acceptable as a permanent condition of life. Yet the betrothal goes ahead, with all its implications. Ravenswood must be prepared to live as a dependent of the Ashtons, to grow into a pot-bellied and grey-headed family man, and to be viewed (not, perhaps, unjustly) as one who has deserted his family's honour to make good prudent connexions by marriage, an opportunist not distinctly different from Ashton, however he may view himself. He actually draws Lucy's attention to this galling interpretation:

"I would impress on you the price at which I have bought your love – the right I have to expect your constancy. I say not that I have bartered for it the honour of my house, its last remaining possession; but though I say it not, and think it not, I cannot conceal from myself that the world may do both."[41]

An interesting touch is this insistence that his love affair is a matter of public interest and public concern (Craigengelt at one point says that "nothing else is spoken of betwixt Lammer Law and Traprain").[42] There is constant pressure within Ravenswood to harmonise his private actions with his public image and his symbolic significance in the community, which repeatedly takes a less flattering view of his actions than he does.

Lucy's affection springs from her flexibility under her father's guidance,[43] and from her romantic imagination: "Lucy Ashton, in short, was involved in those mazes of the imagaintion which are

---

[40] *Op. cit.*, Ch. 19.   [41] *Op. cit.*, Ch. 20.   [42] *Op. cit.*, Ch. 21.
[43] On Lucy's relationship with her father, see Alexander Welsh, "A Freudian Slip in *The Bride of Lammermoor*", in *Études Anglaises*, XVIII (1965) pp. 134–6.

most dangerous to the young and the sensitive."[44] Such a description, with its echoes of Edward Waverley and his various counter-
parts, evokes the ruinous malleability which is the essential source
of her tragedy. By contrast, the Master's responses to Lucy show
a curious detachment and fatalism, combined with something like
contempt for her weakness. The scene of their declaration[45] and
the description of the progress of their love[46] actually reveal that
there is no basis for Edgar's love, nothing like the community of
mild interests Scott shows between Rose Bradwardine and
Waverley, for instance. Indeed, Edgar's love is presented as
growing *despite* the lack of foundation and despite his recognition
that in some ways Lucy is actually unsuitable for him;[47] he seems
oddly self-contained, oddly unaware of Lucy as a person. Contrast
this with Roland Graeme's or Frank Osbaldistone's lively apprehension of the independence and vitality of the girls they love, and
one begins to suspect that Edgar's love for Lucy is fundamentally
a reflexion of his preoccupation with his own problems. As critics
have always charged, the core of the novel is hollow, but that is
part of the point: the love that one would expect to flame through
the centre of the book is replaced by Edgar's subconscious pursuit
of the final tragic consummation of his sense of himself. Scott's
portrait of the lovers is passionless because, finally, it is not love
but self-love that is at the root of the attachment. The Master of
Ravenswood is Scott's most profound expression of the depths
and dangers of selfishness.

The story of Edgar is the story of a war within the self, and
ultimately of self-destruction: again and again it returns to the
Master's divided mind, his repression of his real feelings, his
failure to know himself.

> Had any one at this period told tne Master of Ravenswood
> that he had so lately vowed vengeance against the whole
> lineage of him whom he considered, not unjustly, as author
> of his father's ruin and death, he might at first have repelled
> the charge as a foul calumny; yet, upon serious self-examina-
> tion, he would have been compelled to admit that it had, at
> one period, some foundation in truth, though, according to

[44] B.L., Ch. 5.　　[45] *Op. cit.*, Ch. 20.　　[46] *Op. cit.*, Ch. 21.
[47] *Ibid.*

the present tone of his sentiments, it was difficult to believe that this had really been the case.[48]

"Perhaps," said Ravenswood, "you read me more rightly than I can myself."[49]

"Why, now, you go farther than I do, Caleb," said the Master, drowning a certain degree of consciousness in a forced laugh; "you are for marrying me into a family that you will not allow me to visit, how's this?"[50]

Ravenswood, not allowing himself to give a second thought to the propriety of his own conduct, walked with a quick step towards the stream, where he found Lucy seated alone. . . .[51]

The tumult in Ravenswood's mind was uncommonly great; she had struck upon and awakened a chord which he had for some time successfully silenced.[52]

Edgar has chosen to love Lucy *because* the outcome can only be tragic. "Alas!" says Scott. "What fiend can suggest more desperate counsels than those adopted under the guidance of our own violent and unresisted passions?"[53] Ravenswood's passions are not unresisted, but before he has made his gesture towards life he has so arranged things that it can only lead to death. Our own minds are diabolical enough.

Ravenswood's fate is thus a result of his conviction of fate. Many of the portents that associate themselves with him are the result of his choice. He does not have to stay in Wolf's Crag, he need not dress as he does, and so forth. The use of the supernatural as a manifestation of the subconscious desire of Ravenswood – and probably Lucy – for a tragic death explains a number of apparent coincidences: the repeated association of their love with the Mermaiden's Well, for instance, is surely not accidental. At the beginning of the betrothal scene[54] Lucy is specifically associated with the murdered Nymph of the Fountain, and thus with the Ravenswood family curse. Nor can Henry Ashton's shooting of the raven be a simple coincidence: it seems to be at

[48] *Op. cit.*, Ch. 8.   [49] *Ibid.*   [50] *Op. cit.*, Ch. 18.   [51] *Op. cit.*, Ch. 20.
[52] *Op. cit.*, Ch. 19.   [53] *Op. cit.*, Ch. 1.   [54] *Op. cit.*, Ch. 20.

least partially an expression of a basic, though concealed, Ashton distrust of Ravenswood, instantly covered by Henry's boyish jocularity. Again, Scott makes the Kelpie's Flow move a little before Ravenswood vanishes in it. All we have to believe is that Ravenswood, with no fear of death left, simply omitted to be careful, so that his death is a blend of accident and suicide.

Similarly, old Alice's role is explainable in terms of intuitive understanding. The text offers repeated indications that her intellect and her other senses are sharpened by the loss of her sight, and her ordinary penetration of states of mind is considerable. Her apparition at the Mermaiden's Fountain, however, has always been considered a blemish,[55] and the horse's fear insists that it has some kind of objective reality. This one slip, however, is heavily mitigated by the psycho-supernatural atmosphere of the whole book, and Scott emphasises that the incident is part of the traditional story, which he feels he must insert but which he hesitates to accept. The apparition remains a minor blemish rather than the serious disruption it might easily have become.

Most of the remaining supernaturalism is readily understood as the peasant means of expressing genuine social insights. It does not take supernatural power to predict misfortune for the proud and ruined Tory laird in a country overrun by cunning and ruthless Whigs. It is not difficult to see horror ahead of Lucy as she goes to be wed, the ferocity of her mother behind her, the coarseness of Bucklaw beside her. From time to time Scott interjects a note of wry scepticism: when Lucy and her father are in Wolf's Crag during the thunderstorm, for instance, he reports that "It might seem as if the ancient founder of the castle were bestriding the thunderstorm, and proclaiming his displeasure at the reconciliation of his descendant with the enemy of his house." Then a sentence or two later, he points out that Ravenswood was obliged by the storm to become "engaged in the most delicate and dangerous of all tasks, that of affording support and assistance to a beautiful and helpless being, who, as seen before in a similar situation, had already become a favourite of his imagination, both when awake and when slumbering". Therefore, "If the genius of the house really condemned a union betwixt the Master and his fair

[55] *Edinburgh Monthly Review*, II (1819) p. 168; quoted with approval by Parsons, *Witchcraft and Demonology in Scott's Fiction*, p. 117, n. 37.

guest, the means by which he expressed his sentiments were as unhappily chosen as if he had been a mere mortal."[56]

In all, *The Bride of Lammermoor* offers a beautifully formed tale of tragic pride and the treachery of the self, smoothly interwoven with a Scottish peasant sense of the supernatural based on penetrating insight into the social life of the time and the hidden processes of the mind. With *The Heart of Midlothian*, it is Scott's supreme achievement as a novelist. It represents his most concentrated exploration of several aspects of the Scottish character: pride, superstition, rage and the love of honour have no finer expression in his work. In addition, and off-handedly as it were, it has considerable merit as a historical novel. *The Heart of Midlothian* is in some ways more ambitious, and it comes closer to the hot centre of his impulse as a novelist. But no other of his novels succeeds so fully in its own terms, and as a self-contained work of art, as *The Bride of Lammermoor*.

[56] B.L., Ch. 10.

David Murison

THE TWO LANGUAGES IN SCOTT

It soon becomes obvious even to the most cursory reader who goes through the Waverley Novels in their chronological order that in the first half-dozen at least Scott has two languages, English for the narration and background description, and Scots for the dialogue of those who are natives of Scotland and belong in general to the lower social classes; the exceptions to this last, like the Baron of Bradwardine or Rob Roy or, later on, King James in *The Fortunes of Nigel*, will be accounted for later. A closer examination will reveal subtle variations of style in both languages. For the time being we can say that Scott is fully bilingual and that this is a fairly true reflexion of the speech of Scotland of his own time. To understand this some historical survey of the linguistic situation is necessary.

Anglo-Saxon, from which both the Scots and English of today are descended, was itself broken up into dialects of which one of the most important was the Northern, spoken from the Humber northwards to the Forth and differentiated from the others especially by certain vowel sounds and by a large element of words of Scandinavian origin in its vocabulary. The Norman Conquest which brought French to England (and later to Scotland) also resulted in the expansion of this Northern speech throughout all the Lowlands of Scotland to Moray and Inverness as the vehicle of feudal government. By the fourteenth century, when the political independence of Scotland had been successfully defended, the language of the Scottish Court, based on Edinburgh and the Forth region, had risen to the status of a national tongue, distinct from its Southern cousin in London which had now become the King of England's English. It received further accretions of vocabulary, from the Gaelic which preceded it in the Lowlands, from the Dutch of the Flemings who settled in Scotland as imported craftsmen, and from the French which came from the contacts of the Auld Alliance struck between France and Scotland in 1295; it became the vehicle of a considerable literature and it was approaching its full development as an all-purpose speech in the sixteenth century when the Reformation turned Scotland away from France and towards England. The English Genevan Bible, already conveniently to hand, was adopted by the Kirk and from its use in every church, and in many a home, gradually began to exert an influence on the old speech of Scotland and, more especially, to breed in the minds of the Scots an association of English with what was serious, solemn and formal, and of the vernacular with the more informal, colloquial, sentimental, and humorous aspect of life. To this lowering of the dignity of Scots was added, after 1603, a diminution in social prestige when the Scottish Court, and the nobility in its train, removed to London and adopted the speech of its new milieu. The comings and goings of the Civil War, the Cromwellian occupation, and finally in 1707 the Union of the Parliaments, when the language of Westminster became the official speech of the United Kingdom, brought about the relegation of Scots to the status of a dialect or patois spoken only informally and by a slowly but steadily decreasing number of people, beginning with the gentry and others who had business in England or abroad, and gradually extending downwards in the social scale. Today the decay of the old tongue has gone pretty far but in the eighteenth century its currency was still very wide spread, even in the upper circles of the metropolitan society of Edinburgh.

It is true that the Scottish M.P.'s in their new home were taken aback by the inability of the English to understand them and made valiant efforts to mend their speech in the approved direction; and that, ten years before Scott was born, some of the legal luminaries, chiefly among the Whigs, organised elocution classes in Edinburgh under the playwright Sheridan's father to promote "the Reading and Speaking of the English Language"; and when Dr Johnson passed through in 1773 he noted that "the great, the learned, the ambitious, the vain all cultivate the English phrases and the English pronunciation".[1] Yet Ramsay of Ochtertyre, who made a

[1] Johnson, *Journey* (1st. edn. 1775), p. 380.

special observation of speech, notes that about the same period, new (i.e. English) vocabulary was coming in but accent and pronunciation remained, that there were different qualities of Scots in different speakers, and that there were, in fact, two forms of speech in use, the colloquial and informal Scots "spoken in good company" and the formal and oratorical, approximating to English and used by judges, lawyers, and the clergy in their business but dropped when the social context became more intimate. Some old-fashioned people persisted in speaking a kind of classical Scots; Lord Cockburn tells of old ladies of the period whose language like their habits was "entirely Scotch, but without any other vulgarity, than what perfect naturalness is sometimes mistaken for";[2] and William Craig, writing in the *Mirror*, says "The Scottish dialect is our ordinary suit; the English is used only on solemn occasions. When a Scotsman therefore writes, he does it generally in trammels."[3] This of course was because prose-writing in Scots which had never at any time been so fully developed as writing in verse, had practically died out in the seventeenth century and schools had taken early to teaching English as the vernacular language.

But there had been quite a spectacular revival of Scots as the medium of verse soon after 1707, started off by Allan Ramsay, carried on by others and particularly the Edinburgh poet, Fergusson, and brought to a brilliant climax in the work of Burns. Scots as a *literary* language, at least for verse, acquired a fresh status and, although the general attitude to Scots, among the upper classes anyhow, was by this time equivocal, the triumph of Burns could not be gainsaid and indeed was accepted with national self-satisfaction.

So when Ballantyne expressed doubt about the propriety or likely success of broad Scots in *Waverley*, Scott replied, "Why, Burns, by his poetry, has already attracted attention to everything Scottish and I confess I can't see why I should not be able to keep the flame alive, merely because I write Scotch in prose and he wrote it in rhyme".[4]

[2] J. Ramsay, *Scotland and Scotsmen in the 18th Century*. Edinburgh, 1888 II. pp. 542–5; Lord Henry Cockburn, *Memorials*. Edinburgh 1856, p. 58.
[3] *Mirror* III, p. 74.
[4] J.G. Lockhart, *Memoirs of Sir Walter Scott*. London (MacMillan) 1900, Ch. 33.

In this Scott's motive is quite clear and in accord with that of the rest of his work, to paint Scottish "manners", to show the impact of Scottish history on the Scottish people individually and severally, and to interpret Scotland and the Scottish way of life to the world at large. To make the picture more realistic and complete, he had to introduce characters more genuinely Scots than their social "betters", who had been exposed to cultural influences from beyond Scotland. One indispensable element in the tradition was their Scots speech.

There was of course nothing original in using dialect in a novel. Scott was following the example of Fielding and Smollett before him, not to mention the odd bits of patois that Shakespeare throws into *Lear* or *Henry IV*. Only Scott is much more thorough-going and, as we shall see, subtle and imaginatively creative in his use of it.

It is a truism now to say how very much better he is at Scots than English and how vivid and revealing the one compared with the stilted woodenness of the other:

> "Lord Glenallan told me himself," answered the Antiquary; "so there is no delation – no breach of trust on your part; and as he wishes me to take her evidence down on some important family matters, I chose to bring you with me, because in her situation, hovering between dotage and consciousness, it is possible that your voice and appearance may awaken trains of recollection which I should otherwise have no means of exciting. The human mind . . . is to be treated like a skein of ravelled silk, where you must cautiously secure one free end before you can make any progress in disentangling it."
>
> "I ken naething about that," said the gaberlunzie, "but an my auld acquaintance be hersell, or onything like hersell, she may come to wind us a pirn. It's fearsome baith to see and hear her when she wampishes about her arms, and gets to her English, and speaks as if she were a prent book, let a be an auld fisher's wife. But, indeed, she had a grand education, and was muckle taen out afore she married an unco bit beneath hersell. I mind weel eneugh they made as muckle wark about her making a half-merk marriage wi' Simon

Mucklebackit, this Saunders's father, as if she had been ane o' the gentry."[5]

Scott's English style has received severe handling from critics at all times, sometimes simply for its bad grammar and solecisms. The fastidious Stevenson for example is quite aghast at the sentence "The tune awoke the corresponding associations of a damsel, who, close behind a fine spring about half-way down the descent, and which had once supplied the castle with water, was engaged in bleaching linen."[6]

Then again it is frequently formless and dull, and full of long heavy sentences like a schoolboy's translation of some Roman historian:

> The brow of the hill, on which the royal Life-Guards were now drawn up, sloped downwards (on the side opposite to that which they had ascended) with a gentle declivity, for more than a quarter of a mile, and presented ground, which, though unequal in some places, was not altogether un-favourable for the manœuvres of cavalry, until near the bottom, when the slope terminated in a marshy level, traversed through its whole length by what seemed either a natural gully, or a deep artificial drain, the sides of which were broken by springs, trenches filled with water, out of which peats and turf had been dug, and here and there by some straggling thickets of alders which loved the moistness so well, that they continued to live as bushes, although too much dwarfed by the sour soil and the stagnant bog-water to ascend into trees.[7]

Others disapprove of his clichés and circumlocutions — "romantic scene", "dizzy height", "commanding position", "the last mansion of mortality" for a coffin, "the woman of joints and giblets" for a butcher's wife, "the man of meal and grindstones"

---

[5] *A.*, Border Edition edited by A. Lang. Edinburgh (Nimmo) 1892–4, Ch. 39. All quotations from Scott's novels are from this edition, but the ordinary consecutive chapter numbering has been followed.

[6] *G.M.*, Ch. 41.; R. L. Stevenson, *Memories and Portraits*. Pentland Edition, London (Cassell) 1907, Ch. 15.

[7] *O.M.*, Ch. 15.

for a miller and so on, and his high-flown and often misplaced rhetoric, as in the harangues of Norna Gest;[8] and his contemporary critics complained of the rags and tags of Latin and French and Gaelic, as in *Waverley*, and of Shakespeare, as in *Woodstock*, with which he cluttered up his prose.

Scott himself was the first to admit the truth of such criticisms. His defence was that after all it did not matter so much and in any case he was not likely to mend his ways. "J. G. L[ockhart]" he says in his *Journal* (22 Apr. 1826) "kindly points out some solecisms in my style as 'amid' for 'amidst', 'scarce' for 'scarcely'. 'Whose', he says, is the proper genitive of 'which' only at such times as 'which' retains its quality of impersonification. Well! I will try to remember all this, but after all I write grammar as I speak, to make my meaning known, and a solecism in point of composition, like a Scotch word in speaking, is indifferent to me. I never learned grammar." Earlier in the year (12 February) he had written in the same *Journal*, "I have often been amused with the critics distinguishing some passages as particularly laboured, when the pen passed over the whole as fast as it could move, and the eye never again saw them, except in proof." The fact is that in his earlier novels he wrote more or less as he describes. He was notoriously careless in revising his manuscript (in truth he probably did not have the time) and must bear the consequences from the delicate critics of his century.

Today when style and grammar have been more or less banished from our schools as inhibiting trammels on freedom of expression, Scott may get away with the solecisms – they might not even be recognised as such; what is no longer acceptable is the long-winded padding, the slabs of close description of some antique object, architecture, armoury or the like, or exotic scenery with which he clogs his narrative, like the chapter on Tully-Veolan, the Green Room at Monkbarns, the studies of Triptolemus Yellowley at St Andrews.[9]

Readers brought up on the detective novel with gun battles on every page have little patience with Scott's lumbering procedure, and yet this bumbling constitutes in reality a relatively small proportion of his tales. He thought of himself indeed as a lively and vigorous writer, as again from his *Journal* (16 Jun. 1826): "I

[8] *P.*, Ch. 19.   [9] *Wav.*, Ch. 8; *A.*, Ch. 10; *P.*, Chs. 4, 9.

P

am sensible that, if there be anything good about my poetry or my prose either, it is a hurried frankness of composition, which pleases soldiers, sailors, and young people of bold and active dispositions." In other words he claims to be a writer of action and to match the excitement of the story with the animation of the style.

In general his manner is simple, unsubtle, and at times even bald. His description of the death of Colonel Gardiner at Prestonpans is curiously flat and ends almost in bathos:

> He felt that death was dealing closely with him, and resigning his purpose, and folding his hands as if in devotion, he gave up his soul to his Creator. The look with which he regarded Waverley in his dying moments, did not strike him so deeply at that crisis of hurry and confusion, as when it recurred to his imagination at the distance of some time.[10]

Nor is he good at love scenes and the dialogue of passion and, it will be noticed, tries to avoid them as much as possible. Frequently in scenes between hero and heroine, the girl is on her high horse about something and telling the young man off, like Isabella Wardour to Lovel:

> "I am much embarrassed, Mr. Lovel, by your – I would not willingly use a strong word – romantic and hopeless pertinacity. It is for yourself I plead, that you would consider the calls the country has on your talents, that you will not waste, in an idle and fanciful indulgence of an ill-placed predilection, time, which, well redeemed by active exertion, should lay the foundation of future distinction."[11]

And Edith Bellenden reproaches Henry Morton in a similarly starchy schoolma'amly vein, in fact as if she were composing a cutting letter and not giving unpremeditated vent to anxiety and vexation.[12] Even Catherine Glover in a more happy and playful mood delivers herself of the carefully worded and polished sentiment – "I only meant to say, father, that in choosing Henry Gow for my Valentine, and rendering to him the rights and greeting of the morning, according to wonted custom" (a kiss, in fact, described in the language of feudal conveyancing) "I meant but to

[10] *Wav.*, Ch. 47.   [11] *A.*, Ch. 13.   [12] *O.M.*., Ch. 29.

show my gratitude to him for his manly and faithful service, and my obedience to you."[13]

Much of this is no doubt due to the legacy of the earlier eighteenth century when there was a passion for elegance in style, for the neatly turned phrase, the balanced antithesis, the epigram, and all the other tricks of rhetoric that are to be found in, say, Richardson or Fanny Burney, and even to some extent in Fielding, Smollett or Sterne. Possibly in Scott's case he had picked up this style from some of the numerous manuals on letter-writing such as Elizabeth Rowe's *Letters Moral and Entertaining*, which we know from his *Autobiography* that he used, and which played havoc with the epistolary style of Burns who had also studied it. We can in fact see the letter-writing technique in full in Julia's letters in *Guy Mannering*,[14] and in the rather tedious Fairford-Latimer correspondence in the first half of *Redgauntlet*. Johnson, too, of whom Scott was a devotee, exercised some considerable influence in producing the laboured ponderousness which we have seen, for example, in his descriptive pieces.

Yet in spite of all the verbosity and the padding, once he really gets going on his story, which sometimes admittedly takes a while, he can rise splendidly to the occasion, when action is called for, or a display of the more masculine qualities of courage, resolve or endurance, or when the dramatic crisis is at hand:

> Several of the party began to make ready their slaughter-weapons for immediate execution, when Mucklewrath's hand was arrested by one of his companions.
>
> "Hist!" he said – "I hear a distant noise."
>
> "It is the rushing of the brook over the peebles," said one.
>
> "It is the sough of the wind among the bracken," said another.
>
> "It is the galloping of horse," said Morton to himself, his sense of hearing rendered acute by the dreadful situation in which he stood; "God grant they may come as my deliverers!"[15]

or again later on when Morton speaks incognito to his old nurse:

[13] *The Fair Maid of Perth*, Ch. 5.   [14] *G.M.*, Chs. 17, 18.
[15] *O.M.*, Ch. 33.

While Mrs. Wilson was thus detailing the last moments of the old miser, Morton was pressingly engaged in diverting the assiduous curiosity of the dog, which, recovered from his first surprise, and combining former recollections, had, after much snuffing and examination, begun a course of capering and jumping upon the stranger which threatened every instant to betray him. At length, in the urgency of his impatience, Morton could not forbear exclaiming, in a tone of hasty impatience, "Down, Elphin! Down, Sir!"

"Ye ken our dog's name," said the old lady, struck with great and sudden surprise – "Ye ken our dog's name, and it's no a common ane. And the creature kens you too," she continued, in a more agitated and shriller tone ; "God guide us! it's my ain bairn."[16]

Above all there is the tremendous trial scene in *The Heart of Midlothian* when the defending counsel tries to elicit an answer from Jeanie Deans that her sister had not concealed her pregnancy:

The question was put in a tone meant to make her comprehend the importance of her answer, had she not been already aware of it. The ice was broken, however, and with less pause than at first, she now replied, – "Alack! alack! she never breathed word to me about it."

A deep groan passed through the Court. It was echoed by one deeper and more agonised from the unfortunate father. The hope, to which unconsciously, and in spite of himself, he had still secretly clung, had now dissolved, and the venerable old man fell forward senseless on the floor of the Court-house, with his head at the feet of his terrified daughter. The unfortunate prisoner, with impotent passion, strove with the guards, betwixt whom she was placed. "Let me gang to my father! – I will gang to him – I will gang to him – he is dead – he is killed – I hae killed him!" – she repeated in frenzied tones of grief, which those who heard them did not speedily forget.

Even in this moment of agony and general confusion, Jeanie did not lose that superiority, which a deep and firm

16 *Op. cit.*, Ch. 39.

mind assures its possessor, under the most trying circumstances.

"He is my father – he is our father," she mildly repeated to
those who endeavoured to separate them, as she stooped.[17]

True, there is still the cliché, still the unnecessary clause, the
superfluous moralising, but the tension is well held – indeed the
leisurely style helps to increase it – and the dramatic implications
of Jeanie's correction of herself from "my" to "our" are conveyed
in a master-stroke of word economy, like so many more of Scott's
finest touches, as when the senile Elspeth at her grandson's funeral
wishes the mourners their healths and "often may we hae such
merry meetings".[18]

And there are plenty of scenes written with sober earnestness
and dignity in which language and theme are perfectly attuned,
the last journey of Fergus MacIvor to the scaffold, Macbriar
before the Privy Council, the appalling murder of Morris,[19] the
last chapter of *The Bride of Lammermoor*. It is in such passages,
many of them adaptations of dramatic incidents in Scottish history, that Scott rises to his best. Of *The Tales of a Grandfather*, in
which the same stories are told as straight history, an acute critic
used the word "Homeric" to describe the style,[20] and this gets
pretty near the mark. The plain unadorned starkness and directness are there, which the epic shares with the ballad, and no
doubt it was to his early work on the ballads that Scott owes his
ability to attain to it when the occasion demands. It is for that
matter the common element in the best Scottish literature of all
ages.

Probably the most characteristic and sustained element in
Scott's narrative, and therefore English, style is the sly humour,
often ironical, a kind of badinage with which he analyses a charac-
ter or incident, again often in a few words or brief aside, as when
Mannering and Dandie Dinmont are asked to pronounce on
Pleydell's claret:

[17] *H.M.*, Ch. 23.
[18] *A.*, Ch. 31.
[19] *Wav.* Ch. 49.; *O.M.*, Ch. 35; *R.R.*, Ch. 31.
[20] *Westminster Review*. April, 1829, p. 257. See also R. C. Jebb *Introduction
to Homer*. Glasgow, 1887, pp. 19 sqq.

"It's ower cauld for my stamach," said Dinmont, setting down the glass (empty, however).[21]

Or in the neat turning-off of the verbally enthusiastic Jacobite:

He talked much, indeed, of taking the field for the rights of Scotland and Charles Stuart; but his demi-pique saddle would suit only one of his horses; and that horse could by no means be brought to stand fire. Perhaps the worshipful owner sympathized in the scruples of this sagacious quadruped, and began to think, that what was so much dreaded by the horse, could not be very wholesome for the rider.[22]

Here we are reminded of Fielding before him and Dickens after. It is now generally conceded that when he abandoned for a while the Scotland that had come down to him from the seventeenth and eighteenth centuries, the "Scottish manners, Scottish dialect, and Scottish characters of note, being those with which the Author was most intimately and familiarly acquainted", to write *Ivanhoe*[23] and its immediate successors, *The Monastery*, *The Abbot*, *Kenilworth*, his anxiety to create the atmosphere of the "manners" of the time led him into blunders and grotesqueries of style as well as treatment, into a pseudo-antique diction which he patched up in a slap-dash manner from the more fustian passages of Shakespeare and his contemporary dramatists and of Lord Berner's translation of Froissart written in 1523. Here, for instance, from *Kenilworth*:

"What, ho! John Tapster."
"At hand, Will Hostler," replied the man of the spigot. . . .
"Here is a gentleman asks if you draw good ale," continued the hostler.
"Beshrew my heart else," answered the tapster, "since there are but four miles betwixt us and Oxford. – Marry, if my ale did not convince the heads of the scholars, they would soon convince my pate with the pewter flagon."
"Call you that Oxford logic?" said the stranger.
"Is it logic you talk of, Sir Guest?" said the host, "why then, have at you with a downright consequence – 'The horse to the rack, And to fire with the sack'."

[21] *G.M.*, Ch. 36.   [22] *A.*, Ch. 5.   [23] *I.*, Intro. (1830).

"Amen! with all my heart, my good host," said the stranger; "let it be a quart of your best Canaries."[24]

which is a kind of rag-bag from *Henry IV*.

As for *The Monastery*, which almost on every count is one of his least successful novels, the prose lumbers dreadfully. The monks prate interminably, Sir Piercie Shafton is made to speak in that high-flown antithetical alliterative sixteenth-century fashion known as euphuism (and if Scott's imitation of this is not very authentic, his efforts at least show his interest in linguistic "manners" as well as any other kind), and he cannot make up his mind what form of speech to put in the mouth of Dame Glendinning who switches from Scots to English with no apparent reason or consistency. Thus speaks the Border laird, the Baron of Avenel, to the Protestant preacher:

"Hark ye, Sir Gospeller! trow ye to have a fool in hand? Know I not that your sect rose by bluff Harry Tudor, merely because ye aided him to change *his* Kate! and wherefore should I not use the same Christian liberty with *mine*? Tush, man! bless the good food, and meddle not with what concerns thee not – thou hast no gull in Julian Avenel."[25]

This is the sort of stuff that Stevenson derides as "tushery", though he exploited it himself in *The Black Arrow*,[26] and the danger lies in its being purely artificial and mechanical. It was only when he returned to Scotland for the scene of *St Ronan's Well* and *Redgauntlet* that Scott recovered his ease and naturalness in writing.

"I'm no wanting to learn ony thing at my years," said Meg, "If folk have ony thing to write to me about, they may gie the letter to John Hislop, the carrier, that has used the road these forty years. As for the letters at the post-mistress's, as they ca' her, down by yonder, they may bide in her shop-window, wi' the snaps and bawbee rows, till Beltane, or I loose them. I'll never file my fingers with them."[27]

[24] *K.*, Ch. 1.
[25] *The Monastery*, Ch. 25.
[26] R. L. Stevenson, *Letters*, Tusitala edn. London (Heinemann) 1924, II, pp. 241–2.
[27] *St Ronan's Well*, Ch. 2.

Thereafter the old troubles reappear in *The Betrothed* and *The Talisman*, in which he was again on unfamiliar territory and from 1826, when the crash came and with it illness and exhaustion, the whole story becomes more laboured both in the concept and the telling, though he can still write a striking or moving passage:

> Years rush by us like the wind. We see not whence the eddy comes, nor whitherward it is tending, and we seem ourselves to witness their flight without a sense that we are changed; and yet Time is beguiling man of his strength as the winds rob the woods of their foliage.[28]

Sorrow and trouble have plainly deepened his experience and disciplined his pen.

From the purely linguistic point of view, however, the "tushery" had its good points and results. Scott had a rich and full vocabulary, amounting, it has been calculated, to some 30,000 words drawn from all sources, English and Scots, contemporary, Tudor, including Shakespeare and Spenser, and medieval, like Chaucer and Barbour, out of his omnivorous reading and prodigious memory. Such was the popularity and enthusiasm with which his novels were received and read that from all these he has added nearly 200 words to the English language, few indeed of his own making, for he was not creative linguistically, but merely by reviving or introducing them from some out-of-the-way original and by his use making them acceptable to a generation that had gone all romantic.

A selection of the commoner of these follows with a brief note of the probable source, which will in itself give an idea of Scott's wide and eclectic reading: *awesome* is from his own Scots usage; *bale-fire*, probably from Blind Harry's *Wallace*; *barbican*, from Spenser; *bartizan* is a Scots form of *bratticing*; *basnet*, from Berners; *berserk*, from Norse mythology; *blackmail*, from Scottish history; *bluff* gets its good sense from Scott's charitable interpretation of the character of Henry VIII in the phrase *bluff King Hall*, first used by Horace Walpole; *canny*, *uncanny* and *clanjamfray* are from Scots; *coign* is adopted from Shakespeare; *derring-do* from Spenser; *dour*,

---

[28] *Woodstock*, Ch. 38.

downcome, dree one's weird, forbears and *forgather* are Scots; *following,*
for adherents, is from Jacobite history; *foray* and *foeman* are from
Barbour, *free lance* is his own composition based on the medieval
free companion; *gambade* is straight from French, and *gentrice* at one
remove through Barbour; *glamour* is Scots, also its earlier form
gramarye which came from Percy's *Reliques*; *gruesome* is also Scots;
henchman has a somewhat complicated history, but the immediate
source for Scott was *The Letters from a Gentleman in the North of
Scotland* (*c.* 1730) attributed to one of Wade's officers, Edward
Burt, which he used as a quarry for much of the description of
Highland society in *Waverley*; *fiery cross* was from a military report
from Wade himself; *ilk*, now misused in standard English, came
in from Scotland through Scott; *moss-trooper*, also from Scottish
history; *Norseman* is apparently his own creation; *light o' love* is
from the Elizabethan dramatists and *malison* from general medieval
literature; *onslaught* is originally German, but appears to have
established itself in modern English through Scott's borrowing
from Capt. Monro's *Expedition* of Mackay's Regiment in Germany
in 1637; *pensil* is from Barbour or Berners or both; *popinjay* from
Shakespeare; *raid* and *reiver* come through Border history from
medieval Scots words; *red-handed, scatheless* and *soothfast* are
Scots law terms; *rampage* he got from Ramsay; *sleuth(hound)* and
slogan are from Barbour and Douglas respectively; *stalwart* is also
old Scots; *volte face* is directly from French; *towering passion* and
yeoman service, originally Shakespearean, got a second lease of life
through Scott, and so also *undo*, which Chaucer uses as well; *thew*,
in the sense of sinew, and *warison*, assault-note, are due to a mis-
understanding by Scott of lines of Shakespeare and of the ballad
of *Otterbourne* in Percy; *wraith*, far too "romantic" for Scott to
miss, is from old Scots, probably Douglas's *Aeneis*.

Professor Ernest Weekley considers that of all individual
writers next to Shakespeare, whose formative influence on English
is beyond all comparison, Scott has contributed most to the
English vocabulary.[29] It would be as difficult to prove as to dis-
prove this but it is certainly clear that whatever the faults of
Scott's style there is no question of the richness of his language,
which after all reflects the sheer bulk of his work, its great sweep
and range and the extraordinary variety of its content. This in

[29] *Atlantic Monthly* CXLVII (Nov. 1931), p. 595.

itself is a proof of the vitality he imparted to the words he used and in so many cases effectively recreated.

Among Scott's 30,000-word vocabulary are included some 3,000 words used only in Scotland or having meanings peculiar to Scotland and belonging to the remains of the old Scots language. Scott would have most certainly spoken it himself at the High School and at his uncle's farm at Sandyknowe. He spoke it to his servants at Abbotsford and most likely to friends like Hogg and the old ladies mentioned by Cockburn and Ramsay. There is a local tradition about Selkirk that, when in the midst of a novel he was anxious to find the right word for his Scots dialogue, he would go out to the workmen who were constantly coming and going at Abbotsford and artfully start up a conversation calculated to produce the required word. But that he knew his Scots thoroughly and could reproduce its idioms and cadences perfectly is obvious to anyone who is a native speaker himself. Indeed one of his correspondents, an anonymous Border shepherd, writes to him in 1820 – "I am perfectly astonished how ye have acquired the Scottish dialect and phraseology so exactly. Ye have it as truly as if ye knew no other."[30]

We can also be quite sure that Scott's Scots is actually thicker than it looks. As one might expect, his spellings are irregular and inconsistent but, if they have any tendency at all, it is in the direction of making it more intelligible to an English reader, so that *sore* or *good* or *house* or *heart* or *right* may be written when *sair* or *guid* or *hoose* or *hert* or *richt* are intended. This indeed was in the tradition of the eighteenth-century Scots writer from Ramsay onwards, but it has the unfortunate effect of obscuring the proper pronunciation and rhythm which enhance the author's effects in using this broken language to its maximum capacity. For it is admitted by all critics now, and by most critics in his own day, that when he writes in Scots, the laboured bumbling that so often mars his English disappears and his natural excitement and vigour take command. It is not merely that the Scots dialogue is in the mouth of simple unsophisticated speakers (for we shall see in a moment that they are made to utter some of Scott's most ambitious efforts in style); it is simply that for Scott, born as he was

[30] W. Partington *The Private Letter-Books of Sir Walter Scott*. London (Hodder and Stoughton) 1930, p. 321.

in the capital of Scotland in 1771, English was still essentially a
foreign language, the language he had learned from books, from
Pope, Johnson, Fielding, and the other Augustans. Scots was the
language of his natural expression of action and emotion, the
language of immediacy but not of reflexion in which Scott seldom
shone. Scots was in fact to him what it had been to the most of his
countrymen for nearly a century, by the very reason of its history
in relation to the encroachment of English. But within the shrink-
ing limits thus imposed on it the variety, the nuances, the range of
key that Scott can produce from it are quite astonishing.

Just as he created a whole gallery of characters of all kinds and
conditions, excelled only by Shakespeare, and the Scottish ones
the most memorable, so he rings the changes in their speech in all
sorts of subtle ways. In *The Antiquary* for example, the Laird of
Monkbarns speaks generally in English with an old-fashioned
thou and *thee* to his social inferiors, interlarded frequently, of
course, with Latin as a sign of his learning or pedantry, but in
moments of excitement or rage he falls back into Scots, frequently
to berate some menial who would naturally speak Scots, like the
innkeeper at Queensferry. His spinster sister, living a secluded life
and dealing mainly with servants, speaks Scots – a feminine Scots
full of domestic vocabulary about cookery, furniture, cloth, small
gossip, and traditional tales – as about the ghost in the Green
Room guiding the family lawyer to the vital charter:

> "The ghaist cried aye *Carter, Carter* —".
> "*Carta*, you transformer of languages!" cried Oldbuck. . . .
> "Weel, weel, *carta* be it then, but they ca'd it *carter* that
> tell'd me the story. It cried aye *carta*, if sae be that it was
> *carta*."[31]

The full idiomatic flavour of this, especially the last clause, will
appear probably only to a Scot who knows the argumentative
reluctance of his fellow-countrymen to admit a mistake in matters
of erudition. Grizel Oldbuck therefore is the typical rustic gentle-
woman of the time who in her youth (about 1745) had received the
second-rate education reserved for women, whose somewhat
deficient English is amply recorded in the letters and household
books of the period.

[31] *A.*, Ch. 9.

Elspeth of the Craigburnfoot who, as we have seen, "was a weel-educate woman", speaks Scots in the character of the old fisherman's widow to her own family but in the character of the Glenallan family retainer and sibyl speaking to the Earl as last of the line uses a kind of apocalyptic English mixed with some Scots, much in the same style as Meg Merrilies, but when the beggar Ochiltree is set on to try to worm the secret out of her she continues her story in Scots in answer to Edie's voice that has succeeded in penetrating through her delirium to her subconscious.[32] In this Scott shows a remarkable comprehension of the complex speech-associations of the Scot. We may also note in passing the speech of the Aberdonian, Francie Macraw, in the dialect of the North-East, which Scott reproduces with tolerable accuracy. There is another similar Aberdonian, "Davie Dingwall, the writer" in *The Bride of Lammermoor*, but Scott does not venture on reproducing Shetland dialect in *The Pirate* though he introduces a few Shetland words in his text like *bismar, lipsund, haaf-fish, Ranzelman, tuscar, jagger, voe, air, geo*, and so on. For good thick rural Scots consistently spoken the classic example is Cuddie Headrigg in *Old Mortality*.

The Fortunes of Nigel is another novel which illustrates the switching about from Scots to English. The scene is London and the characters in the main an enclave of Scots, from the King downwards strangers in a strange land. The Scots banker, Heriot, who is obviously doing well in the South, uses formal English to all about him but breaks out into Scots when he hears the voice of Richie Moniplies from his native Edinburgh. Ramsay, the clock-maker, expatiates on his trade in the language of the text-books on chronometry but on his own personal affairs speaks his mother Scots. The King himself is made to accommodate himself to his audience and mood. In moments of excitement, as in the stag-hunt in Greenwich Park, or when speaking to Scottish courtiers, he reverts to Scots; in Court, he speaks a formal pedantic Latinate English, laced however with some Scots, especially when he is being facetious, an attempt no doubt to represent him in his popular character as a mixture of scholar and clown.

"This Dionysius of Syracuse caused cunning workmen to

---

[32] *Op. cit.,* 33.

build for himself a lugg. – D'ye ken what that is, my Lord Bishop?"

"A cathedral, I presume to guess," answered the Bishop.

"What the deil, man – I crave your lordship's pardon for swearing – but it was no cathedral – only a lurking-place called the king's lugg or ear, where he could sit undescried and hear the converse of his prisoners."[33]

Possibly Scott is reminding his readers that Scotland once had a national language of its own – the King's Scots. Of the latter he has to say in his Introduction to *The Chronicles of the Canongate* (1827) in describing the old Edinburgh lady, Mrs Bethune Baliol, a character supposed to be modelled on a kinsman of his own, much in the same terms as we have seen in Ramsay of Ochtertyre:

... the peculiarity of the dialect which Mrs. Baliol used. It was Scottish, decidedly Scottish, often containing words and phrases little used in the present day. But then her tone and mode of pronunciation were as different from the usual accent of the ordinary Scotch *patois*, as the accent of St. James's is from that of Billingsgate. ... It seemed to be the Scottish as spoken by the ancient court of Scotland, to which no idea of vulgarity could be attached."[34]

Unfortunately in the event he does not attempt to reproduce this for Mrs Baliol speaks English throughout, and we have to turn to a different type of Scotswoman for a different kind of Scots with distinctive elements of its own. Jeanie Deans is in fact the only heroine who speaks Scots. But it is a Scots of varied register or intensity. To her father and sister it is the ordinary speech of the Lothian peasant; to comparative strangers like Saddletree and Staunton it is much more anglicised; when she is in England she is obviously trying to make herself intelligible in English, though the occasional Scots word drops out; when she first meets the Duke of Argyll she is as formal as her school English will permit but when, to set her at her ease, he speaks of Scotland, the familiar topic brings out her Scots more and more. But the antithesis is not merely between high society English and low society Scots.

[33] *F.N.*, Ch. 33.
[34] *Chronicles of the Canongate*, Ch. 6.

When Jeanie, in her nocturnal interview with her sister's seducer, is brought face to face with the moral dilemma of telling a lie under oath or of destroying her sister's chance of acquittal, first comes the Scots of her emotion:

> "I wad ware the best blood in my body to keep her skaithless," said Jeanie, weeping in bitter agony; "but I canna change right into wrang, or make that true which is false."

But as Staunton presses her to forswear herself:

> "He has given us a law," said Jeanie, "for the lamp of our path; if we stray from it we err against knowledge. I may not do evil, even that good may come out of it. But you – why do not you step forward and bear leal and soothfast evidence in her behalf, as ye may with a clear conscience?"[35]

This is the second language of Scotland, the heritage of the sixteenth century, of the English Bible and Calvinist theology – with which every Scottish peasant was familiar and which he could reproduce in varying degrees of accuracy in proportion to his own intelligence and articulateness in moments of moral reflexion.

So the light-hearted Effie coming home "sae late at e'en" singing her ballad about "The Elfin Knight" and parrying her sister's questions about where she had been with "What needs ye be aye speering then at folk? I'm sure, if ye'll ask nae questions, I'll tell ye nae lees," brings down a diatribe on dancing from her father, couched, as Scott himself admits, in the language of a Cameronian tract of 1728, and mentally resolves "I'll no gang back there again. I'll lay in a leaf of my Bible, and that's very near as if I had made an aith that I winna gang back." But the same Effie in the condemned cell, showing Jeanie the passage in Job where the leaf had by chance been folded down, thus applies it to herself:

> "Isna that ower true a doctrine? isna my crown, my honour removed? And what am I but a poor wasted wan-thriven tree, dug up by the roots and flung out to waste in the highway, that man and beast may tread it under foot?"[36]

[35] H.M., Ch. 15.
[36] Op. cit., Ch. 20.

And it is in this style that Scott words the greatest purple patch of the novel, Jeanie's speech to the Queen, which its author himself seems to have thought a good piece of work ("This is eloquence," said her Majesty)[37].

Scott adopts, sometimes to excess, the obvious method of giving linguistic verisimilitude to his characters by introducing metaphors from their trade or occupation, Cuddie Headrigg from the work of a ploughman, Maggie Mucklebackit from fishing, Dugald Dalgetty from soldiering in continental wars, with scraps of French and German thrown in, the Fairport wives from the vocabulary of their various tradesmen husbands, and Andrew Fairservice in *Rob Roy*:

> "Nae doubt I should understand my trade of horticulture, seeing I was bred in the parish of Dreepdaily, where they raise lang-kale under glass, and force the early nettles for their spring kale. And to speak truth, I hae been flitting every term these four-and-twenty years; but when the time comes, there's aye something to saw that I would like to see sawn, or something to maw that I would like to see mawn, – or something to ripe that I would like to see ripen, – and sae I e'en daiker on wi' the family frae years's end to year's end."[38]

From which we learn a lot more about Andrew than just that he was a gardener.

There are subtleties also in the quality of the Scots as between speakers to which Scott himself draws the reader's attention:

> "'Ow, ay, sir! a bra' night,' replied the lieutenant, in broad Scotch of the most vulgar description; the broad coarse Scotch that is spoken in the Cowgate of Edinburgh, or in the Gorbals;[39]

and he draws similar fine distinctions in regard to his Highland characters whose native language would be Gaelic but who could also speak Scots and, according to their station in life, good or indifferent English as well. Servants, retainers, and such, like Ewan Dhu in *Waverley*, the Dougal cratur in *Rob Roy*, and Duncan Campbell in *The Heart of Midlothian*, speak a kind of pidgin Scots,

[37] *Op. cit.*, Ch. 37.   [38] R.R., Ch. 6.
[39] *Wav.*, Ch. 39; H.M., Ch. 48.

full of "oichs" and "her nainsels", which was a literary tradition for Highland speech, though quite unauthentic, long before Scott. With more exalted Highlanders he refines considerably – even between Roy Roy and his wife:

> Nor was there the least tincture of that vulgarity, which we naturally attach to the Lowland Scottish. There was a strong provincial accentuation, but otherwise the language rendered by Helen MacGregor, out of the native and poetical Gaelic, into English, which she had acquired as we do learned tongues, but had probably never heard applied to the mean purposes of ordinary life, was graceful, flowing and declamatory. Her husband, who had in his time played many parts, used a much less elevated and emphatic dialect, – but even his language rose in purity of expression, as you may have remarked, if I have been accurate in recording it, when the affairs which he discussed were of an agitating and important nature; and it appears to me in his case, and in that of some other Highlanders whom I have known, that, when familiar and facetious, they used the Lowland Scottish dialect, – when serious and impassioned, their thoughts arranged themselves in the idiom of their native language; and in the latter case, as they uttered the corresponding ideas in English, the expressions sounded wild, elevated and poetical.[40]

Unfortunately, being innocent of Gaelic, Scott had to make do with the theatrical inflated English he puts in the mouth of Helen MacGregor; nor is he very consistent about her husband, who speaks Scots when he is most animated. Seldom has more racy vigorous dialogue been written than in the scene in Glasgow Tolbooth between Rob Roy and Bailie Nicol Jarvie.[41] Scott himself maintains his belief in the superiority of dialogue over description in his argument with himself in the first chapter of *The Bride of Lammermoor* and Scots from the very nature of its status in the eighteenth century is admirably adapted for colloquial purposes. One can recall also the argument between Mause Headrigg and Lady Bellenden,[42] the chaffering between King James and George Heriot over the gold plate;[43] the sinister conclave of the hags at the wake of Alice Gray: "Dead deal will never be laid on his

[40] R.R., Ch. 35.   [41] Op. cit., Ch. 23.   [42] O.M., Ch. 7.   [43] F.N., Ch. 5.

back; make you your market of that, for I hae it frae a sure hand."[44]

The echo of witchcraft in the last phrase brings us close to the world of the folk, their beliefs and superstitions, and their traditional wisdom as it is expressed in their similes, sayings, and proverbs, Scott makes a liberal use of these to create the atmosphere of "manners" as in the following phrases: "The clartier, the cosier"; "ance wud and aye waur"; "a tout on a bawbee whistle"; "welcome to a tune on your ain fiddle"; "there's sma sorrow at our parting, as the auld mear said to the broken cart"; "to come to their hand like the bowl o' a pint stoup"; "to rout like a coo in a fremd loaning"; "jouk and let the jaw gae bye"; "like a hen on a het girdle"; "our ain fish guts to our ain sea-maws". He improves on the ordinary version by alliteration in "To steek the stable door when the steed's stolen." He also borrows, as we have seen, phraseology, much of it actually historical, from earlier writers, like Patrick Walker, Burt, Pennant, Pinkerton, and the Master of Sinclair, and of course incorporates many historical or traditional sayings ("Tak up your bonnie bridegroom; he fought for his ain hand"), snatches of ballads and folk-songs, like those of Effie Deans, not to mention cant and slang among the gipsies and smugglers in *Guy Mannering* and *Redgauntlet* and the flash-talk of Alsatia in *The Fortunes of Nigel*.

For Scott, in the final analysis, the strength of Scots at its best lay in its simplicity and directness (and here again we can see the influence of the ballad on him). In a letter of 2 January 1824 to Henry Mackenzie, criticising Galt for "out-Scottifying the Scotch dialect",[45] he says "Our Doric dialect is only beautiful when it is simple," a point he had already made more fully in his Preface to *The Antiquary* in 1816: "I agree with Mr. Wordsworth that they [the peasantry] seldom fail to express their feelings in the strongest and most powerful language. The antique force and simplicity of their language, often tinctured with the Oriental eloquence of Scripture, in the mouths of those of an elevated understanding give pathos to their grief and dignity to their resentment," and in the novel itself he translates this into memorable discourse, as in

[44] B.L., Ch. 23.

[45] Galt, in fact, not only uses Scots for his dialogue but experiments with a Scotticised English in his narrative, especially in *Ringan Gilhaize* (1823).

Q

the storm scene with the three figures huddled desperately on the wave-lashed crag:

> "Good man," said Sir Arthur, "can you think of nothing? – of no help? – I'll make you rich – I'll give you a farm – I'll —".
> "Our riches will soon be equal," said the beggar, looking out upon the strife of the waters – "They are sae already; for I hae nae land, and you would give your fair bounds and barony for a square yard of rock that would be dry for twal hours";[46]

or when Monkbarns comes on Saunders Mucklebackit mending the boat in which his son was drowned:

> "What would ye have me to do, unless I wanted to see four children starve, because ane is drowned? It's weel wi' you gentles, that can sit in the house wi' handkerchers at your een when ye lose a friend; but the like o' us maun to our wark again, if our hearts were beating as hard as my hammer."[47]

It is in such passages that Scott gets pretty near the root of the matter.

But Scott occasionally attempts even more, in the famous oracular malediction of Meg Merrilies:[48]

> "Ride your ways, Laird of Ellangowan – ride your ways, Godfrey Bertram! ? This day have ye quenched seven smoking hearths – see if the fire in your ain parlour burn brighter for that. Ye have riven the thack off seven cottar houses – look if your ain roof-tree stand the faster. – Ye may stable your stirks in the shealings at Derncleugh – see that the hare does not couch on the hearthstane at Ellangowan . . ."

Coleridge condemned the diction of Meg Merrilies as "falsetto", but this is hardly the point here. The passage is a set piece in which Scott is really experimenting with Scots to see how far it will go in the direction of poetic prose. The subtleties of its construction, its symmetries and rhythm, were fully analysed by A. W. Verrall who appropriately enough translated the whole speech into Greek tragic iambics.[49] It is in fact no mean attempt to

---

[46] *A.*, Ch. 7.   [47] *Op. cit.*, Ch. 34.
[48] *G.M.*, Ch. 8. There is another passage in the same key in Ch. 53.
[49] *Quarterly* (July 1910), p. 33, *Cambridge Compositions* (Cambridge University Press) 1904, p. 329.

extend the range of the old tongue from the cramping limits which history has imposed on it, much like the achievement of Burns in his most inspired moments with the folk-song he turned into art-song.

But the masterpiece in this line of course is Wandering Willie's Tale in *Redgauntlet*,[50] a certain inclusion in all anthologies of short stories on every count. As a piece of Scots prose it is equally meritorious; the vocabulary, the grammar, the word-order, the idioms, the similes, the proverbs, the historical allusions, the speech-rhythms, are all there to perfection, and in it we catch a fascinating and tantalising glimpse of what Scottish literature might have been if the events of 1560, 1603, and 1707 had taken a different turn.

[50] R., Letter 11. Stevenson paid it the best compliment by writing a palpable imitation of it in Tod Lapraik's Tale in *Catriona*.

F. A. Pottle

THE POWER OF MEMORY IN BOSWELL AND SCOTT[1]

"The Wizard of the North" is a title no serious critic would care to employ nowadays: it has a flavour of the sentimental or the comic or both together – something like the Wizard of Oz. Yet it is hard to see what epithet could fit Scott better. A wizard is a man who casts a spell: he enchants a country and it all seems changed. One walks dryshod where the map shows a river, and ascends mountains where uneasy memory records a fen. A wizard breaks the comfortable shackles of time, and the familiar scene, as in that disquieting narrative of the two ladies at Versailles, is frequented by forms that belong there, no doubt, but not now. Scott did precisely that to Scotland, and the spell has not lifted. For better or worse, Scotland as it is seen today is largely the creation of Walter Scott. And the best existing means of testing the extent of this transformation is the journal of James Boswell.

By an indiscriminate attention to significant and superficial resemblances, it would be possible to prove that James Boswell and Walter Scott were practically identical. Both were born in Edinburgh and spent the greater part of their lives there; both attended the University of Edinburgh; both were sons of lawyers, both became advocates and curators of the Advocates' Library; both were Tories, both were Masons, both belonged to The Club; both preferred the forms and doctrine of the Church of England to those of the Kirk; both had fine estates in the country; both wrote a great deal more than anybody knows, and are

[1] Reprinted from *Essays on the Eighteenth Century Presented to David Nichol Smith* . . . Oxford (Clarendon Press) 1945 pp. 168–89.

remembered today merely as literary men, and both, in their own time, would have been offended at being classed as authors by profession.

It would be possible to go on for a long time extending the parallels, but such activity would be mere ingenuity, not criticism. There are, indeed, a surprising number of respects in which Boswell and Scott resemble each other to such a degree that by knowing the character of one it would be possible to predict the attitude of the other on a given issue. The similarity of their attitude towards the law is very striking. Perhaps the best evidence of this is the inexhaustible usefulness of Scott's novels in annotating Boswell's journal. Neither Scott nor Boswell was so constituted as to become really prominent at the bar, but the reason was not any lack of aptitude. It was simply that both had other interests and were not willing to give them up. Men who wish to acquire fame and fortune as advocates must study in the vacations of the courts; they must not rush off the day the court rises on jaunts to London or raids into Liddesdale. Both Scott and Boswell (to use the words of one of them) defied the jealousy of the goddess Themis towards any fliration with the Muses, but neither ever really meant to apostatise. Boswell groaned for manumission, not from the law but from the petty routine of the Court of Session and the General Assembly; always before his eyes hung the mirage of splendid success at the English bar. That mirage, at the age of forty-six, he characteristically pursued. Scott, a more hard-headed man who worked his romance off in best-sellers, accepted appointment as one of the principal clerks in the Court of Session. Both remained lawyers. Boswell, a year before his death, was outlining a legal education for his eldest son and chatting to him as one lawyer to another, while the sharpest letter Scott ever wrote to *his* eldest son was occasioned by some disparaging remarks which that young man had made about lawyers.[2]

[2] "The question which you put . . . is shrewd, and makes me believe you have a good law head" (Boswell to Alexander Boswell, 13 Mar. 1794, *The Private Papers of James Boswell from Malahide Castle, in the Collection of Lt.-Colonel Ralph Heyward Isham*, Ed. Godfrey Scott and F. A. Pottle, privately printed, 1928–34, 18 vols., Vol. 18, p. 325; "DEAR WALTER, I have your letter of May 6th, to which it is unnecessary to reply very particularly. I would only insinuate to you that the *lawyers* and *gossips* of Edinburgh, whom your military politeness handsomely classes together in writing to a lawyer

Scott continued his regular attendance in the Court of Session until 1830, and never did resign his sheriffship.

The politics of Boswell and Scott are also of a piece. Scott deflates his own self-importance with humour in a way that shows a great advantage beside the stiffness and pompousness of the political notes in the *Life of Johnson*, but like Boswell he was a deadly serious intuitive Tory. Scott cherishing in his coat-tail the whisky-glass which the royal lips of George IV had touched, is hardly to be distinguished from Boswell melting in the seraphic smile of George III. And the touching scene of Scott on the Mound, bursting into tears and resting his head on the coping until he should have recovered his composure, when his Whig friends had tried to make a joking matter out of proposed reforms in the administration of justice in Scotland, is matched by Boswell in the vale of Glenmoriston weeping over Culloden.[3]

In their attitudes towards family and landed property they again see eye to eye. It is true that Boswell came of a long-established family, whereas Scott was establishing one himself; true also that Boswell could not bear to *live* on his property, whereas Scott was not completely happy anywhere else. But Boswell's tendency "to think with sacred reverence and attachment of his Ancestors and to hope to aggrandize the Family" quite matches Scott's, and his appetite for land was little less reckless and insatiable. Everyone knows that Scott overreached himself in his expenditure at Abbotsford and brought himself and his connexions to spectacular ruin, but it is not so well known that Boswell did what a lesser man could to involve his affairs. In order to purchase Knockroom ("I am willing to give more than any person whatever . . . I will *restrict* myself to any degree rather than fail") he had to borrow at a time when his affairs were "sadly straitened". In 1792, presumably to consolidate his debts, he granted a heritable bond for £4,000 on his lands of Dalblair to Quintin McAdam of Craigen-

[3] *Memoirs*, Vol. 7, pp. 53–5, Ch. 56; *Private Papers*, Vol. 15, pp. 100–1; *Memoirs*, Vol. 2, p. 328, Ch. 15, at end; *Journal of a Tour to the Hebrides*, ed. Pottle and Bennett, initials, place, date, pp. 106–7 (1 Sept. 1773).

. . ." (Scott to Cornet Walter Scott, 15 May 1821, *Memoirs of the Life of Sir Walter Scott* by J. G. Lockhart, 2nd ed., 1839, 10 vols. [Chapter references apply to any abridged edition after the first.] Vol. 6, p. 316, Ch. 51.

gillan. The bond, falling due on his death, could not be met, and Dalblair was lost for the mere sum of the debt. Sixty years later it sold for £17,300.[4]

To many this comparison will seem sophistical, if not in bad taste. It would be if we were concerned with the central practical issue. Scott from the earliest period at which we can discern him was a man of character: manly, courageous, confident to the point of rashness, self-controlled, and extraverted. So far as I can see, he had no vices at all, but my feeling for him has always been that of the sentimental pig, and perhaps is not to be trusted. Boswell in certain respects was a moral weakling: his vices are notorious, self-confessed, and unattractive. They all spring, unless I am mistaken, from a fundamental sense of insecurity, from a basic lack of confidence, caused by, or at least accompanied by, an extreme form of introversion. Here, certainly, the two men are dia-metrically opposed, and opposed in the most important respect. My concern in this essay, however, is not with conduct, but with a lesser matter, art; and I hope the reader will not be shocked if I say that in the sort of analysis which I propose to make of Boswell and Scott moral differences are largely irrelevant.

Scott, as I have said, cast a spell on the world; we know it by the world which Boswell has preserved for us. Between the two men there occurred tremendous acceleration in the shift of sensibility which gradually transformed what we call the neo-classic mind into the romantic. A detailed and objective description of the essential differences between the sensibility of Boswell and the sensibility of Scott should be of some utility, for it would be material for a properly controlled generalisation as to the nature of the neo-classic and the romantic expressions of the world. *Material*, of course, not a complete or trustworthy generalisation. No one should expect to define romanticism except by extended historical statement, and one should not expect any particular author to be either completely "neo-classic" or completely "romantic". These terms name imaginary or ideal embodiments of average characteristics.

A thorough study of the kind I propose would go far beyond the limits imposed upon this essay. I can give only a sketch. And

[4] *Private Papers*, Vol. 14, p. 17, vol. 18, p. 287, 288 n.; James Paterson, *History of the Counties at Ayr and Wigton*, Vol. 1, pp. 201–2.

the sketch will violate strict propriety of method. Though my purpose is in the main descriptive, I shall suggest rather more in the way of generalisation than the material presented justifies.

It may be felt that the comparison is rendered futile at the start by the fact that Scott was a writer of fiction, Boswell a biographer and journalist. And indeed, unless one is willing to grant the fundamental assumption of the Crocean position – that all expression is art, and that the difference between a novel and a journal like Boswell's is a difference of degree and not of kind – there will seem to be no justification for the present study. It is precisely that assumption that will be made in what follows: that in analysing Boswell's journal we are concerned not merely with perception and memory, but also with imagination. To distinguish Scott from Boswell merely in the workings of the imagination is useful, but I should like to go farther back and see if even more interesting results could not be obtained if we began at the level of perception and continued on through the stage of memory. It may well be that memory will prove to be the most useful differential of all.

Did Boswell and Scott perceive the same sort of world to begin with? We have, as it happens, documents which should be capable of answering the question. They are Boswell's *Journal of a Tour to the Hebrides* and the journal of the tour to the Shetlands, Orkneys, and Hebrides which Scott made in 1814. The material is all similar in nature, and some of it – rather less than one would have expected – is quite parallel. Boswell's original manuscript has been recovered and printed; Scott's, so far as I know, is accessible only in the text given by Lockhart in the *Memoirs*, which seems to show some subsequent manipulation by Scott or his editor, but has probably not been sophisticated in any way injurious to our purpose.[5]

From Boswell's journal as a whole, it appears that his central interests were strongly humanistic. His perception was keen and

[5] "Within the castle [of Dunvegan] we saw a remarkable drinking-cup . . . which I have described particularly elsewhere" (*Memoirs*, Vol. 4, p. 304, Ch. 31). The "elsewhere" is Note xii to *The Lord of the Isles*, of which the pertinent portion must have been written later than the journal. Lockhart, finding the description of the Dunvegan cup rather long and dull, probably modified the text at this point so that he could eliminate it from his printing of the journal.

full for all varieties of human nature (Johnson was merely his best subject), for social customs and practices, for human antiquities, for history and legends. For landscape and merely natural curiosities it was relatively languid. He remarks more than once that he has no skill in depicting natural objects, a clear indication that he did not see them with much detail. No author I know is more completely free from picturesque writing. Not that his perception of landscape is purely utilitarian, for he sometimes remarks aesthetic values in it. Landscape, however, is not by him perceived as involved in history and symbolic of it. It is probable that human antiquities such as Dunvegan or the ruins of Iona, though symbols of history, were perceived by him as *disconnected* from it, elements of a storied past gone beyond recall, a past which existed verbally but not in visual imagery tied to the scene.

Lockhart says that Scott's journal draws his character fully: "We have before us, according to the scene and occasion, the poet, the antiquary, the magistrate, the planter, and the agriculturist."[6] It is easier to illustrate the antiquary, the magistrate, the planter, and the agriculturist than the poet. Scott shows the eager interest one would expect in brochs, tombs, drinking-cups, legends, trees, and crops – indeed, his interest in agriculture causes him to be much more detailed and intelligible on that topic than Boswell ever is – but the poetry of the journal is very low-pitched, so much so as to be almost a matter of inference. We see it because we come to the journal fortified with those passages from his autobiographical fragment which describe his early "love of natural beauty, more especially when combined with ancient ruins, or remains of our fathers' piety or splendour", and his power to fill an old castle or a field of battle "with its combatants in their proper costume".[7]

In his journal, as one would expect, he gives a great deal of space to remarkable and terrific scenes: the Cave of Smoo, Loch Coruisk, "Macallister's Cave" (Spar Cave), and Staffa – several extended and serious attempts at picturesque writing. And that, oddly enough, is just about what they remain. Loch Coruisk may have been overrun by tourists as a result of *The Lord of the Isles*, as

[6] *Memoirs*, Vol. 4, p. 371, Ch. 33, beginning.
[7] *Op. cit.*, Vol. 1, pp. 55, 72, Ch. 1.

Loch Katrine undoubtedly was because of *The Lady of the Lake*, but the passage in Scott's journal would not have effected such a result.

Similarly when Scott comes upon "remains of our fathers' piety or splendour" (this particular tour was relatively barren in historical monuments) we sense the heightened interest we should have predicted. The best example is perhaps those ruins at Scalloway and Kirkwall connected with Patrick Stewart, Earl of Orkney.[8] But these, though extremely interesting, do not strike the reader as being intensely poetic.

The fact is that the two journals show much less difference in immediate perception of the world than one would have predicted. Boswell favours conversation (and would have even if Johnson had not been his companion), Scott favours scenery. But the central interests are so similar that not merely sentences but whole paragraphs could be interchanged without being detected by a casual reader. The two journals do not show respectively a typically "neo-classic" and a typically "romantic" perception of the world. Scott's throughout has the shrewd, humane, humorous tone of common sense that we associate with the eighteenth century.

Shall we conclude that the Wizard of the North was a charlatan, or at least an extraordinarily clever and deliberate showman –that he naturally and habitually *saw* Boswell's world, but by conscious literary devices tricked other people into seeing something else? That would be too simple a description of a very complex situation. Scott *did* perceive a normal, average world just about like Boswell's. But he constantly perceived another world behind and through it: the romantic world into which it could be transformed. He could hardly have written his description of Loch Coruisk without seeing it as sympathetic landscape for the meeting of Bruce and Cormac Doil – or at least for some melodramatic encounter; and it is safe to infer that when he saw Earl Patrick's ruined castle at Scalloway he was conscious of the lively presence of that rapacious prince in a way that Boswell would have considered enthusiastic. He does not *record* the romantic perception because he is recording fact, and he believes the romantic perception to be make-believe. It is very interesting to see at the

[8] *Op. cit.*, pp. 213–15, 247–9, Chs. 28, 29.

basis of his artistic activity this clear, sharp, undistorted, "realistic" perception of things, and his determination to keep it clear from the play of free imagination. It is the source of his strength and at the same time of his greatest weakness. One becomes impatient with an artist who is so genuinely convinced that fiction is merely make-believe that he can do himself justice only when the fiction sweeps him off his feet. But when it does, we get an imaginative presentation of such solidity and power as our language elsewhere hardly affords.

It is only when we turn to the *uses* that Scott made of his perceptions that we discern a sharp and striking difference between his mind and Boswell's. His memory works very differently. It will be easier to show this if we say something of Boswell first. The nature of Boswell's memory has been made the subject of a brilliant investigation by Geoffrey Scott, unfortunately in a work of limited circulation.[9] In what follows I shall draw freely on his conclusions, not pausing to indicate the places where I have modified and extended them.

Given the right kind of jog to his memory, Boswell had something that looks like total recall. If he failed to make a written record soon after a series of events, he seems to have lost those events permanently, or at least to have had no greater power of recall than the next person. But given his written clue, and given time and patience, he could reconstruct accurately and in minute detail an account of practically everything that ever happened to him. The clues he relied on (when he did not write a full journal immediately) were rough and abbreviated notes jotted down on odd scraps of paper, often on the backs of envelopes. In these notes, which are in the highest degree fragmentary and cryptic, there appears to be no attempt to select what is important. Boswell simply jots down whatever rises first to his consciousness, knowing that one sort of hint will serve as well as another.[10] Once fixed in this fashion, the events may be recalled at will, the fullness of the recovery depending less upon the interval of time than upon his patience and ability to concentrate his attention.

The journal is generally written from these notes, after a lapse

[9] *The Making of the Life of Johnson*, vol. 6 of the *Private Papers*.
[10] "A hint like this will serve to bring back to me all that past, though it would be useless to any one else" (Boswell's journal in the *Private Papers*).

of time varying from days to years. When the notes and journal are compared (which is seldom possible, for Boswell's usual practice was to destroy his notes as soon as they had served their purpose), it will generally be found that something – sometimes a great deal – turns up for which there was no sort of hint in the notes, and not infrequently that some hints in the notes are ignored.[11] Suppressions of this kind in the journal I take to be due to several causes: inability to read the note; lack of time or patience to bring the scene back fully; deliberate rejection of remembered material as not worth recording. The material which turns up in the journal without warrant in the notes I can only conclude to have been *remembered*. It is of exactly the same sort as the material for which the notes furnish hints, and is just as circumstantial. When the circumstances are of a sort that will permit verification, they prove to be correct.

The process of recollection does not stop with the journal, but is still going on in the *Life of Johnson*. For one thing, the greater part of the extended Johnsonian conversations in which several speakers take part seems never to have been expanded in the journal at all. The only record Boswell had was frequently the rough note written many years before.[12] And even when he had before him a journal version which could have been transferred almost without change into the *Life*, one constantly finds additions

[11] Good examples will be found in Geoffrey Scott, *The Making of the Life of Johnson, Private Papers*, VI. For the brilliant account of the evening at Lord Mansfield's, 11 April 1773 (pp. 107–11), the notes have only "Lord Mans. Jenkins [on] there – Had him afterwards an hour alone. Etourdi again. Felt still that greatness and cold command can confuse me." The journal gives a report of the hour's conversation, 750 words on six different topics, all highly detailed and circumstantial. For examples of hints recorded but not made use of, see the notes for 3 June 1784 (*op. cit.* 53–6).

[12] 11 April 1773 exists in the journal in a form fuller, if anything, than the version in *Boswell's Life of Johnson*, Ed. G. B. Hill and revised L. F. Powell, Oxford Vols. 1–4, 1934. Vols. 5–6, 1950., 13 April 1773 of the *Life* was written as late as 1787 from a rough note merely. In both cases (wages of female servants, 11 April; law reports, 13 April) Johnson is credited with remarks for which there is no warrant in the notes. A great deal, no doubt, depended on the fullness of the note. When, as in the latter portion of the *Journal of a Tour to the Hebrides* (ed. Pottle and Bennett, p. 346), Boswell complains of lack of freshness and fullness, he may have had only very brief notes to work from.

which can only be explained, in my opinion, by assuming that even here he relived the scene as he copied it and recollected matter which had eluded him at the time he wrote the journal, or which he had then suppressed.[13]

The qualities which make the recall of Boswell remarkable are its wealth of detail and its circumstantial accuracy. Memory in people of education, particularly in artists, is usually a very inaccurate affair and deals cavalierly with circumstances. Very few people, moreover, can distinguish between what they have actually witnessed and what they have been told. Adults, no less than children, frequently convince themselves that they were spectators of events which for a time they were content to relate on the authority of others.

Yet the kind of memory here ascribed to Boswell, if it were merely a matter of detail and accuracy, would be no very rare thing. We have all met people who could remember everything, and we have shunned them. Who does not number among his acquaintance a narrator who bores his audience with interminable circumstantial detail, often of events of the remote past? We do not doubt the accuracy of the detail or the power of the narrator, having got hold of this thread, to unravel it to the end of time. But accuracy of that sort is tedious. What we want, as we say, is for him to come to his *point*. We want selection; that is, we want him to pick out a few important things and sink the rest. To repeat, the memory which is tenacious of circumstantial detail is not uncommon, but it is usually associated with a low order of intelligence or a primitive culture.

The really remarkable feat of Boswell is that he has combined the full recall of the savage or the moron with the selectivity of the

[13] In the nature of things, these additions are seldom of a sort to permit verification. One remarkable exception occurs in the account of 3 June 1784 as given in the *Life*. We are told there that Mrs and Miss Beresford were Americans; that they were going to Worcestershire, where they resided; and that Mr Beresford had been a member of Congress. None of this is recorded in the note (which happens to have survived) nor in the journal. But it is all correct. After a searching review, I have been unable to detect any difference in authenticity between expansions which Boswell made in the *Life* and those that he made in the journal; or, to state the problem more precisely, between additions made after an interval of years and additions made after an interval of days or months.

artist. His record, by its wealth of circumstantial detail, convinces us of its firm basis in reality, while by coming to the point he keeps us interested: that is, persuades us that what he is saying is significant.

What gives the peculiar quality of solidity and trustworthiness to Boswell's accounts is that he always presents his scenes in terms of average or normal experience. It begs the question to say that he presents things as they really were. There is a certain area in which all minds agree or in which agreement is ideally possible. The circumstantial detail which we have mentioned falls in this area. A particular conversation occurred on Thursday 3 June 1784 in the Oxford coach, or it did not; the ladies who accompanied Johnson were named Beresford, were Americans, were going to Worcestershire, or they were not; Mr Beresford was a member of Congress or he was not. We may not always be able to verify things like this, but we shall agree that they are capable of verification and that only one answer is right. This is selection (for many more details could have been given) but it is not interpretation. When it comes to what Johnson *said* on any subject if it was a matter of more than a sentence or two, it is obvious that Boswell gives us not merely selection but also interpretation, for you cannot condense or epitomise speech without deciding what, on the whole, it means. Boswell's interpretation moves on the plane of average or normal experience, with the result that in him we seem to see the past through no kind of medium at all, or at most through plate glass. The style that can achieve this result is one of the rarest things in literature. Much more common is the medium which colours or distorts – Carlyle's, let us say, or Scott's.

Boswell seems not in his own lifetime to have been regarded as a prodigy. Though he himself remarks with awe on the "stretch of mind" which had enabled him to recover extended conversations, most readers of the *Life*, then as now, have thought of him as a stenographer. Scott's memory, on the contrary, was an object of general astonishment from the time he was six years old.[14] Like most memories which history chooses to distinguish as prodigious his was essentially verbal and literary. He never pretended to be able to remember circumstantial details of his own experience or

[14] *Life*, vol. 1, p. 6 (Advertisement to the First Edition); *Memoirs*, Vol. 1, pp. 118–20, Ch. 2.

to report at length general conversations which he had once heard. But from childhood he could repeat from memory, without any conscious effort at memorisation, a "really marvellous quantity" of stanzas from the *Faerie Queene*, or ballads, or pages of history – in short, in any part of the field of his passionate antiquarian interest, to read or to have heard and to remember were the same thing.[15]

We have seen that Boswell, if he had a hint or clue, could recall past scenes of his life with remarkable fullness and accuracy. The clue he depended on was a *written* note; nothing else would serve. Scott seems never to have formed the habit of systematic notation. But we do have the tantalising business of the notched twigs, and a great misfortune it is that we do not have from Scott himself a more satisfactory account of these extraordinary memoranda. Our authority is Robert Shortreed, Scott's companion in the Liddesdale raids. He was nine years older than Scott and predeceased him, but his son in 1824 had taken down his recollections in his own racy dialect. The passage about the notched sticks must be quoted in full:

> J. E. S. "Did Sir Walter keep a memorandum-book or take any notes, during your tours?"
> FATHER. "None that I ever saw. We had neither pens, nor ink, nor paper. But we had *knives* and they served the turn just as weel, for we took bits o' Cuttings wi' them, frae a broom Cowe, or an aller, or a hazel-bush, or whatever else might be at hand, and on thae bits o' stick (maybe tway or three inches lang they were) he made a variety o' notches, and these were the only memoranda I ever saw him take or have, of any of the memorable spots he wished to preserve the recollection of, or any tradition connected wi' them. And when he had notched them they were just slipt into our pockets, a' heads and thraws. When we cam hame frae some o' our trips, I hae seen us have a'maist haill wallets fu' o' them – wud aneuch to mend a mill as Burns says. I couldna think what he meant by this at first, and when I asked him what a' thae marked sticks were for, he said, 'these are my log-book, Bob!'"

[15] *Memoirs*, Vol. I, pp. 50, 53, Ch. I.

J. E. S. "This is most amazing – And are you aware that he ever made any after use of them?"

FATHER. 'Yes I can satisfy ye on that point too. For I was frequently wi' him at his Father's house in Edinr. when he was preparing the Minstrelsy for publication, and I know, *for I saw it*, that as he went along he very often had recourse to *the notched sticks*. He had them a' hanging in their order above him, by a string alang the ceiling o' his room – (as you'll see Rhubarb in a gardener's house) – wi' mony mae o' the same kind about the Highlands, for ye ken he used often to gang on travels there too, about that time. I never saw a pen in his hand nor a piece o' paper a' the times we were in Liddesdale thegither, or in any other o' our Border rides, but twice, and that was when he took the two sketches that he made o' Hermitage Castle, and the one sheet o' paper he got frae Dr. Elliot, the other frae Willie o' Millburn."[16]

It is very odd that Lockhart, who had Shortreed's manuscript before him and used it for other information, did not quote this highly interesting passage. He may have thought that it made mystery of a very simple matter. It has not, I think, been noted that there is a reference to the twigs by Scott himself in the autobiographical fragment which does seem on a careless reading to reduce them to the status of mere souvenirs. After relating his inability to learn to sketch the scenes that interested him, Scott says:

I endeavoured to make amends for my ignorance of drawing, by adopting a sort of technical memory respecting the scenes I visited. Wherever I went, I cut a piece of a branch from a tree – these constituted what I called my log-book; and I intended to have a set of chessmen out of them, each having reference to the place where it was cut – as the kings from Falkland and Holy-Rood; the queens from Queen

16 W. E. Wilson, "The Making of the Minstrelsy", in *Cornhill Magazine*, n.s. cxlvi, p. 281 (July–Dec. 1932). As Mr Dobie has pointed out (*Transactions of the Edinburgh Bibliographical Society*, vol. 2, Part 1, p. 68 n.), there is at least one slight inaccuracy in Shortreed's account: the *Minstrelsy* was not planned until after Scott had left his father's house. But he had been recording ballads for a long time before he formed any plan of publication.

Mary's yew-tree at Crookston; the bishops from abbeys or
episcopal palaces; the knights from baronial residences; the
rooks from royal fortresses; and the pawns generally from
places worthy of historical note. But this whimsical design
I never carried into execution.[17]

Scott's "technical memory" is, I think, equivalent to the "artificial
memory" which the *Oxford Dictionary* defines as "a system of
mnemonic devices", and illustrates from Hoyle (1747): *A Short
Treatise on the Game of Whist . . . To which is added, An Artificial
Memory: Or, An easy Method of assisting the memory of those that play
at the Game.* The intention of making chessmen out of the twigs
was probably second thought.

There is not much doubt, I think, that we have here a very
interesting means of differentiating the modes of memory possessed by Boswell and Scott. Boswell had to consult verbal clues,
and was unable or unwilling to reconstruct the past unless he was
properly buttressed and limited by circumstance. Landscape he
saw with little detail and made little or no effort to recall. For
verbal material, Scott demanded no clues, but confidently constructed it out of his head as he wanted it. Picturesque landscape
was a different matter. If he were to recall this, he must have some
kind of clue. Written descriptions, such as those of the journal of
1814, would serve, but when he was in the field he was generally
too busy enjoying himself to do any writing. He would have been
willing to dash off a sketch, but drawing was something he could
not master. The notched sticks were *landscape* memoranda, and
served well enough for the broad effects he was partial to. But it
is not likely that such memoranda could have furnished the circumstantial detail which ensures accuracy of memory.

And the fact is that Scott's memory, as contrasted with Boswell's, is wildly inaccurate. Imaginative construction is at work in
it, and at work in the same way as in his fictions. Indeed, it is fair
to say that the only difference between Scott's fictions and his
anecdotal memories is that in the one case imagination is at work
consciously and in the other it is not.

Consider first an instance where the professed object was
merely to recall events and scenes of the tour of 1814. In the last

[17] *Memoirs*, Vol. I, pp. 72–3, Ch. I.

R

of the *Letters on Demonology* (1830) he speaks of his experience in
the haunted apartment at Dunvegan. The experience was in fact
disappointing: the setting was impressive but nothing happened.
What he has to say, therefore, concerns itself almost entirely with
setting:

> An autumnal blast, sometimes clear, sometimes driving
> mist before it, swept along the troubled billows of the lake,
> which it occasionally concealed, and by fits disclosed. The
> waves rushed in wild disorder on the shore, and covered with
> foam the steep pile of rocks, which, rising from the sea in
> forms something resembling the human figure, have obtained
> the name of Macleod's Maidens, and, in such a night, seemed
> no bad representatives of the Norwegian goddesses, called
> Choosers of the Slain or Riders of the Storm. [He goes on to
> mention the ancient battery of cannon on the platform beneath
> his window, the view of the two flat-topped mountains called
> Macleod's Dining Tables, and the noise of the cascade known
> as Rorie More's Nurse.][18]

This is impossible, even granting that one could discern features
of the landscape so clearly at twelve o'clock of a misty night.
Macleod's Maidens are not visible at Dunvegan; they stand eight
miles away as the crow flies on the southern shore of Duirinish;
that is, on the other side of the Dining Tables. Scott did not
actually see them until the day *after* his experience of the haunted
chamber. His memory has here done just what his imagination
would have done if he had been constructing a fiction: that is, has
blended a collection of impressive objects and given something
more striking and romantic than actual fact. Scott himself once
described his habit of modifying everything that went through
his brain in a phrase that will serve as a sort of witty summary of
the nature of his constructions, whether deliberate or unconscious:
[Clerk] is continually saying that I change his stories, whereas in
fact I only put a cocked hat on their heads, and stick a cane into
their hands – to make them fit for going into company."[19]

Consider a group of recollections that are of particular importance for a comparative study of Scott and Boswell: the Boswellian

[18] Quoted by Lockhart in *Memoirs*, Vol. 4, p. 306, Ch. 31.
[19] *Op. cit.* Vol. 1, p. 276, Ch. 7.

anecdotes which Scott wrote for Croker's edition of the *Life of Johnson*. Here we have Scott in Boswell's own field. It is true that we cannot be entirely certain of the extent of his variations, for he gives an oral source for one of the stories and none at all for the others. An analysis of two of them, however, should convince any one that even if he had had his stories from Boswell himself, they would have come back riddled with "circumstantial inaccuracy".[20]

In the much-quoted note on the Douglas Cause Scott represents Boswell ("I know not on what authority") as having "headed the mob which broke the windows of some of the judges, and of Lord Auchinleck, his father, in particular".[21] I think I can name his authority: it was his friend John Ramsay of Ochtertyre, one of the originals of Jonathan Oldbuck. Ramsay left voluminous manuscript collections, of which a substantial portion has since been published under the title *Scotland and Scotsmen in the Eighteenth Century*. Scott's Boswellian anecdotes may derive from Ramsay's conversation, but I think it more likely that they go back to the manuscript.[22] There, in a chapter of reminiscences of Lord Auchinleck, Ramsay gives an account of the window-breaking which is circumstantial and plausible. But of course it does not say that Boswell broke his father's windows, for the good reason that Lord Auchinleck, who had voted *for* Douglas, was one of the heroes of that riotous evening. It was the windows of the Lord President and the other judges who had voted *against* Douglas that suffered. What Ramsay had written was that Boswell "headed the mob which broke the judges' windows, and insulted them in the most licentious manner".[23] Scott, knowing that Lord Auchinleck

---

[20] I omit consideration of the account (which he ascribes to Professor John Miller) of an altercation between Johnson and Adam Smith at Glasgow in Oct. 1773. Croker himself reprobated his anecdote, though not until after Scott's death. See *Life*, Vol. 5, p. 369 n. 5.

[21] *The Life of Johnson . . . by James Boswell*, ed. J. W. Croker, 1831, Vol. 3, 48 n.

[22] See the statement made by Dr Gleig, an acquaintance, to Ramsay's editor: "The MSS. which you are preparing for the press had been his recreation for years, and he never failed to read a portion of them to every visitor whom he could prevail upon to listen" (*Scotland and Scotsmen*, Vol. 1, p. xix).

[23] *Ibid*, p. 173.

was one of the Fifteen, and knowing furthermore that he was not on the best terms with his son, constructed a memory which was more dramatic than actual fact. This is a clear case of the cocked hat.

The longest and most famous notes, besides giving a good deal of miscellaneous information about Lord Auchinleck, record two of his remarks. The first expresses Lord Auchinleck's low opinion of Boswell's Corsican adventures and of Johnson: "There's nae hope for Jamie, mon. Jamie is gaen clean gyte. – What do you think, mon? He's done wi' Paoli – he's off wi' the land-louping scoundrel of a Corsican; and whose tail do you think he has pinned himself to now, mon? A *dominie*, mon – an auld dominie; he keeped a schule, and cau'd it an acaadamy." The second describes confidently the altercation at Auchinleck between Johnson and Lord Auchinleck which Boswell had suppressed. It seems that Johnson asked Lord Auchinleck what good Cromwell had ever done to his country, and the old judge replied, "God, doctor! he gart kings ken that they had a *lith* in their necks."[24]

When we read in Ramsay that Lord Auchinleck was offended with Boswell for going to Corsica, and that in 1774 he told Ramsay "with more warmth than common, that the great Dr Johnson . . . was just a *dominie*, and the worst-bred dominie he had ever seen", we need have little doubt that we have found the source of all that is genuine in the first of these famous speeches. But Ramsay's manuscript furnishes nothing that could have served as the kernel of the second. "Very different accounts," he says, "were given of their famous altercation at Auchinleck. All that could be collected was that the disputants were equally hot and bigoted."[25] Here, I think, Dr G. B. Hill has given us the needed clue. "Lord Auchinleck's famous saying had been anticipated by Quin, who . . . had said that 'on a thirtieth of January every king in Europe would rise with a crick in his neck'."[26] Anticipated indeed! My firm conviction is that Scott's account rests on nothing whatever except his memory of Boswell's own text and that anecdote about Quin. I do not mean that he consciously invented it. Knowing

[24] *The Life of Johnson* . . . *by James Boswell*, ed. J. W. Croker, 1831, Vol. 3, pp. 78–9 n.

[25] John Ramsay, *op. cit.* (see p. 182, n. 2), Vol. 1, 172 n. 2, 175–6, 176 n.

[25] *Life*, Vol. 5 p. 383 n.

from Boswell that the altercation concerned Cromwell and Charles I, his mind played with the problem, searching for something appropriate. Sooner or later Quin's remark came into his consciousness, was reshaped slightly, and fitted in. The result was a brilliant historical fiction which, after telling it once or twice, he remembered as a fact.[27]

Yet I should not like to give the impression that Scott never remembered accurately. It has seemed to me that I could distinguish areas in which the unconscious creative impulse was very active, and others in which it was relatively inhibited. Scott always shows the greatest licence in dealing with chronology, and with the names and traits of historical personages, but he cleaves to what he believes to be literal fact in costume, architecture, and topography. Contrast, for example, the mass of literal detail of costume and architecture in *Marmion* with the melodrama of the plot; or the extraordinary manipulations of chronology and identity in *Kenilworth* with the insistence that the reader follow the story with an actual ground-plan of the castle in his hand. This cleavage is exactly what one would expect, but we can discuss it better after a somewhat general consideration of the relations of perceiving, remembering, and imagining.

Perceiving is not a simple mechanical process operating similarly in two minds faced with an identical situation.[28] It is shot through with imagining, with valuing, even with judging. "It is directed by interest and by feeling, and may be dominated by certain crucial features of the objects and scenes dealt with." That is, some features of the situation will stand out over the others, and will form a sort of nucleus about which the rest of the detail will shape itself. Temperament, interests, and attitudes often determine what will be perceived. And a great part of what is believed to be perceived is in fact inferred. Social conventions may affect powerfully not merely what one imagines but even what one perceives.

[27] The practice of taking a telling speech or phrase from one context and fitting it into another is so characteristic of Scott's method in the novels that it hardly needs illustration. It was this trait of Scott's, no doubt, which caused Hazlitt, somewhat unjustly, to say that where Shakespeare *created*, Scott *compiled*.

[28] The psychological theory in what follows is from F. C. Bartlett, *Remembering, A Study in Experimental and Social Psychology*, Cambridge, 1932, especially pp. 31-3.

A shift of sensibility such as that which separates Pope from Wordsworth does not mean merely a different taste in poetry; it means ultimately the perception of a different world.

At the basic level of perception Scott and Boswell show less difference than one would have expected. Scott still perceived the world with eighteenth-century eyes. But we infer that he must have had a double vision: side by side with the world which he would have agreed with Boswell in calling the "real" world was another which he would probably have called the world of romance. The romantic vision did not completely cover the field of the "real" world; there were some features (features corresponding to Scott's strong antiquarian and collecting interests) which appear in only one mode. Scott, like Byron, held the romantic mode to be "a factitious state";[29] he published romances because they amused people and made him money, but he made no claim to be considered a seer or a teacher.

We commonly think of the brain as a storehouse, and memory as the setting forth of things actually stored. Every specific event, on this assumption, makes a literal, physical trace in the substance of the brain, which recollection somehow gets at and re-excites. If recollection cannot get at the trace, we say a person has "forgotten". If what is presented as recall is demonstrably at variance with historical fact, we say that the person has "imagined" it.

So long as it was believed that Boswell was a stenographer who took down conversations verbatim on the spot, there was no great difficulty in accepting his records for what they purported to be. But when the recovery of his materials made clear in the most unequivocal manner that his first or basic notations were generally hints or clues, his claim to have remembered so amply and with such detail naturally roused incredulity. Some scholars have believed that a good part of the *Life of Johnson* is not "memory" but "imagination". The notes or journal, it is said, furnished him with an outline which he filled in much as a playwright expands a scenario. The problem of defining Boswell's use of imagination is the most difficult and delicate of this entire study. I have no doubt that the pages of the *Life are* an imaginative reconstruction, but I wish to differentiate his controlled use of imagination from that free imaginative play that results in fiction. I wish, in short,

[29] *Don Juan*, Vol. 4, p. xix.

to maintain that a man can use his imagination and yet remember "accurately".

What is not realised, I think, by those who have written about Boswell's memory is that certain distinguished modern students of psychology believe that imagination inevitably plays a part in *all* remembering, just as it does in all perceiving. The theory of literal traces in the brain is now sharply attacked. Recollection, according to F. C. Bartlett, "is an imaginative reconstruction, or construction, built out of the relation of our attitude towards a whole active mass of organized past reactions or experience, and to a little outstanding detail which commonly appears in image or in language form". The outstanding detail gains its prominence through a valuation of items, depending upon the person's interests. Memories do not come out of a storehouse; they are *constructed* as we need them, and in most cases they do not correspond at all closely to historical fact.[30] But granted an overwhelming *interest* in a certain kind of details, and granted the right kind of "organised setting", the imaginative construct would reproduce history. Boswell himself said that at first he had some difficulty in recalling Johnson's conversation, but that after he got himself "strongly impregnated with the Johnsonian aether" he could retain and recollect it "with more facility and exactness".[31] This is only a witty and literary way of putting Bartlett's theory. Granted the purity of the "Johnsonian aether", the imaginative reconstruction could be trusted to be not merely appropriate but as close to what Johnson really said as any condensed or selective report could be. Details in which Boswell was strongly interested would be sharply and fully perceived, and would furnish the nucleus for his recollection. Through his method of notation this detail, by being early verbalised, would become even more strongly anchored, so that the imaginative reconstruction would operate within an area which was at once rich in material and restricted in scope. The principal difference between recall and constructive imagination is that in recall one specially organised mass remains central, while in constructive imagination no particular scheme is central, and there is freer range from interest to interest. Boswell's detail kept him anchored to his central setting and kept his

[30] *Op. cit.* (see p. 184, n. 1), pp. 213–14.
[31] *Life*, vol. 1, p. 421, 1 July 1763.

imagination to the limits within which "accurate" reconstruction is possible. The vividness of his writing shows that imagination has been at work, while his circumstantial accuracy shows how scrupulously he has limited its operation.

For Boswell was one of those extremely rare persons who have a conscience about anecdotes and will discard the results of constructive imagination when reference to an earlier recording shows that the story has developed into something better than the truth. His awareness of the progressive improvement of stories is constant, and his honesty in trying always to get back to unimproved versions is remarkable.[32] Compare him with his rival Lockhart – I use the word deliberately, for I am not sure sometimes that I do not *like* Lockhart's book better than Boswell's. Pick out a succession of passages from Lockhart that you want to read aloud to people: the run keg of brandy and the young minister ruefully closing the Bible; the moving hand in the candlelight piling up the pages of *Waverley*; the sentimental pig; the furious letter about Blackwood's proposed alterations of *The Black Dwarf*; the deathbed[33] – they are all wonderful and you cannot trust any of them. You know that if you investigate them, they will evaporate. It will turn out that there is some truth in them, but that things didn't "really" happen that way. Circumstantial detail has been altered for striking effect. But when you read one of the Johnsonian conversations which Boswell gives on his own authority, you know that so far as any human testimony can be trusted, that can.

Scott felt a clear distinction between the products of what I have called average or literal perception and those of constructive imagination, and derived the keenest pleasure from the juxtaposition of the two. No other English author, I should suppose, has ever taken such delight in exposing his *sources*: here are the real facts, here is what I made of them. Wordsworth furnishes a strong contrast. *The White Doe of Rylstone* is based upon matter precisely like that which Scott used in *The Lay of the Last Minstrel*, and, if it

[32] See the testimony of Dugald Stewart, quoted in G. B. Hill, *Johnsonian Miscellanies*, Vol. 2, p.425. For a typical example from Boswell himself, see *Life*, Vol. 5, 339 n. 5.

[33] *Memoirs*, Vol. 1, pp. 270–1, Ch. 7; 4, pp. 171–3, Ch. 27; 6, pp, 239–42, Ch. 49; 5, pp. 157–9, Ch. 37; 10, pp. 217–18, Ch. 83.

had been written by Scott, would have been accompanied by voluminous antiquarian notes, showing in detail just how the original history had been cooked. Wordsworth was rather angry when Scott offered to send him a batch of this material while he was at work on the *Doe*: he did not wish his conception of the poem to be affected by it, and he certainly did not intend to print it.[34] But Scott, having presented a romance, seems almost to feel under obligation to deflate it by parallel columns of history. It is a paradox something like Byron's alternations of romance and satire in *Don Juan*.

But we cannot say "history" and leave it at that. Scott was more a child of the new sensibility than he himself realised. He was not aware of the fact that much of the matter in his parallel columns was coming out of his memory, and that his memory had already romanticised it strongly. No man wrote more pleasant or vivid notes than Scott, and for a good reason: they were often half fiction. In fact, to a mature reader the professed fictions often suffer by comparison with the unacknowledged ones. I have never been able to free myself from a feeling that the Introduction to *The Bride of Lammermoor* steals the show.

How far, one asks in conclusion, dare one go in generalising from these observations? Have we anything more than a description of two highly unrepresentative individuals? Is Scott's imaginative memory any different from that of the anecdotist of any period? And was not Boswell so much *sui generis* that it would be futile to take him as typical of anything?

The objection as concerns Boswell seems the stronger. The mental organism with which he was endowed was certainly abnormal. And no other writer of whom we have record seems to have followed his peculiar method of journalising or to have submitted his memory to so much deliberate self-discipline. As Mr Bronson has pointed out, there are the youthful exercises in mimicry;[35] there are the reiterated memoranda to himself urging restraint and reasonableness; there are the regular notations in his collection of anecdotes, "I was present"; finally there is the

[34] Wordsworth to Scott, 84 May 1808 (*The Letters of William and Dorothy Wordsworth: The Middle Years,* ed. E. de Selincourt, Vol. 1, p. 458 e).

[35] B. H. Bronson, *Johnson and Boswell,* University of California Publications in English, Vol. 3, pp. 404-5.

s

life-long discipline of the journal, in some respects the most ambitious ever undertaken. Of what other journalist can it be said that he sat up four entire nights in one week recollecting and writing in his journal what he thought worthy of preservation?[36] If any one would train himself by the Boswellian system, would take notes persistently and consult them scrupulously, he would certainly astonish himself and his friends by the richness and accuracy of his circumstantial recall.

Yet if we indulge for a moment in a game of speculation, I think we shall agree that it would be most remarkable to find a man pursuing such discipline in the nineteenth century but not at all surprising to find one doing it in the eighteenth. All the devices leading to circumstantial memory: the note-taking, the journalising, the review and re-review, are as much symptoms as causes. People then were generally *interested* in personal detail. Boswell is the extreme example, but he fits into his time. There was tremendous social pressure on the individual mind to perceive in the average mode and to eschew free imagination in recall. Any scholar who has attacked biographical problems in both centuries knows how different in quality the basic materials for the two periods are. It is hardly too much to say that, given time enough, one can find the answer to any factual question concerning an eighteenth century author. The records, both manuscript and printed are abundant and trustworthy. Men and women then wrote informative letters and kept detailed journals. Newspapers and magazine accounts were factual, and though they swarmed with faked news, the genuine and the spurious were not blended. People really feared the dangerous prevalence of the imagination. In the nineteenth century, biographical material is often scanty, sometimes voluminous to the point of embarrassment, and never trustworthy. If Byron had lived fifty years earlier, is it conceivable that we should be in doubt as to the nature of his deformity, even as to which of his feet was deformed? Could an author of the prominence of Shelley present so many unsolved biographical riddles if he had been a contemporary of Gray? The power to admire the average, the norm, the area of sanity in human experience; the power to hold this by a kind of memory in which the

[36] *Life,* Vol. 1, p. 461, 30 July 1763. "An exertion", he continues, "which during the first part of my acquaintance with Johnson, I frequently made."

imagination was made to work within the limits of literal circumstances; finally, the power to express this in words – these things were given Boswell by his time. In many respects wildly romantic, he was in his re-creation of the past the fullest expression of the Age of Reason.

The characteristic mode of the Romantic period is strongly imaginative recall: Wordsworth's *Prelude*. There is no longer powerful social pressure in favour of average perception and "accurate" memory. It becomes not merely permissible but praiseworthy to mingle a larger amount of inference in perception, as of imagination in recall. "Facts" of life become less important than what is conceived to be their "real" meaning.

In this Scott is a bridge figure, much less advanced in his sensibility than Wordsworth, but with enough of the new temper to understand and like the people on both sides of him. While his perception is rooted firmly in the eighteenth century, his imagination in the mode of fiction has freed itself completely from the restrictions which that century imposed. But he does not, like the more advanced Romantics, believe in the creative imagination as revelatory of truth. Fiction, for him, is make-believe and amusement. Hence, even in his most magnificent writing, he seldom escapes a tone of humorous self-exposure. It was in the mode of memory, where the workings of the imagination were unconscious, that his mind was most completely at one with itself.

SELECT BIBLIOGRAPHY

I. BIBLIOGRAPHIES

See *The Year's Work in English Studies*; the *Subject Index to Periodicals* (up to 1962); the *Annual Bibliography of English Language and Literature*; *MLA International Bibliography of Books and Articles in the Modern Languages and Literatures*; and the *British Humanities Index*. Also the following:

The Cambridge Bibliography of English Literature, 5 vols. Cambridge (University Press) 1940–57. (See vols. III, 369 ff; v, pp. 616–17.)

CORSON, J. C. *A Bibliography of Sir Walter Scott. A Classified and Annotated List of Books and Articles Relating to his Life and Works*, 1797–1940. Edinburgh (Oliver & Boyd) 1943.

JACK, I. "Sir Walter Scott: A Select Bibliography" in *Sir Walter Scott*, Writers and Their Work 103. London (Longmans Green) 1958.

———Select Bibliography in *English Literature 1815–1832*. Oxford (Clarendon Press) 1963. (See pp. 603–9.)

RENWICK, W. L. Select Bibliography in *English Literature 1789–1815*. Oxford (Clarendon Press) 1963. (See pp. 282–3.)

RUFF, W. A. "Bibliography of the Poetical Works" in *Transactions of the Edinburgh Bibliographical Society*, I (1937–8).

WORTHINGTON, G. *Bibliography of the Waverley Novels*. London (Constable) 1931.

II. TEXTS

The best edition of Scott's poems and novels is the Dryburgh Edition, London (A. & C. Black Ltd) 1892–4. It consists of *Poetical Works*, 2 vols, ed. A. Lang, 1895; and *Waverley Novels*, 25 vols, 1892–4. Separate works by Scott, referred to in this volume are included in *Quarterly Review* and *Foreign Quarterly Review*. Other works include:

The Journal of Sir Walter Scott, eds. J. G. Tait and W. M. Parker, 3 vols. Edinburgh (Oliver & Boyd) 1939–46; 1 vol., 1950.

Letters on Demonology and Witchcraft. London, 1830.

The Letters of Sir Walter Scott, eds., H. J. C. Grierson, *et al*, 12 vols. London (Constable) 1932–7.

The Lives of the Novelists, 1821–4), Everyman Edition. Introduction by George Saintsbury. London (J. M. Dent) 1910; New York (E. P. Dutton).

The Minstrelsy of the Scottish Border, ed. T. F. Henderson, 4 vols. Edinburgh (William Blackwood & Sons) 1902; reprinted 1932. Ed. T. Henderson. London (G. G. Harrap) 1931.

Miscellaneous Prose Works, 3 vols. Edinburgh, 1848.

Miscellaneous Prose Works, 28 vols. Edinburgh and London, 1834–6.

Poems and Plays, Everyman Edition, 2 vols. London (Dent) 1905.

Poetical Works, ed. J. Logie Robertson. London (Oxford, complete edition: Henry Frowde.) 1904.

III. CRITICISM

a. *Articles*

BATHO, E. C. "Scott as Medievalist", in *Sir Walter Scott Today*, ed. H. J. C. Grierson. London (Constable) 1932.

BIGGINS, D. *"Measure for Measure* and *The Heart of Midlothian"*, in *Études Anglaises*, XIV (1961), pp. 193–205.

BOATRIGHT, M. C. "Demonology in the Novels of Sir Walter Scott", in *University of Texas Bulletin*, Studies in English, No. 14 (1934).

BRANDL, A. "Walter Scott über sein dichterisches Schaffen", in *Sitzungsberichte der Preussischen Akademie der Wissenschaften*, XXX (1925), pp. 356–64.

BUSHNELL, N. S. "Walter Scott's Advent as Novelist of Manners", in *Studies in Scottish Literature*, I (1963), pp. 15–34.

CECIL, D. "Sir Walter Scott", in *Atlantic Monthly*, CL (1932), pp. 277–87, 485–94.

CRAIG, D. "*The Heart of Midlothian*: its Religious Basis", in *Essays in Criticism*, VIII (1958), pp. 217–25.

DAICHES, D. "Scott's Redgauntlet", in *From Jane Austen to Joseph Conrad. Essays Collected in Memory of James T. Hillhouse*, eds. R. C. Rathburn and M. Steinmann, Jr., Minneapolis (University of Minnesota Press) 1958, pp. 46–59.

DAVIE, D. "The Poetry of Sir Walter Scott", in *Proceedings of the British Academy*, XLVII (1961) pp. 60–75.

DEVLIN, D. D. "Scott and *Redgauntlet*", in *Review of English Literature*, IV (1963), pp. 91–103.

DOBIE, M. R. "The Development of Scott's Minstrelsy", in *Transactions of the Edinburgh Bibliographical Society*, II (Pt. I, 1940), pp. 65–87.

ERSKINE, JOHN. "The Waverley Novels", in *The Delight of Great Books*. London (Eveleigh, Nash and Grayson) 1928.

FISHER, P. F. "Providence, Fate and the Historical Imagination in Scott's *The Heart of Midlothian*", in *Nineteenth Century Fiction*, X (1955), pp. 99–114.

GORDON, R. C. "*The Bride of Lammermoor*: a Novel of Tory Pessimism", in *Nineteenth Century Fiction*, XII (1957), pp. 110–24.

GORDON, R. K. "Scott's Prose", in *Transactions of the Royal Society of Canada*, XLV (1951), pp. 13–18.

GORDON, S. STEWART. "Waverley and the 'Unified Design' ", in *English Literary History*, XLVIII (1951), pp. 107–22.

GRIERSON, SIR HERBERT. "History and the Novel", in *Sir Walter Scott Lectures 1940–8*, ed. W. L. Renwick, Edinburgh (University Press) 1950.

HENDERSON, T. F. "The Vernacular of the Waverley Novels", in *Glasgow Herald* (5 Sept. 1907), p. 10.

LYNSKEY, W. "The Drama of the Elect and Reprobate in Scott's *Heart of Midlothian*", in *Boston University Studies in English*, IV (1960), pp. 39–48.

MAYHEAD, R. "*The Heart of Midlothian*: Scott as Artist", in *Essays in Criticism*, VI (1956), pp. 266–77.

MAYO, R. D. "The Chronology of the Waverley Novels", in *Publications of the Modern Language Association of America*, LXIII (1948), pp. 935–49.

MONTGOMERIE, W. "The Twa Corbies", in *Review of English Studies*, n.s. (1955), pp. 227–32.

———"Sir Walter Scott as Ballad Editor", in *Review of English Studies*, n.s. (1956), pp. 158–63.

NOYES, A. "Scott's Poetry", in *Quarterly Review*, CCXC (1952), pp. 211–15.

OGILVIE, R. M. "Sir Walter Scott and Livy", in *The Listener* (3 Nov. 1960), pp. 792–5.

OLIVER, J. W. "Scottish Poetry in the Earlier Nineteenth Century", in *Scottish Poetry: A Critical Survey*, ed. J. Kinsley. London (Cassell) 1955, pp. 212–30.

PARSONS, C. O. "The Dalrymple Legend in *The Bride of Lammermoor*", in *Review of English Studies*, XIX (1943) pp. 51–8.

PITTOCK, J. "The Critical Forum", in *Essays in Criticism*, VII (1957), pp. 477–9.

RALEIGH, J. H. "What Scott Meant to the Victorians", in *Victorian Studies*, VII, 1 (1963).

ROBERTS, P. "Scott's Contribution to English Vocabulary", in *Publications of the Modern Language Association*, LXVIII (March 1953), pp. 189–210.

SMITH, D. NICHOL. "The Poetry of Sir Walter Scott", in *University of Edinburgh Journal*, XV (1949–51), pp. 63–80.

STEPHEN, LESLIE. "Some Words about Sir Walter Scott", in *Hours in a Library* (First Series). New York, 1875.

TILLYARD, E. M. W. "Scott's Linguistic Vagaries", in *Études Anglaises*, XI (1958) 112–18. Also in *Essays Literary and Educational*. London (Chatto and Windus) 1962, pp. 99–107.

WILSON, W. E. "The Making of the Minstrelsy", in *Cornhill Magazine*, n.s., CXLVI (July-December 1932), pp. 266-83.

YOUNG, G. M. "Scott and the Historians", in *Sir Walter Scott Lecture*: 1940-8, ed. W. L. Renwick. Edinburgh (University Press) 1950.

b. *Books*

BALL, M. *Sir Walter Scott as a Critic of Literature*. New York (Columbia University Press) 1927.

BATHO, E. C. *The Ettrick Shepherd*. Cambridge (University Press) 1927.

BOS, K. *Religious Creeds . . . in Sir Walter Scott's Works . . .* Amsterdam (H. J. Paris) 1932.

BUCHAN, JOHN. *Sir Walter Scott*. London (Cassell) 1932.

CECIL, D. *Sir Walter Scott*. London (Constable) 1933.

CROCKETT, W. S. *The Scott Originals*. London and Edinburgh (Foulis) 1912.

DAVIE, D. *The Heyday of Sir Walter Scott*. London (Routledge and Kegan Paul) 1961.

ELLIOTT, W. F. *Further Essays on Border Ballads*. Edinburgh (Andrew Elliot) 1910.

FISKE, C. F. *Epic Suggestion in the Imagery of the Waverley Novels*. New Haven, Conn. (Yale University Press) 1940.

GRIERSON, H. J. C. *Sir Walter Scott, Bart*. London (Constable) 1938.

GRIEVE, C. M. ("Hugh MacDiarmid"). *Lucky Poet*, London (Methuen) 1943.

HART, FRANCIS R. *Scott's Novels, The Plotting of Historical Survival*. Charlottesville (University of Virginia Press) 1966.

HILLHOUSE, J. T. *The Waverley Novels and their Critics*. Minneapolis (University of Minnesota Press) 1936.

LANG, A. *Sir Walter Scott and the Border Minstrelsy*. London (Longmans) 1910.

LOCKHART, J. G. *The Life of Sir Walter Scott*, 10 vols. (2nd edn.) Edinburgh 1839.

MUIR, E. *Scott and Scotland*. London (Routledge) 1936.

PARSONS, C. O. *Witchcraft and Demonology in Scott's Fiction*. Edinburgh and London (Oliver & Boyd) 1964.

PARTINGTON, W. *The Private Letter-Books of Sir Walter Scott*. London (Hodder and Stoughton) 1930.

POPE-HENNESSY, U. *The Laird of Abbotsford*. London (Putnam) 1932.

———*Sir Walter Scott*. London (Home and Van Thal) 1948.

SCOTT, A. *The Story of Sir Walter Scott's First Love.* Edinburgh, 1896.

Sir Walter Scott Today, ed. H. J. C. Grierson. London (Constable) 1932.

STEIGER, OTTO. *Die Verwendung des schottischen Dialekts in Walter Scotte Romanen.* (Doktor-dissertation Giessen.) Darmstadt, 1913.

TWEEDSMUIR, BARON. *See* BUCHAN, JOHN.

VERRALL, A. W. Translation of Scott in *Quarterly* (July 1910) and in *Cambridge Compositions.* Cambridge (University Press) 1904.

Sir Walter Scott Lectures 1940–8, ed. W. L. Renwick. Edinburgh (University Press) 1950.

WELSH, A. *The Hero of the Waverley Novels.* New Haven, Conn. (Yale University Press) 1963.

IV. OTHER RELEVANT WORKS

ADOLPHUS, J. L. *Letters to Richard Heber, Esq.* (2nd edn.). London, 1821.

ALLEN, WALTER. *The English Novel.* London (Phoenix House) 1954.

From Anne to Victoria, ed. B. Dobrée. London (Cassell) 1937.

BAKER, E. A. *The History of the English Novel,* 10 vols. London (H. & F. Witherby) 1924–39.

BARTLETT, F. C. *Remembering, a Study in Experimental and Social Psychology.* Cambridge (University Press) 1952.

From Blake to Byron, ed. B. Ford. Harmondsworth (Penguin) 1957.

BOSWELL, JAMES. *The Private Papers of James Boswell from Malahide Castle, in the Collection of Lt. Colonel Ralph Heyward Isham,* eds. Geoffrey Scott and F. A. Pottle, 18 vols. Privately printed, 1928–34.

Boswell's Life of Johnson, ed. G. B. Hill and revised by L. F. Powell, 6 vols. Oxford (Clarendon Press) 1950.

BOWRA, C. M. *The Romantic Imagination.* London (Oxford University Press) 1950.

BRADLEY, A. C. *Oxford Lectures on Poetry.* London (Macmillan) 1909.

BRONSON, B. H. *Johnson and Boswell.* Berkeley and Los Angeles (University of California Publications in English), Vol. 3, No. 9.

Works of Robert Burns, ed. J. Currie, 4 vols. Liverpool, 1800.

BUTTERFIELD, H. *The Historical Novel.* Cambridge (University Press) 1924.

CARLYLE, T. *Critical and Miscellaneous Essays,* 7 vols. London, 1888.

CHILD, F. J. *The English and Scottish Popular Ballads.* London, 1882–98; New York (Houghton, Miflin) 1904, reprinted 1957, 5 vols. as 3.

COCKBURN, H. *Memorials of his Time.* Edinburgh, 1856.

COLERIDGE, S. T. *Biographia Epistolaris,* ed. A. Turnbull, 2 vols. London (G. Bell & Sons) 1911.

COLERIDGE, S. T. *Coleridge's Miscellaneous Criticism*, ed. T. M. Raysor. London (Constable) 1936.

COLLINGWOOD, R. G. *The Idea of History*. Oxford (Clarendon Press) 1946.

CRAIG, D. *Scottish Literature and the Scottish People, 1680–1830*. London (Chatto and Windus) 1961.

CROCE, B. *European Literature in the Nineteenth Century*, tr. D. Ainslie. London (Chapman and Hall) 1924.

CROSS, W. L. *The Development of the English Novel*. New York 1899.

DAICHES, D. *A Critical History of English Literature*, 2 vols. London (Secker and Warburg) 1960.

DE QUINCEY, T. *Collected Works*, ed. D. Masson, 14 vols. London 1888–90.

EDGAR, PELHAM. *The Art of the Novel*. New York (Macmillan) 1933.

ELTON, O. *Survey of English Literature, 1780–1830*, 2 vols. London (Edward Arnold) 1912.

The English Romantic Poets and Essayists: A Review of Research and Criticism, ed. Carolyn Washburn Houtchens and Lawrence Huston Houtchens, New York (Modern Language Association) 1957.

English and Scottish Popular Ballads, eds. H. C. Sargent and G. L. Kittredge. Boston and London (Houghton, Miflin) 1904.

FORSTER, E. M. *Aspects of the Novel*. London (Edward Arnold) 1927; Harmondsworth (Penguin) 1962.

FOX, R. *The Novel and the People*. London (Laurence and Wishart) 1937; reprinted London, 1948.

FRYE, N. *Anatomy of Criticism*. Princeton, N.J. (University Press) 1957.

GALT, JOHN. *Ringan Gilhaize*. Edinburgh, 1823.

HAZLITT, W. *Collected Works*, ed. P. P. Howe, 21 vols. London and Toronto (Dent) 1930–4.   . .

HENN, T. R. *The Apple and the Spectroscope*. London (Methuen) 1951.

HILL, G. B. *Johnsonian Miscellanies*, 2 vols. Oxford, 1897; new edition, London (Constable) 1966.

HODGART, M. J. C. *The Ballads*. London (Hutchinson) 1950.

JEBB, R. C. *Introduction to Homer*. Glasgow 1887.

JEFFREY, F. *Contributions to the Edinburgh Review,* 3 vols. London 1844 (1 vol, 1850).

JOHNSON, SAMUEL. *A Journey to the Western Islands of Scotland* (1775), ed. R. W. Chapman. London (Oxford University Press) 1930.
——*The Rambler*, No. 151.

KETTLE, A. *Introduction to the English Novel*, 2 vols. London (Hutchinson) 1953.

KIRK, R. *The Conservative Mind.* London (Faber) 1954.

KROEBER, K. *Romantic Narrative Art.* Madison (University of Wisconsin Press) 1960.

The Life of Johnson by James Boswell, ed. J. W. Croker, London, 1831.

LUBBOCK, PERCY. *The Craft of Fiction.* London (Jonathan Cape) 1921.

LUKÁCS, G. *Studies in European Realism (c.* 1938), tr. E. Bone. London (Merlin Press) 1950.

MATHIESON, WILLIE. MSS. in School of Scottish Studies Archives, University of Edinburgh.

MILES, J. *Eras and Modes in English Poetry.* Berkeley and Los Angeles (University of California Press) 1957.

MONTGOMERIE, W. *Bibliography of the Scottish Ballad Manuscripts 1730–1825.* Unpublished Ph.D. thesis, Edinburgh 1954.

MUIR, E. *The Structure of the Novel.* London (Hogarth Press) 1928.

NEFF, E. *The Poetry of History.* New York (Columbia University Press) 1947.

PATERSON, JAMES. *History of the Counties of Ayr and Wigton.* Edinburgh 1863.

PRITCHETT, V. S. *The Living Novel.* London (Chatto and Windus) 1946.

RAMSAY, J. *Scotland and Scotsmen in the 18th Century,* Edinburgh, 1888.

SENIOR, N. W. *Essays in Fiction.* London 1864.

SHARPE, C. K. *Letters,* ed. A. Allardyce, 2 vols. Edinburgh 1888.

STEVENSON, R. L. *Memories and Portraits,* Pentland Edition. London (Cassell) 1907.

——*Letters,* Tusitala Edition. London (Heinemann) 1924.

TAVE, STUART M. *The Amiable Humorist. A Study in the Comic Theory and Criticism of the Eighteenth and Early Nineteenth Centuries.* Chicago (University Press) 1960.

TILLYARD, E. M. W. *The Epic Strain in the English Novel.* London (Chatto and Windus) 1934.

VAN GHENT, D. *The English Novel.* New York (Rinehart) 1956.

Westminster Review, April 1829.

WITTIG, K. *The Scottish Tradition in Literature.* Edinburgh & London (Oliver & Boyd) 1958.

WORDSWORTH, W. *The Letters of William and Dorothy Wordsworth,* ed. E. de Selincourt. Oxford (Clarendon Press) 1935.

INDEX

Abbotsford, 13, 14, 28, 220, 232.
Abercorn, Lady, 5.
Adelchi, 129.
Adolphus, J. L., 185 *note*, 192 *note*.
Ahnen, 124.
Alice, "old", 186, 200, 204.
Argyle, Duke of, 122, 126, 127, 223
Ashton, Henry, 203, 204.
Ashton, Lady, 198, 204.
Ashton, Lucy, 197–204.
Ashton, Sir William, 197–9, 201, 204.
Auchinleck, Lord, 245, 246.
Avenel, Baron of, 217.

Baker, E. A., 185 *note*.
Balderstone, Caleb, 22, 45, 87, 88, 197, 198.
Baliol, Mrs Bethune, 223.
Ball, M., 11 *note*.
Ballantyne, James, 10, 13.
Ballantyne, John, 10, 11, 13, 208.
Balzac, 93, 97, 99, 102, 105–8, 121.
Barbour, 218, 219.
Bartlett, F. C., 247 *note*, 249.
Belinski, 98, 115
Bellenden, Edith, 159, 191, 212.
Bellenden, Lady, 226.
Bellenden, Major, 40.
Belsches, Williamina, 5, 6, 14.
Beresford, Mr, Mrs, and Miss, 239 *note*, 240.
Berners, 216, 219.
Bertram, Godfrey, 174, 178, 179.
Bertram, Harry, 189.
Bertram, Lucy, 177.
Biographia Literaria, 22.
Birrenswork, Herries of, 53.
Bittlebrains, Lord, 186.
Blake, William, 8.
Bleak House, 70, 71, 167.
Blenkensop, Lady, 186.
Blind Harry, *see* Harry, Blind.
Boatright, M. C., 186 *note*, 194, 194 *note*.
Bonnie Dundee, *see* Claverhouse.
Bos, K., 185 *note*.
Boswell, Alexander, 231 *note*.
Boswell, James, 230–53.

Bothwell, 40.
Bradwardine, Baron, 22, 25, 31, 32, 38, 62, 90, 91, 137, 206.
Bradwardine, Rose, 26, 33, 62, 78, 202.
Branksome, Margaret of, 6.
Bronson, B. H., 251.
Brown, 175, 177, 178.
Bruce, 236.
Bucklaw, 199, 204.
Bürger, 10.
Burgundy, Duke of, 113.
Burke, Edmund, 18, 56.
Burley, Balfour of, 40, 41, 47, 51, 102, 104, 172, 191, 194.
Burney, Fanny, 213.
Burnes, William, 4.
Burns, Robert, 4.
Burt, Edward, 219, 227.
Butler (friend of Jeanie Deans), 160.
Butterfield, H., 75 *note*.
Byron, Lord, 11, 96, 139, 248, 251.

Carlyle, Thomas, 72, 72 *note*, 101, 240.
Campbell, Duncan, 225.
Campbell, General, 48, 77, 183.
Carpenter, Charlotte, 5, 6.
Caxon (wig-maker), 39, 68.
Caxton, 130.
Cedric (Saxon Nobleman), 102, 115.
Cervantes, 25, 133.
Charles I, 247.
Charlie, Prince, 47, 75, 77, 122, 136, 137, 140, 180–3, 190, 216.
Chartreuse de Parme, La, 93, 107.
Chateaubriand, 128.
Chaucer, Geoffrey, 218.
Claverhouse, 40, 41, 172.
Cleishbotham, Jedediah, 11.
Cockburn, Lord, 4 *note*, 208, 208 *note*, 220.
Colburn, 185 *note*.
Coleridge, S. T., 7, 22, 89, 165, 228.
Collingham, R. G., 83 *note*.
Constable, Archibald, 13, 14, 27.
Cooper, 98, 107, 134.
Crabbe, 145 *note*, 146.

Craig, David, 15, 15 *note*, 18, 18 *note*.
Craig, William, 208.
Craigburnfoot, Elspeth of the, 222.
Craigengelt, 199, 201.
Crawford, Thomas, ix, x 75 *note*, 168 *note*, 172, 172 *note*.
Croce, B., 10, 10 *note*, 234.
Croker, J. W., 245, 245 *note*, 246 *note*.
Crosbie, Provost, 47, 52, 57, 77, 91.
Cromwell, Oliver, 101, 118, 247.
Crutwell, P., 7 *note*.
Currie, J., 4 *note*.

Daiches, David, x, 18, 19, 19 *note*, 56, 59, 85 *note*, 88, 91, 91 *note*.
Dalgetty Dugald, 22, 46, 92, 225.
Davie Donald, 18, 18 *note*, 78, 78 *note*, 79.
Davie, Douce, 172.
Davy, Sir Humphrey, 81.
Deans, Davie, 169, 170, 171, 172.
Deans, Effie, 127, 168, 171, 224, 227.
Deans, Jeanie, 21, 22, 82, 118, 119, 127, 151, 160, 214, 223–5.
de Laclos, *see* Laclos.
de Worde, Wynken, *see* Worde.
Dhu, Evans, *see* Maccombich.
Dickens, Charles, 54, 70, 71, 133, 145, 167, 168, 216.
Dingwall, Davie, 88, 222.
Dinmont, Dandie, 35, 36, 177, 179, 186, 215, 216.
Dobie, 242 *note*.
Dobrée, B., 7 *note*.
Doil, Cormac, 236.
Donald Bean Lean, *see* Lean.
Don Quixote, 25.
Douglas, Earl of, 122.
Douglas, Gavin, 219.
Dousterswivel, 68.
Dryburgh, 6 *note*.
Dryden, John, 7, 19.
Dryfesdale, Jasper, 190.
Dumas, A., 23.
Durward, Quentin, 113.

Eckermann, 120.
Edinburgh Review, 4.
Egmont, 117.
Elizabeth I, 95, 101.
Ellangowan, 174, 178, 182.
Eliott, T. S., 14 *note*.
Elspeth (Old Elspeth), 69, 70.
Engels, 121, 123, 124.
Erskine, John, 189.
Evandale, Lord, 40, 41.

Evan Dhu, *see* Maccombich.
Ewart, Nanty, 181, 182.

Faerie Queene, The, 241.
Fairfold Alan, 47, 48, 53, 58, 59, 77, 84, 181, 183.
Fairford, Saunders, 22, 47, 181.
Fairservice, Andrew, 22, 39, 42, 44, 84, 225.
Falkner, Meade, 178.
Faust, 159.
Fergusson, 208.
Fielding, Henry, 61, 79, 84, 131, 133, 209, 213, 216, 221.
Fiske, G. F., 2 *note*.
Flaubert, 184.
Forster, E. M., 16, 16 *note*, 17, 198.
Fox, Ralph, ix, 17, 17 *note*, 68.
Freytag, Gustav, 124.
Froissart, 216.
Froude, 154.
Frye, Northrop, 16, 16 note.

Galt, John, 52, 193, 193 *note*, 227, 227 *note*.
Gardiner, Colonel, 212.
Geddes, Joshua, 60, 76, 77, 182, 183.
Gellatley, Davie, 31, 90.
George III, 232.
George IV, 25, 27, 232.
George Sand, *see* Sand.
Gibbon, 57.
Gibbon, Lewis Grassic, 52.
Gleig, Dr, 245 *note*.
Glen, James, 28.
Glenallan, Countess of, 69.
Glenallan, Earl of, 69, 71, 222.
Glendale, Sir Richard, 183.
Glendinning, Dame, 217.
Glennaquoich, Laird o', 33.
Glossin, Gilbert, 173–8.
Glover, Katherine, 212.
Goethe, 3, 93, 97, 99, 105, 106, 117–20, 128–30, 158–60.
Gordon, R. C., 185 *note*.
Gordon, Stewart, 19, 19 *note*.
Gourlay, Ailsie, 187.
Gow, Henry, 122, 212.
Graeme, Roland, 140, 141, 202.
Gray, Alice, 226.
Gray, Thomas, 252.
Greenleaf, Gilbert, 196.
Grierson, H. J. C., Sir Herbert, 4 *note*, 5 *note*, 11 *note*, 12, 12 *note*, 13, 13 *note*, 28, 74, 74 *note*, 186 *note*.

Grieve, C. M., (Hugh McDiarmid), 16, 16 *note*, 17, 17 *note*, 18, 20.
Gurth, 115.

Hardy, Thomas, 167.
Harry, Blind, 218.
Hart, Francis R., 83 *note*.
Hatteraik, Dirk, 173, 179.
Hazelwood, Sir Robert, 37, 177.
Hazlitt, William, 146, 247.
Headrigg, Cuddie, 40, 41, 222, 225.
Headrigg, Mause, 226.
Hegel, 98, 99, 103, 112, 120, 123, 128, 129, 130.
Heine, 123.
Henry IV, 31, 32.
Henry VIII, 154, 258.
Heriot, George, 222, 226.
Herries of Birrenswork, *see* Birrenswork.
Hilderbrand, Sir, 45.
Hill, Dr G. B., 238 *note*, 246.
Hillhouse, James T., ix, 16 *note*, 185 *note*.
Humphrey Clinker, 61, 64.
Hurd, Bishop, 27.
Hogg, James, 220.
Holderlin, 111.
Homer, 104, 111, 123, 137.
Hood, Robin, 102, 115, 119.
Hoyle, 243.
Hume, 123.

Iliad, The, 104, 129.
Inglewood, Mr Justice, 25.
Ivanhoe, 96, 115.

James I and VI, 206, 226.
Jarvie, Bailie Nicol, 22, 42–5, 52, 83, 84, 91, 125, 226.
Jebb, R. C., 215, 215 *note*.
Jefferson, D. W., x.
Jeffrey, (contemporary of Scott) 4, 27.
Johnson, Dr Samuel, 7, 14, 78, 207, 207 *note*, 235, 245 *note*, 246, 249, 252 *note*.
Jonson, Ben, 59.
Joseph Andrews, 84, 85 *note*.
Joyce, James, 15.

Keats, John, 7.
Keeper, Lord, 185.
Kettle, Arnold, 18, 82, 82 *note*.
Kidnapped, 23.
Kirk, Russel, 18, 18 *note*.

Laclos, Choderlos de, 97.

Laird o' Glennaquoich, *see* Glennaquoich.
Latimer, Darsie, 25, 47, 48, 50, 51, 53–6, 178–81, 190.
Latouche, 106.
Lean, Donald Bean, 62.
Lenin, 109.
Leo, 106.
Le Sage, 133.
Letters on Chivalry and Romance, 27.
Lewis, M. G. ("Monk"), 10.
Leyden, John, 7.
Life, by Lockhart, *see* Lockhart.
Lockhart, J. G., 2 *note*, 5, 5 *note*, 6, 6 *note*, 9 *note*, 11 *note*, 27, 31, 140, 208 *note* 211, 232 *note*, 234, 235, 242, 250.
Louis XI, 101, 122, 125.
Louis XIV, 107.
Lovel, 38, 39, 65, 66, 212.
Lubbock, Percy, 70, 70 *note*, 71.
Lucan, 121.
Ludwig, Otto, 110, 111.
Lukács Georg, 19, 19 *note*, 60, 63, 63 *note*, 75 *note*, 82, 82 note, 83, 83 *note*, 85 *note*, 93 *note*.
Lyrical Ballads, 22.

McAdam, Quintin, 232.
McAulay, Allan, 195.
Macbriar, 40, 215.
Maccombich, Evan Dhu, 31–3, 62, 115, 116, 225.
McCrie, Thomas, 40.
"MacDiarmid, Hugh", *see* Grieve, C. M.
MacGregor, Helen, 23, 43, 52, 226.
MacGregor, Rob Roy, 25, 26, 42–5, 81, 83, 84, 86, 102, 110, 119, 125, 126, 189, 190, 206, 226.
MacIntyre, Edie, 67, 68, 70.
MacIntyre, Hector, 67, 68, 70.
MacIvor, Fergus, 31–3, 35, 40, 62, 91, 215.
MacIvor, Flora, 26, 31, 62, 86, 151, 159, 160.
Mackenzie, Henry, 227.
Macleuchar, Mrs, 65.
Maclure, Bessie, 41.
MacMorlan, 177.
Macraw, Francie, 222.
Macwheeble, Bailie Duncan, 31–3, 62, 91.
Mailsetter, 84.
Mannering, Colonel, 34, 37.
Mannering, Guy, 143, 174, 176, 177.
Manzoni, 97, 129.
Margaret of Branksome, *see* Branksome.
Marx, Karl, 123.

Mary Stuart, Queen of Scots, *see* Stuart.
Matilda, 7.
Maxwell of Summertrees (Pate-in-Peril), *see* Summertrees.
Mayo, R. D., 12, 12 *note*.
Mazarin, 107.
Menteith, 195.
Merrilees, Meg, 34, 35, 39, 52, 143, 144 174, 175, 177, 179, 222, 228.
Mervyn, 177.
Middlemarch, 167.
Minstrel of Satchells, *see* Scott.
Moniplies, Richie, 222.
Monkbarns, 64–8, 70, 221, 228.
Monro, Captain, 219.
Montrose, Duke of, 126, 127.
Moonfleet, 178.
Morgan, 123.
Morley, Henry, 187 *note*.
Morris, 215.
Morton, Henry, 40–2, 51, 96, 172, 194, 212.
Mortsheugh, Sexton, 186.
Mucklebackit, Maggie, 66–71, 225.
Mucklebackit, Saunders, 228.
Mucklebackit, Steenie, 38, 39, 67, 68, 69.
Mucklewrath, 84.
Muir, Edwin, 14, 15, 15 *note*, 16, 16 *note*, 17, 24, 48.
Murray, Regent, 140, 141.
Musgrave, 92.

Napoleon, 108.
Neff, E., 18, 18 *note*.
Newman, Cardinal, 18.
Nibelungenlied, 130.
Nixon, Cristal, 182.

Ochiltree, Eddie, 22, 39, 65, 143, 186, 222.
Ochtertyre, Ramsay of, 207, 208 *note*, 223, 245, 246 *note*.
Odyssey, The, 129.
Old Alice, *see* Alice, "old".
Oldbuck, Grizel, 221.
Oldbuck, Jonathan, 38, 39, 45, 245.
Olmsted, 134.
Omen, The, 193.
Osbaldistone, Frank, 25, 26, 43, 44, 84, 96, 202.
Osbaldistone, Sir Hilderbrand, 86.

Parish Register, The, 145, 145 *note*.
Parsons, Coleman O., 19, 186 *note*, 188, 188 *note*, 194, 194 *note*, 196, 204 *note*.

Partington, W., 220 *note*.
Pate-in-Peril, *see* Summertrees.
Paterson, James, 233 *note*.
Patrick, Earl, 236.
Pattieson, Peter, 11.
Peebles, Peter, 53, 54, 59, 60, 87, 181, 182.
Pelham, Edgar, 185 *note*.
Pennant, 227.
Percy, Bishop, 70, 219.
Pickwick Papers, The, 184.
Pinkerton, 227.
Pleydell, Councillor, 35, 36, 45, 52, 175–7, 181, 215.
Pope, Alexander, 221, 248.
Pope-Hennessy, Dame Una, 6, 6 *note*, 12, 12 *note*, 18, 18 *note*, 185 *note*.
Polwarth, Alick, 33.
Poundtext, 40.
Porteous, 168.
Powell, L. F., 238 *note*.
Pride and Prejudice, 167
Prince Charlie, *see* Charlie, Prince.
Pushkin, 93, 96, 97, 99, 120.

Quin, 246, 247.

Rabelais, 59.
Raleigh, J. H., 85 *note*.
Ramsay, Allan, 208, 219, 220.
Ramsay, John, *see* Ochtertyre.
Ramsay (the clock-maker), 222.
Rashleigh, 45, 84.
Ratcliffe, 143.
Ravenswood, 45, 46, 86–8, 161, 185, 197–204.
Redgauntlet, 25, 47, 48, 51, 52, 56, 77, 81, 86, 87, 91, 179–83, 190.
Regent Murray, *see* Murray, Regent.
Ritson, Joseph, 7, 70.
Richard I, *Coeur de Lion*, 101, 115, 152, 153.
Richardson, Samuel, 213.
Richelieu, Cardinal, 107.
Rob Roy, *see* MacGregor, Rob Roy.
Rousseau, 97.
Rowe, Elizabeth, 213.
Ruskin, 14, 14 *note*.

Saddletree, Bartoline, 169, 170, 171, 171 *note*, 172, 173, 223.
Sage, Le, *see* Le Sage.
Saintsbury, G., 200 *note*.
Sand, George, 114.
Scott, Captain Robert, 9.

Scott, Geoffrey, 237, 238 *note*.
Scott, Lady, 14.
Scott, Minstrel of Satchells, 2.
Scott, Oldham, 6.
Scott, Sir Walter. Works:
  Abbot, The, 122, 140, 141, 154, 190, 216.
  Antiquary, The, 24, 34, 37–9.
  Auchindrane or the Ayrshire Tragedy, 11.
  Autobiography, 213.
  Ballads and Lyrical Pieces, 10.
  Betrothed, The, 12, 218.
  Black Dwarf, The, 250.
  Border Antiquities of England and Scotland, 11.
  Bridal of Triermain, The, 6, 11.
  Bride of Lammermoor, The, 12, 24, 45, 46, 73, 86–8, 185–205, 215, 222, 226, 251.
  Castle Dangerous, 12, 196.
  Chronicles of the Canongate, 12, 12 *note*, 188, 223.
  Doom of Devergoil, The, 11.
  Essays on Chivalry, 11.
  Fair Maid of Perth, The, 12, 122, 124, *213 note*.
  Field of Waterloo, The, 11.
  Fortunes of Nigel, The, 206, 222, 227.
  Guy Mannering, xi, 24, 34, 37, 39, 162, 173, 175, 177–80, 184, 189, 213, 215, 227.
  Halidon Hill, 11.
  Harold the Dauntless, 11.
  Heart of Midlothian, The, x, 19, 21, 24, 26, 45, 118, 122, 168, 168 *note*, 172, 205, 214, 225.
  Ivanhoe, 46, 73, 76, 78, 80, 102, 115, 130, 152, 216.
  Journal, 6 *note*, 8, 27, 211.
  Kenilworth, xi, 216, 247.
  Lady of the Lake, The, 10, 11, 138, 139.
  Lay of the Last Minstrel, The, 7, 10, 14, 250.
  Legend of Montrose, A, 24, 46, 92, 125–6, 188, 195, 195 *note*.
  Letters of Sir Walter Scott, 6 *note*.
  Letters of Demonology and Witchcraft, 11, 191, 192 *note*, 194, 195, 195 *note*, 244.
  Life of Bage, 199.
  Life of Napoleon, 11.
  Lives of the Novelists, 11.
  Lord of the Isles, 11, 235, 236.
  Macduff's Cross, 11.
  Marmion, 8, 10, 247.
  Minstrelsy of the Scottish Border, 27, 54.
  Monastery, The, 216, 217, 217 *note*.

  Old Mortality, xi, 18, 24, 39, 40, 42, 46, 74, 102, 172, 186, 191, 222.
  Pirate, The, x, 190, 222.
  Quentin Durward, 125.
  Redgauntlet, 7, 12, 19, 21, 24–6, 38, 46, 48, 50, 53, 56, 56 *note*, 57, 59, 61, 75–7, 84, 91, 178, 180, 182, 184, 190, 213, 217, 227, 229.
  Rob Roy, xi, 7, 24, 25, 42–4, 83, 84, 91, 120, 124, 125, 225.
  Rokeby, 7, 11.
  St Ronan's Well, 217.
  Sir Tristrem, 10.
  Tales from Benedictine Sources, 12, 12 *note*.
  Tales of a Grandfather, xi, 11, 215.
  Tales of my Landlord, 11, 46.
  Tales of the Crusades, 12, 12 *note*.
  Talisman, The, x, xi, 23, 218.
  Translations, 10.
  Vision of Don Roderick, The, 11.
  Waverley, 11, 13, 19, 24, 29–32, 34, 35, 61, 73, 76, 78, 79, 83, 102, 115, 122, 125, 136, 189, 211, 225, 250.
  Waverley Novels, The, 9, 11, 14, 56, 78, 90, 132–6, 170 *note*, 171, 188, 189 *note*, 190, 206.
  Woodstock, 211.
Serlo, 105.
Shafton, Sir Piercie, 217.
Shakespeare, William, 31, 32, 51, 93, 142, 159, 180, 209, 211, 218, 219, 221.

Sharp, Archbishop, 191, 194.
Sharpe, C. K., 7.
Shelley, P. B., 156, 156 *note*, 252.
Sheridan, Thomas, 207.
Shortreed, Robert, 5, 241, 242 *note*.
Sinclair, Master of, 227.
Smith, Adam, 147, 245.
Smollett, Tobias, 61, 67, 133, 209, 213.
Spencer, Edmund, 218.
Staunton, 223, 224.
Steenson, Steenie, 91.
Stendhal, 93, 96, 107.
Stephen, Leslie, 81, 81 *note*, 185 *note*.
Sterne, Laurence, 59, 67, 213.
Stevas, Norman St John, 133 *note*, 152 *note*, 159 *note*, 162 *note*, 164 *note*.
Stevenson, Robert Louis, 23, 52, 70, 210, 210 *note*, 217, 217 *note*, 229.
Stewart, Dugald, 3.
Stuart, Charles Edward, *see* Charlie, Prince.
Stuart, Mary (Mary Queen of Scots), 101, 113, 122.
Sue, Eugnèe, 107.
Summertrees, Maxwell of, 57, 58, 182.

Swift, Dean, 7, 11, 19.

Taine, 96, 114.
Tait, J. G., 187 *note*.
Talbot, Colonel, 31, 63, 91.
Taming of the Shrew, The, 38.
Tave, Stuart M., 64, 64 *note*.
Thierry, 123.
Thiers, 165.
Thomas the Rhymer, 188.
Tolstoy, 98, 107, 108, 114, 121.
Tom Jones, 187.
Trumbull, Thomas, 181, 182.
Turntippit, Lord, 186.
Tweedsmuir, Lord, 44.

Vernon, Diana, 7, 26.
Verrall, A. W., 228, 228 *note*.
Vich Ian Vohr, *see* Vohr.
Vico, 98.
Virgil, 123.
Vohr, Vich Ian, 81, 86, 102, 104, 115.

Wade, General, 219.
Walker, Patrick, 227.
Walpole, Horace, 218.

Wamba, 115.
Wandering Willie, *see* Willie, Wandering.
Wardour, Isabella, 39, 65, 159, 212.
Wardour, Sir Arthur, 37–9, 46, 65, 67, 172.
Waverley, Edward, 25, 26, 30–4, 40, 61–3, 78, 84, 86, 89–91, 96, 100, 116, 136, 137, 160, 202.
Weekley ernest, 219.
Weir of Hermiston, 52.
Wellington, The Duke of, 140, 141.
Welsh, Alexander, 18, 18 *note*, 19, 81, 81 *note*, 201 *note*.
Werther, 97.
Wilhelm Meister, 105.
Willie, Wandering, 47, 50, 52–6, 91, 181, 183, 193.
Will the Bolsheviks Retain State Power?, 109.
Wilson, W. E., 242 *note*.
Worde, Wynken de, 130.
Wordsworth, William, 7, 22, 227, 248, 250, 251, 253.
Wuthering Heights, 167.

Young, G. M., 10 *note*, 72, 73 *note*.
Young Pretender, The, *see* Charlie, Prince.

TEXT CORRIGENDA

p. 2, fn. 3: *The title of C. F. Fiske's book is 'Epic Suggestion in the Imagery of the Waverley Novels'.*

p. 18, line 23: *Footnote signal should be* 55.

p. 19, first fn.: *For* 59 *read* 57.

p. 24, fn. 2: *For* 1956 *read* 1936.

p. 26, lines 17–18: *Should read* (we are told in an . . .

p. 56, fn. 2, last line: *Should read* Steinmann, Jr., Minneapolis (University of Minnesota Press) 1958, p. 58.

p. 82, line 21: *For* complex *read* complete.

p. 132, fn. 1, line 3: *Should read* N. St John Stevas.

p. 186, fn. 6, line 1: *For* 1927 *read* 1827.

p. 193, fn. 21, line 2: *For* 1834–61 *read* 1834–6; *for* p. 351 *read* p. 352.

p. 228, line 22: *For* burn brighter *read* burn the blyther.

p. 232, fn. 3, lines 2–3: *Should read* eds. F. A. Pottle and C. H. Bennett. London (Heinemann) 1936, pp. 106–7 (1 Sep. 1773).

p. 233, fn. 4, line 2: *For* at *read* of.

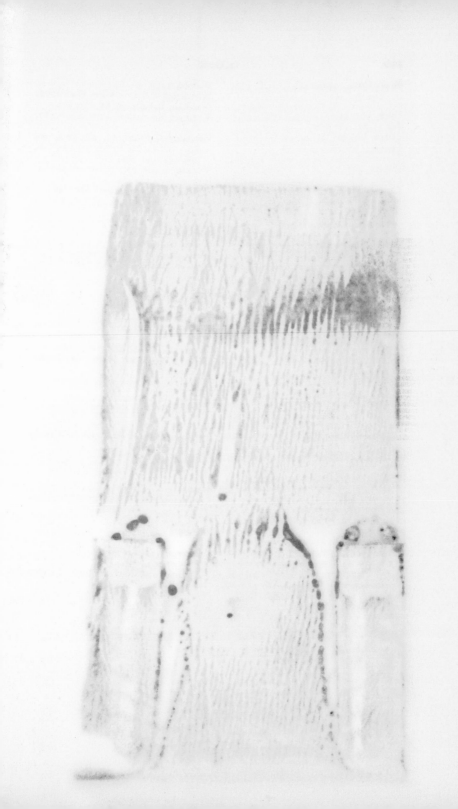